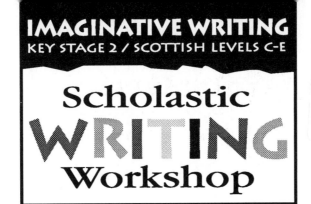

IMAGINATIVE WRITING
KEY STAGE 2 / SCOTTISH LEVELS C-E

Scholastic
WRITING
Workshop

C000293779

Aspects of the craft of

WRITING

SUE ELLIS &
GILL FRIEL

Scholastic WRITING Workshop

Published by Scholastic Ltd,
Villiers House,
Clarendon Avenue,
Leamington Spa,
Warwickshire CV32 5PR
Text © 1995 Sue Ellis and Gill Friel
© 1995 Scholastic Ltd
567890   01234

Authors
Sue Ellis and Gill Friel

Editor
Kate Banham

Assistant Editor
Sophie Jowett

Series Designer
Joy White

Illustrations
Robin Lawrie and Peter Wilks

Cover illustration
Margaret Chamberlain
(From *The Man Whose Mother Was a Pirate* by Margaret Mahy,
published by J.M Dent)

Designed using Aldus Pagemaker

British Library Cataloguing-in-Publication Data
A catalogue record for this book is
available from the British Library.

ISBN 0-590-53466-1

Scholastic WRITING Workshop

Contents

ACKNOWLEDGEMENTS

The publishers gratefully acknowledge permission to reproduce the following copyright material:

Andersen Press for 'Mrs Cole's House' from *I'll take you to Mrs Cole!* text © Nigel Gray 1985, illustrations © Michael Foreman 1985 . First published by Andersen Press London, 1985. All rights reserved; Frederick Covins for 'The woodland meeting' from *The Battle for Badger's Wood* by Frederick Covins © 1973 (Cassell and Co) (Reprinted 1983-84 PEP Limited); Victor Gollancz for 'Huge Red Riding Hood' from *The Topsy-Turvy Storybook* by Dick King-Smith. Text copyright © Fox Busters Limited 1992 (1992, Victor Gollancz); HarperCollins Publishers for an extract from *Voyage of the Dawn Treader* and *The Silver Chair* by C.S. Lewis (1974, HarperCollins), 'Salford Road' from *Song of the City* by Gareth Owen (1985, Fontana Lions an imprint of Harper Collins Publishers Limited), 'The Princess and the Frog' and 'The Three Bears and Goldilocks' by Jonathan Langley from *The Collins Book of Nursery Tales* (1993, HarperCollins Publishers Limited), an excerpt from *Homecoming* by Cynthia Voigt (1984, HarperCollins) and from *Tree by Leaf* (1989, Armada Lions, an imprint of Harper CollinsPublishers Limited); Helen Cresswell for 'Lizzie Dripping' from *Lizzie Dripping and the Orphans* (BBC Books); David Higham Associates Limited for an except from *The Weirdstone of Brisingamen* by Alan Garner (1965, HarperCollins Publishers Limited) and 'Whitewash' from *A Child's Christmas in Wales* by Dylan Thomas (1986, Dent Paperbacks); Macdonald Young Books for extracts from *Matthew and the Sea Singer* by © Jill Paton Walsh (1992, first published by Macdonald Young Books, formerly Simon and Schuster Young Books); Marilyn Malin for 'Jack Bobbin' from *Jack Bobbin* by © Jill Bennett 1990. First published by Orchard Books London; the Trustees of the Literary Estate of the late Dr Alfred Noyes for 'Daddy fell into the pond' from *Alfred Noyes: Collected Poems* (1952, Sheed and Ward Inc.); Oxford University Press for permisson to use an extract from *The Three Little Pigs* by Val Biro (1990, Oxford University Press), an extract from *The Wedding Ghost* by Leon Garfield (1985, Oxford University Press); Penguin Books Limited for an extract from *Thunder and Lightnings* by Jan Mark (1976, Puffin), 'Lenny Fraser' from 'Lenny's Red Letter Day' from *I'm Trying to Tell You* by Bernard Ashley (1982, Penguin), 'After the quarrel' from *A Pack of Liars* by Anne Fine (1988, Hamish Hamilton), the excerpt from *Charlotte's Web* by E.B. White (1952, Hamish Hamilton), the extract from *Dragon Ride* by Helen Cresswell (1987, Viking Kestrel), the extract from *Simon's Challenge* by Theresa Breslin (1988, Blackie) and 'Angela Mitchell' from *The Fiend Next Door* by Sheila Lavelle (1983, Armada Lions); Peters, Fraser and Dunlop Group Limited for 'Dumb Insolence' from *Take Me Like I Am* by Adrian Mitchell. None of Adrian Mitchell's work should be used in any examination whatsoever; Murray Pollinger for 'The eye-smiler' from *Danny Champion of the World* by Roald Dahl first published in 1975 by Jonathan Cape Limited and Penguin Books Limited; Random House UK Limited for 'Uncle Owen's room' from *Charlie Moon and the Big Bonanza Bust Up* by Shirley Hughes (1982, Bodley Head), the Estate of Ian Serrailler for an extract from *The Silver Sword* by Ian Serrailler (1960, Johnathan Cape), an extract from *Over Sea Under Stone* by Susan Cooper (1968, Bodley Head) and an extract from *The Night Swimmers* by Betsy Byers (1982, Bodley Head); Reed Consumer Books for the extract from *The Village of Round and Square Houses* by Ann Grifalconi (1986, Methuen Children's Books), 'The Selfish Giant's garden' from *The Selfish Giant* by Oscar Wilde (1982, Picture Puffin), 'On the mountain' from *The Snow Spider* by Jenny Nimmo (1986, Methuen Children's Books), the extract from *The Writing on the Wall* and *The King in the Garden* by Leon Garfield (Methuen); Scholastic Limited for two poems from *Mind Your Own Business* by Michael Rosen (1974, Andre Deutsch); The Society of Authors and the Literary Trustees of Walter de la Mare for 'Snow' by Walter de la Mare from *The Complete Poems of Walter de la Mare* (1969, USA 1970); Watson, Little Limited for 'The Old Field' from *Rhyme Times Rhyme* by D.J. Enright (1974, Chatto and Windus), Jane Wright for an extract from *BB Wolf – My Story*.

Every effort has been made to trace the copyright holders for the works reproduced in this book and the publishers apologise for any inadvertent omissions.

The authors would like to thank the children of St Patrick's Primary School, Kilsyth, Killermont Primary School, Bearsden, and Fintry Primary School, Fintry, who helped in the development of these writing ideas.

Scholastic
IMAGINATIVE WRITING
Workshop

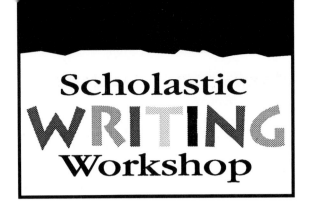

Scholastic WRITING Workshop

Chapter One

INTRODUCTION

TEACHING IMAGINATIVE WRITING

Subject knowledge does make a difference and effective teachers know how to select content and to identify key points. They know how to present topics to children in ways that they understand... Where subject knowledge is richer, deeper and better-integrated, it is more likely that the teacher will be confident and more open to children's ideas, contributions, questions and comments.

(Aubrey, 1994)

This resource aims to help teachers teach imaginative writing in a way that:
• is flexible and responsive to the children's needs and interests;
• is reflective and analytical, focusing on key issues in teaching, learning and content;
• results in confident, enthusiastic and enquiring children who find story-telling and writing both challenging and satisfying.

A balanced approach

The publication of the National Curricula for England and Wales and for Northern Ireland, and the 5–14 Guidelines for Scotland, has focused attention on the role and organisation of subject knowledge in the primary school curriculum. Discussion papers such as *Curriculum Organisation and Classroom Practice in Primary Schools* (Alexander *et al.* 1992) have further fuelled the debate by highlighting the importance of subject-focused knowledge, understanding and skills to ensure coherence, progression and differentiation within the curriculum.

Yet all children, particularly young children, need contexts for learning that harness their enthusiasm and encourage them to integrate new knowledge and skills with those they have already acquired from school and home. Only this can ensure effective education; the real understanding based on 'deep learning' that makes a difference to how children understand and operate in their world.

The aim of the *Scholastic Writing Workshops* is to help teachers introduce and develop specific aspects of the writer's craft within learning contexts that are exciting and meaningful and that encourage children to use their own knowledge and skills in new and powerful ways.

Content knowledge for teaching imaginative writing

Traditionally, advice to teachers on teaching imaginative writing has focused on how to identify story topics and create contexts that are exciting and meaningful to children. While teachers have been told that they comment on surface features such as spelling and handwriting at the expense of other things, they have been given little specific help in identifying how else to focus their efforts – which craft aspects to look for, how to teach these and how to work with young writers.

The 'process writing' approach advocated by researchers such as Donald Graves and Lucy Calkins has highlighted the importance of the following:
• The writer's intention: purpose, voice and audience ('I have a story to tell. It is important to me, and I want you to enjoy reading it.')
• Awareness of the craft skills involved ('These are the techniques I can use to create vivid pictures in your mind.')
• Awareness of how writers work and of personal work patterns and techniques ('This is how I need to work to ensure my writing is as effective as possible.')

The writing/reading link

Effective teaching produces children who are 'good writers'. They are confident in their writing. They know that the stories they write are important and that others will read their work. They think carefully about how to tell their stories and know that it is sometimes necessary to experiment with several ways to find the best. They can transcribe their ideas quickly on to paper, and recognise when neatness and spelling are a priority and when they are not.

When children become enthusiastic and analytical writers, they begin to take an insider's view of reading and to 'read with the eye of a writer' (Calkins, 1986). They begin to notice, and are keen to investigate further, some of the specific strategies and techniques that writers use to 'tell a good story' – how other writers convey characterisation, set the scene or create a particular mood. They want to find out about the use of dialogue and how to develop the plot effectively.

Their developing interst in how writers and writing work adds a new dimension to their reading; they begin to appreciate not only the stories they read, but also how they have been told.

SCHOLASTIC WRITING WORKSHOPS

Scholastic Writing Workshops provide resources both for teaching specific craft skills and for extended writing projects in which children develop a story over a period of time.

The resources provide teachers with:
• the knowledge and the analytical framework necessary to teach children how to write well.
• the strategies to motivate children to write.
• the guidance necessary to respond appropriately and constructively to children's strengths and weaknesses as writers.

Why use a workshop approach?

The term 'writing workshop' reflects beliefs about the nature of writing and the nature of learning to write well. It does not reflect a particular form of classroom organisation. The workshop approach recognises that writing is a practical and an intellectually creative activity and that the challenge lies in doing it; that writers learn through effort and enquiry.

The *Scholastic Writing Workshops* recognise that children need opportunities for individual experiment, but also that they learn by working beside others and benefit from being shown how to achieve particular effects. It implies that there will be times when children are engaged in private struggles and times when they share difficulties or reflect on their work and on the work of others. Above all, the term 'workshop' implies that everyone is intellectually and practically engaged in the craft of writing.

The approach is flexible and can be used with different classroom organisations, including composite classes and team teaching situations.

The materials provided encourage teachers to be responsive to the children's needs and interests and to use their knowledge of the class to decide which aspects of writing to target. Children at different stages or of different abilities can work on the same writing technique or strategy, but with materials that offer differentiated support.

What is needed for the workshop approach?

The single most important thing that children require is a classroom ethos that recognises the value of their ideas and provides a supportive, enthusiastic environment in which to learn.

It is also helpful if the following have been explained to the class:
• where and how to store work in progress;
• where to put work that is finished;
• where to find books that are particularly useful for ideas or models;
• how to use tools such as thesauri and dictionaries and where these may be found;
• how to get access to writing materials;
• how to get access to computers for writing;
• how to get access to basic art materials.

The teacher must decide on the materials to be used for the various writing activities, but it is a good idea to issue children with a small jotter in which they can record ideas for personal writing projects and possible stories.

Teachers may also want to consider how best to use the available display space for writing and the degree to which the children will be involved in deciding what should be displayed, and how. If the children are to take responsibility for presenting their work, it may be helpful to have somewhere for them to see a variety of presentation ideas.

Individual work and group work

The *Scholastic Writing Workshop* activities involve children working individually, but also with writing partners and in groups.

Children undoubtedly need space and silence to work on their own stories and develop their own style. However, they also need to share ideas and understandings with others. Collaborative work can:
• deepen motivation and involvement;
• help children to organise their thoughts;
• help children to understand what the reader needs to know;
• let children test out ideas on others;
• encourage children to explain ideas in different ways to find the most effective;
• encourage originality and diversity by providing a variety of origins and routes for inspiration and development of ideas;
• help children to make reading–writing links;
• deepen learning by encouraging children to explain ideas in their own words, thereby understanding and remembering them better;
• encourage reflection and awareness of what children know and what they need to learn;
• encourage children to take control and responsibility for their work;
• encourage children to be confident, self-aware and sensitive to others;
• help children understand how others can help them to scaffold their ideas.

TEACHING CONTENT

	Planning for writing	Drafting	Myself as a writer	Evaluation and reflection	Imagery: simile, metaphor, personification	Voice, speech and dialogue	Emotive descriptions	Descriptive detail	Description – action
CHARACTERISATION	31	32			3, 4, 30, 33, 35	12, 13, 14, 15, 16, 17, 18, 19, 25, 36	3, 4, 5, 6, 7, 8, 14, 32	1, 2, 4, 11, 15, 22	8, 9, 10, 11, 13, 14, 15, 28, 29
SETTING THE SCENE	9				10, 15, 16, 17, 18, 19, 20, 23, 26, 30, 36	23	1, 4, 6, 7, 8, 9, 10, 11, 12, 13, 14, 21, 24, 26, 28, 29, 30, 32, 35, 36, 37	1, 2, 3, 5, 6, 7, 8, 9, 21, 25, 27, 31, 32, 33	22, 24, 26, 27, 34, 37
STORY STRUCTURE	2, 3, 19			9, 26, 27, 29, 38	38	13, 14, 15, 16, 17, 18, 25, 27, 33, 34	38	30	19, 26
THE WRITING PROCESS	8, 9, 19	9, 10, 11, 12	1, 2, 3, 4, 5, 6, 7, 8, 18, 19, 20, 21	3, 4, 7, 9, 10, 13, 19, 20, 21					

Points of view	Character study	Selecting and structuring description	Sequencing and structuring a story	Turning points and cliff-hangers	Beginnings	Endings	Titles and headings	Layout, chapter divisions, prologues and epilogues	Proof-reading and editing	Reflecting on collaboration
6, 8, 12, 14, 28, 29	20, 21, 22, 23, 24, 26, 31, 34	1, 2, 7, 10, 11, 19, 20, 22, 26, 32		23		38		38		
14, 34		1, 4, 5, 6, 7, 8, 9, 14, 24, 25, 28, 29, 31, 32, 33	1, 7, 22 3, 33							
14, 15, 16, 32	25, 34	37	1, 4, 5, 6, 21, 31, 33, 35, 38	2, 3, 5, 9, 33, 35, 37	7, 8, 9, 10, 30, 36	11, 12, 29	23, 34, 40	18, 20, 21, 22, 28, 31, 35		
		10							14, 15	5, 12, 13, 16, 17, 18, 19, 20, 21

COMPONENTS OF THIS WORKSHOP

• *Aspects of the Craft of Writing* – a teachers' resource book containing:
– ideas for short, focused activities on techniques for developing characterisation, setting, story structure and the writing process;
– photocopiable activity sheets;
– photocopiable anthology section;
– ideas and photocopiable pages for assessment and record-keeping.
• *Writing Projects* – a teachers' resource book containing:
– ideas and lesson plans for ten extended writing projects;
– photocopiable activity sheets;
– ideas for presentation and publishing of children's work including useful resources for calligraphy and illuminated letters;
– ideas and photocopiable pages for assessment and record-keeping.
• Nine high-quality children's books that provide models of excellent writing.
• A 60-minute audio cassette of interviews with and readings by four of the authors whose books are included in the workshop.

Aspects of the Craft of Writing

This volume contains lesson outlines to introduce children to specific aspects of the writer's craft. It consists of four chapters:
• Characterisation;
• Setting the scene;
• Story structure;
• The writing process.
The first three chapters reflect the centrality of characters, locations and problems in driving stories forward, controlled by the structural decisions made by the writer. The fourth chapter focuses on aspects of the writing process and the different ways in which writers work.

Activities in the characterisation chapter explore particular strategies writers can use to portray and develop characters: appearance; actions; speech; lifestyles, friends and environments.

The chapter on setting contains activities that highlight how writers focus and structure a description to convey a sense of place; how they use it to predispose the reader to particular emotional reactions; how they use specific devices such as similes and personification.

The activities in the structure chapter draw attention to decisions writers make on plot and structure; beginnings and endings; viewpoint and dialogue; divisions, layout and titles.

The process chapter contains activities to encourage understanding of how writers work in general, reflection on personal work patterns and how to give and learn from the honest, thoughtful and analytical response of other writers. The activities are divided into three sections: the writer's self-knowledge; aspects of process and helping each other.

The writing activities

The activities have been designed to enable teachers to target children in Key Stage 2 of the National Curricula for England and Wales and Northern Ireland, and at levels C–E of the Language 5–14 Guidelines for Scotland.

The following information is given by symbols at the beginning of each activity:
Level of difficulty is indicated by star ratings. One-star activities are easiest in terms of content level and the support given. Three-star activities are the most difficult and are aimed at older, more able children. Where the content or type of activity is new, one-star activities provide starting points for older and more able children.
Time required gives an idea of how long each session may take. Obviously, this can only be a very rough guide and much depends on individual teachers and classes.
Class organisation shows how children work: individually, in pairs, in groups, or as a class.

The activities are then laid out clearly under the following headings:
Teaching content explains the main teaching objectives of each activity.
What you need details at a glance the resources required for the session.
What to do explains how to present each lesson. The explanations for some tasks indicate how they can be altered to give more or less challenge for particular children or groups.

Many of the activities are linked to photocopiable pages and these are cross-referenced under 'What you need'.
Development/homework tasks give ideas for further development at the end of an activity and can be done in class or as homework tasks.

Recent research (McBeath and Turner, 1990) has stressed the role of homework in developing understanding and in promoting links between parents and schools. However, the type of task is crucial; it must be meaningful and build on, or feed into, classwork.

The anthology

This consists of photocopiable pages of additional fiction and poetry, linked to one or more activity. This extends children's experience of quality literature and can be used to prompt creative and analytical reflection so that the children begin to use their experiences as readers to improve their writing.

Writing Projects

This volume gives ideas and lesson sequences for individual and collaborative extended writing projects. Each project is structured to provide support at strategic points, but most importantly, they allow children to 'live' with a story for long enough to become emotionally involved with it and committed to writing it well. The projects let children think, feel and behave as writers. They involve children in deciding how best to tell their stories, and encourage them to read and learn from each other's work, discovering their own recipes for success. The projects allow teachers and children to celebrate writing as both a process and a product.

The children's books

The children's books support work in both of the teachers' resource books. They have been chosen as examples of excellent writing that will appeal to the whole class, but it is intended that children should read the books as *writers*. They should recognise and appreciate *how* the story has been told, as well as the storyline.

Many of the books are easy to read and some children may have read them already. However, they should not be dismissed as purely for younger readers. Older children will find that a deeper understanding of the writer's craft allows them to appreciate the books in new ways.

Three books are used in each of the chapters on characterisation, setting and structure, and are presented in order of difficulty.

The books included in this workshop are:
The Man Whose Mother Was a Pirate by Margaret Mahy
A Lion at Bedtime by Debi Gliori
The Guard Dog by Dick King-Smith
The Village of Round and Square Houses by Ann Grifalconi
Dinner Ladies Don't Count by Bernard Ashley
Fair's Fair by Leon Garfield
3 Billy Goats Gruff by Ted Dewan
Nice/Nasty Neighbours by Terence Blacker and Frank Rodgers
Matthew and the Sea Singer by Jill Paton Walsh

The audio cassette

The cassette contains lively interviews with and readings by four of the well-known children's authors whose books are included in this workshop. They talk informally about themselves as writers and how they work, and each reads an extract from their book. The authors and passages read are:
- Dick King-Smith reading Chapter 1 of *The Guard Dog*
- Bernard Ashley reading Chapter 4 of 'Dinner Ladies Don't Count'
- Jill Paton Walsh reading Chapters 1 to 3 of *Matthew and the Sea Singer*
- Frank Rodgers reading the opening pages of each story in *Nice/Nasty Neighbours*.

The interviews contain advice and raise specific issues which are used as the basis of some of the activities.

Many of the issues will be of general interest to the children, who may enjoy listening to the interviews as a prelude to reading the book by that particular author.

USING THE SCHOLASTIC WRITING WORKSHOPS

Classroom management and planning

The *Scholastic Writing Workshops* are a resource not a scheme. The materials have been devised in the belief that it is the quality, content and appropriateness of the learning activities and the interactions between the teacher and the children that are important in teaching writing.

The writing workshops can be used with any classroom organisation. Each teacher can, and should, decide how best to organise the classroom space and time.

Only the teacher can decide when children will benefit from studying particular craft aspects or writing processes in depth. The activities in this volume help children to become aware of techniques they can, or maybe already, use.

But children also need to experience the complete writing process – to select and develop their own ideas, and to decide how best to tell their story. They need to put time and effort into publishing their stories and to enjoy seeing them read. The longer projects detailed in the *Writing Projects* volume are ideal for this.

Some teachers will plan the work of the class around a writing project, using teaching activities from *Aspects of the Craft of Writing* in a fairly *ad hoc* manner as specific issues arise. Other teachers may prefer to plan focused teaching on a series of specific aspects and intersperse, or run concurrently, a writing project within the class.

Where do I start?

This depends on the attitudes and needs of the class, and on how well the class and teacher know each other. Donald Graves (1983) recommends that teachers use just a class list to audit their knowledge about the writing interests of each child. Teachers may want to extend this idea, recording any knowledge of each child's specific interests, strengths, needs and opinions about writing and stories

This can highlight gaps in the teacher's knowledge of the children as individuals, but can also be extremely helpful in deciding where and how to start with a class.

The projects encourage children to become highly involved and enthusiastic about their work. They can be good starting points for:
• a newly-formed class that has not yet 'gelled';
• a teacher new to the class who does not know the children well;
• children who are not keen on writing;
• children inexperienced in extended writing.

Each writing project allows the teacher to observe the children and to find out about their interests and what they find easy or difficult. The collaborative nature of much of the work allows the teacher to learn about the children through the issues they raise with each other. They also offer opportunities for the teacher to talk with the children and to look analytically at their work, asking such questions as:
• What is most important about this story for the child?
• What was difficult/satisfying?
• What does this child know and what does she need to know?

Teachers who know the children and their writing well may immediately recognise activities in this volume that will address specific needs, or appeal to particular interests.

Planning across year groups

The graded activities on characterisation, setting and structure help teachers to plan appropriate work for the different ability groups in a class and to ensure progression from one year-group to the next. School staff need to discuss the balance between writing projects and work on the craft aspects of characterisation, setting and structure. However, whole-school policies must ensure that individual teachers retain sufficient flexibility to plan an appropriate and balanced scheme of work that meets:
• the children's needs as writers;
• the children's interests;
• the time available;
• issues covered in other curriculum areas.

Bibliography

Alexander, Rose and Woodhead (1992) *Curriculum Organisation and Classroom Practice in Primary School – A Discussion Paper*, HMSO
Aubrey, C. (1994) 'Overview of advances in understanding of learning and teaching of subject knowledge' in *The Role of Subject Knowledge in the Early Years of Schooling* (ed. Carol Aubrey), Falmer Press
Calkins, L. (1986) *The Art of Teaching Writing*, Heinemann
Graves, D. (1983) *Writing: Teachers and Children at Work*, Heinemann
McBeath, J. and Turner, M. (1990) *Learning Out of School: Homework Policy and Practice*, Scottish Education Department

KEY TO SYMBOLS

 level of difficulty of the activity

approximate duration of the activity in minutes (a blank clock indicates an untimed activity)

 photocopiable page for classroom use

each child in the group working individually

children working in pairs

 a small group collaborating

whole class or larger group working together

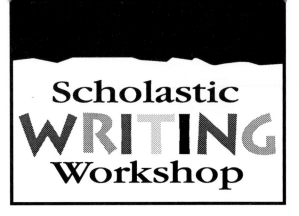

Scholastic
WRITING
Workshop

Chapter Two

ASSESSMENT

ASSESSMENT

If my tennis coach simply watched where my ball went, calling 'Against the net!' or 'Out!' this would not be helpful. If I am going to improve my game, I need help with the process rather than simple evaluations of the products. So my coach watches *how* I play the game, noticing what works and what does not work for me. 'You are stepping away from the ball' he says. 'Try stepping into it.' If we, as writing teachers, watch how our students go about writing, then we can help them develop more effective strategies for writing.
(Lucy Calkins, 1986)

This section should be read in conjunction with the section on assessment in the *Writing Projects* resource book.

The nature of assessment in writing

Assessment in the *Scholastic Writing Workshops* is used to:
- help teachers select appropriate learning activities;
- help children identify their own strengths, weaknesses and progress.

To teach effectively and accurately target the children's needs, teachers must explore and assess the thinking that underpins each child's work. It is not enough simply to identify the ideas, skills and strategies evident in a piece of writing; a teacher needs to know:
- why the child decided to tell it in this way;
- which parts were difficult or easy;
- how the child feels about the story;
- which parts the child thinks are particularly successful or weak.

Progression in writing

Assessment and record-keeping should benefit both children and teachers, helping them to appreciate progress that has been made and decide on the direction of future work.

However, progression in all the aspects of writing is complex. All children will have evolved personal strategies for telling a good story. It is the teacher's job to:
- broaden the range of strategies from which the child draws;
- help the child become more aware of how and when particular strategies are used;
- encourage the child to experiment and take risks in writing.

Progression may be seen in terms of the children's ability or willingness to use a wider range of strategies, in their choice of how and when to use different strategies, or in their increasing awareness of what they (and other writers) do, and how. It is often not the case that one strategy is more difficult than another, or that strategies should be taught in a particular order, but rather that children must learn how and when to use and combine strategies to craft an effective piece of work.

General assessment and record-keeping photocopiable pages

Four types of generic assessment and record-keeping systems are provided for the activities in this book. They are intended to link with, and complement, those in the *Writing Projects* volume.

Class/group notes (pages 16–18)

The class/group notes provide a format for teachers to remind themselves of particular children who stood out during each lesson and why. They are intended as an informal record for the teacher's personal use. Children may stand out for any number of reasons:
- because they found something hard;
- because they found something easy;
- because they said or did something that showed great insight;
- because they produced a piece of work that was surprising;
- because they showed particular enthusiasm or reluctance, sudden understanding or lack of it whilst doing the task.

The format reflects the organisation of the workshop materials into the three aspects of characterisation, setting and structure, and the strategies associated with each. Teachers should copy the relevant sheet(s) and, as the class or group complete activities, simply jot down under the relevant section, the activity number, the date and any general notes on the group/class, plus comments about how specific children coped.

As activities are completed and added to the sheet, the class/group notes provide a running record of the craft aspects and strategies that have been covered. It shows the overall balance of learning activities at a glance, as well as a rough record of how the class in general, and some children in particular, coped with the work. The class/group notes can thus provide a useful basis for planning.

These pages also highlight and help teachers

to analyse general patterns in how the children are coping with the work. They show when particular strategies generate more interest or difficulty than others – something that should be considered when planning future work for the class.

They also allow teachers to spot children who feature very regularly or, just as importantly do not feature at all, in their comments on lessons. If particular names keep cropping up, teachers must consider whether the work is pitched at an appropriate level. Similarly, teachers will want to be sure that if some names never feature this is not because these children find the work too easy, or are being overlooked in a busy classroom. At times, teachers may want to make a decision to focus on specific children who appear to be coping well and finding quiet satisfaction in the work.

There is no photocopiable assessment sheet for the activities covered in the process chapter as process cannot be divorced from context. The extended contexts offered in the *Writing Projects* resource book provide a framework in which to observe and assess the aspects of process highlighted in this chapter.

Pupil's record and evaluation sheet (page 19)

This has been designed to be completed by the children and provides a record of the activities covered by each child, along with a very brief indication of the child's reaction in terms of interest, level of difficulty and level of achievement. It has been designed to be attached to the front of each child's writing jotter or folder so that it can be completed as each activity is finished.

It is useful in highlighting individual patterns of strengths, needs, interests or attitudes, as well as in providing an individual record of work for each child. As a list of work completed, it can provide a basis which children can use to recollect and reflect on their writing over a period of time.

Writing review form (page 20)

This has been designed to provide a format for teachers and/or children to review writing over a period of time, and identify which pieces of work have been particularly successful, either as an effective end product, or as an effective learning experience.

The forms provide a format for children to review all their work – published stories from the *Writing Projects* and the shorter pieces written in response to activities in *Aspects of the Craft of Writing* – and reflect on their progress to date.

This may be particularly useful before a parents' evening or home report.

Overall class record of activities: *Aspects of the Craft of Writing* (pages 21–22)

This record of activities can follow the class as it moves through the school, providing a record of what has been covered in each year. Along with the *Writing Projects* overall class record, it can help teachers find a starting point with a new class and facilitate progression between year groups.

CHARACTERISATION

Strategies

Characterisation through appearance:

Characterisation through action:

Characterisation through speech:

Character study:

Children's book activities

SETTING THE SCENE

Strategies

Straight description:

Emotive description:

Language use:

Children's book activities

STRUCTURE

Strategies

Plot and structure:

Beginnings and endings:

Point of view and dialogue:

Divisions and layout:

Children's book activities

| (NAME) _____ **'S RECORD** |

◆ Fill in the chart for each activity you complete. Use the symbols below –
or make up your own.

Date	Activity	Did I enjoy it?	Was my work good?	Was it easy?

(NAME) _____ **'S WRITING REVIEW**

The best pieces of work I have done are:

These are good because:

These things about my writing have improved:

What I have enjoyed most about writing over this period is:

What I have enjoyed least about writing over this period is:

I would like to do more of the following kind of writing:

Something different I would like to try is:

CLASS RECORD OF ACTIVITIES: ASPECTS OF THE CRAFT OF WRITING

Activities	Y3/P4	Y4/P5	Y5/P6	Y6/P7	Activities	Y3/P4	Y4/P5	Y5/P6	Y6/P7
Characterisation					38. Epilogues...				
1. Guess who?					*Setting the scene*				
2. Identity parade					1. Picture poem				
3. Eye shades					2. Tell me about...				
4. Eyes – windows...					3. View from my window				
5. Fairy-tale appearances					4. The street where I live				
6. Monster mistakes					5. Capture the essence				
7. Gentle giants					6. Preparations				
8. Hidden personalities					7. Fresh eyes...				
9. Handsome is...					8. Through the keyhole				
10. What are they like?					9. The play park				
11. Reluctant arrivals					10. Rooms: cold...				
12. So I said to myself...					11. Music mood writing				
13. Inside out					12. Playground...				
14. Tom and Anne...					13. Miss Rickets...				
15. Secret thoughts					14. A place to play				
16. 'I'll say it *my* way'					15. The sun...				
17. I want ...					16. Who am I?				
18. Don't do that!					17. Similes				
19. Mornings					18. The sea				
20. Schooldays...					19. Trees				
21. Character detective					20. Dangerous waters				
22. Bedrooms					21. The arrivals				
23. Character change					22. Thunderstorm fights				
24. Wanted!					23. Horrible visitors				
25. Ahoy m'hearties					24. Childhood places				
26. Instant impressions					25. Angry world				
27. Writing a character					26. Places I know				
28. Pesky child!					27. Book Corner				
29. Who is this lion?					28. Violent verbs				
30. Fearful movements					29. Danger alert				
31. Character planning					30. Our class				
32. Night-time fears					31. The worst street				
33. His bark is worse...					32. An unexpected turn...				
34. Writing a character...					33. Straight from...				
35. Give a dog...					34. The homecoming				
36. Meeting outside...					35. Snow				
37. Good things come...					36. Dumb animals?				

CLASS RECORD OF ACTIVITIES:
ASPECTS OF THE CRAFT OF WRITING

Activities	Y3/P4	Y4/P5	Y5/P6	Y6/P7	Activities	Y3/P4	Y4/P5	Y5/P6	Y6/P7
Story structure					32. More flipper stories				
1. Going for a dip					33. Lou the footballer...				
2. The end of the holiday					34. Supermarket mayhem				
3. The finding					35. Endings...				
4. A serial story					36. Word detective				
5. The end of the rainbow					37. Happy thoughts				
6. A race against time					38. The dry side...				
7. It's a cracking...					39. Writing trailers				
8. New beginnings					40. Finding the title				
9. Spotlight on...					*The writing process*				
10. A hand...					1. My history as a writer				
11. They all lived happily...					2. Picture a writer...				
12. The end					3. The stories I tell				
13. The lost kitten					4. It's a good story...				
14. Inside a bear's skin					5. That's easy, that's hard!				
15. The voice of the teller					6. Ideas analysis				
16. Perspectives on...					7. Common errors				
17. Stop!					8. The story ideas bank				
18. 'Save my puppy!'					9. My poem's...				
19. A story in the life of...					10. Five line poems				
20. Pause for breath!					11. Only you				
21. A publisher drops...					12. Music poems				
22. How would you say it?					13. Responding to writing				
23. Titles to make...					14. Proof-reading for errors				
24. Favourite titles					15. Find the error				
25. Who said that?					16. How do you feel?				
26. 'STOMP STOMP...'					17. Reading for a friend				
27. 'Billy Goat footsteps...'					18. Perfect writing partner				
28. Layout and lettering					19. Writing partner...				
29. Fairy-tale endings					20. When to talk				
30. Doors into new worlds					21. What I learn from others				
31. Editors in action									

Scholastic WRITING Workshop

Chapter Three

CHARACTERISATION

INTRODUCTION

Why is characterisation important?

Characters are essential to stories. Believable characters underpin the success of stories such as *The Lion, the Witch and the Wardrobe.*They hook the reader's interest and emotions, making the most unbelievable, magical events become real and important. It is the characters that prompt the reader to respond to the story, with admiration, irritation, incredulity or simply by identifying: 'I know someone like that...' or even 'I'm a bit like that...' This reader response is what makes stories emotionally satisfying and worth reading, and characters are central to it. Without characters, stories become lists of events, devoid of human interest.

Characters in real life

In real life, we notice myriad things about the characters we meet. First impressions based on what people look like and how they dress often give us basic information about them. What people say and what they do in particular situations, however, is more powerful evidence of their character, and this often overrides our first judgement.

Children need to be helped to become more observant of people, and more aware of how they draw conclusions about them. The observations may provide 'raw material' for stories, but the heightened awareness and self-knowledge that comes from analysing how and why they draw conclusions about others will develop their understanding, change their thinking and raise the quality of all their work.

Teaching characterisation

Children know from their reading that characters are important to stories. They often have a strong sense of character stereotypes and know that characters may develop as the story unfolds.

Children can be helped in three main areas:
• creating characters that are rounded and consistent;
• handling character development and change in a story;
• developing techniques for conveying characterisation within the story.

All these need to be tackled in the context of children creating and writing their own stories, but single lesson activities can raise their awareness of characterisation and of some useful techniques and strategies writers use.

Sometimes, particularly when children are very involved with the events in the story they are writing, they take the reader's knowledge of the characters for granted. Such stories faithfully relate what happens, but fail to capture the reader's emotions. They read like reports.

Often, teachers *react* to poor characterisation in children's stories, rather than taking active steps to help children develop characters and reveal them though the story. When characterisation is only discussed *after* the story has been written, the discussion tends to result in details (usually physical descriptions) being inserted without too much structural change to what has been written. Children need help with characterisation from the outset, when they are creating the characters and deciding what will happen and what they will do and say. When this happens, children begin to use characterisation to move the story forward, rather than as an additional layer to it. The desire to portray the character accurately inspires the storyline and drives the writing process.

Inventing and developing characters

Character consistency and character change can be a difficult area for children. Often, when children begin writing stories without having considered their main characters in sufficient detail, the character undergoes rapid, unexplained changes in the middle of the story. Children should know that writers get new ideas and insights into their characters as the story unfolds, but also that they need *some* clear ideas at the start about what the character looks like and how the character talks, behaves and lives. It is paradoxical that successful writers begin with clear ideas, yet change and develop them as the story and characters emerge. Children need to reflect on stories they have read to appreciate how, although characters may grow and develop, changes must be explained, either by events in the story, or by reference to events outside the story.

In talking to children about their characters, teachers should be wary of focusing attention too quickly on the details that will feature in the story itself. Initially, children need to think about their main characters in fairly broad terms. This helps the child to decide how a character may behave at different points in the story and how to show this to the reader.

However, children with more experience of stories know that physical descriptions can be used in more sophisticated ways. The writer can lure the reader into making judgements about a character and then show that these are quite wrong – the beast in *Beauty and the Beast* or Bilbo and Frodo Baggins in *The Hobbit*, for example. The activities in this section target using appearance to indicate character and also using appearance to surprise the reader.

CONTENTS AND ORGANISATION

Children need to be aware of and encouraged to use a variety of strategies to convey characterisation. Activities to target four common strategies are detailed in this chapter:
• characterisation through physical descriptions – making and breaking stereotypes;
• characterisation through actions;
• characterisation through speech and dialogue;
• characterisation through portraying lifestyles, friends and environments.

Physical description/appearance is not everything

Writers often use physical descriptions to show what a character is like; the Troll in the *Three Billy Goats Gruff*, or Cinderella and the Ugly Sisters are all given features that match their characters. Even very young children can list typical physical attributes of various characters.

Actions speak louder than words

In life, the strongest evidence of what people are like comes from what they do and say. Children need to be encouraged to use this in their writing. Thus, instead of saying 'Snow White's stepmother was cruel', the writer should describe a situation in which she shows her cruelty. This engages the readers' emotions and involves them in actively making judgements about the character.

The use of speech and dialogue

In life, our impressions of people are influenced by what they say, how they express it and how they speak. Activities here help children to consider how they might use speech and dialogue to develop and portray characters. Writers can also choose to allow the reader to hear what the character says to herself, thus indicating what she *really* thinks or feels. This mechanism is open *only* to writers. In real life, we can only guess at someone's real emotions or motives and writers of plays and films have to use special strategies that interrupt the action of the story. Only story writers can use thoughts as action, as a way of moving the story on.

Character studies

Children need to learn how to use character studies as part of the planning process for a story. Some children imagine more then they could ever write about their characters and need to clarify what is important for the reader to know. Others think about their characters only in superficial ways and need to create more rounded characters. Writing notes, or completing quick character studies, draws attention to the importance of characterisation in stories and helps children to decide what is important so that they can draw and describe their characters with care.

Lifestyles, friends and hobbies

The environments that people create for themselves provide important clues to their personality. Friends are a major influence and can help to explain why we are as we are. Often writers can use friends, hobbies or environments to draw attention to particular character traits.

The children' books

The three children's books chosen as excellent models of characterisation are *The Man Whose Mother Was a Pirate* by Margaret Mahy, *A Lion at Bedtime* by Debi Gliori and *The Guard Dog* by Dick King-Smith.

The Man Whose Mother Was a Pirate is a warm, funny story which hinges on the contrast between Sam, a small, thin, restrained accountant, and his mother, a large, colourful ex-pirate. The characters are keenly observed – there is a bit of Sam and his mother in each of us – and are drawn with wit and skill.

Debi Gliori's *A Lion at Bedtime* tells the story of Ben, a young boy whose night-time fears are personified as a lion. The characterisation of both Ben and his lion is warm and affectionate, quietly capturing a variety of perceptions, to make a story that is witty and comforting.

The third book, Dick King-Smith's *The Guard Dog*, is the story of a tiny dog who is perceived by other characters in the book as a toy pet but who recognises its own talent for being a fierce guard-dog. The children may find it interesting to listen to the interview with Dick King-Smith on the audio cassette, where he talks about his work and reads from the book.

Helping children with characterisation

Teachers can help children develop their understanding of characterisation by:
• making them aware of how character judgements are made in real life and in stories;

• encouraging children to read stories in an informed and analytical way;
• encouraging children to talk and speculate about their characters; what they would do and say, their choice of friends and how they would live, not just focusing on physical appearance;
• discussing the need for the reader to make judgements about characters; the writer should provide evidence rather than make assertions.

The following are some important points for teachers to recognise:
• Often children do need to think in more detail and breadth about their main characters, but should not be encouraged to build a visual image at the expense of all else.
• Discussion needs to focus both on what the characters are like, and on how this can be shown in the story.
• Informal talk about people well known to everyone in the class can help build awareness of character. Children begin to view life with the eye of a writer, seeing stories in everyday incidents and characters.

Activity	Teaching Content	Star rating	Group size	Photo copiable
PHYSICAL APPEARANCE/DESCRIPTION IS NOT EVERYTHING				
1 Guess who?	Developing descriptive vocabulary	∗	1⇨2	✓
2 Identity parade	Detailed observation and physical description	∗∗	1	A
3 Eye shades	Eyes can distinguish characters; writing similes	∗	W⇨1	✓
4 Eyes – windows on to the soul	Close description	∗∗	W⇨1	✓+A
5 Fairy-tale appearances	Using appearance to indicate character; introducing stereotyping	∗∗	1⇨2	✓+A
6 Monster mistakes	Using art to create a character; physical appearance does not always reflect character	∗∗	1	✓
7 Gentle giants	Using appearance to build reader expectations of character	∗∗	2	✓
ACTIONS SPEAK LOUDER THAN WORDS				
8 Hidden personalities	Revealing personality through what others say about a character and what the character does	∗∗	2	✓
9 Handsome is as handsome does	Appearance rarely provides an accurate indication of character; writers often indicate personality through what a character does and says	∗∗	W⇨1	
10 What are they like?	Characterisation through actions and thoughts	∗∗	2⇨4	A
11 Reluctant arrivals	Body language can indicate a character's attitudes	∗	W⇨2⇨1	✓
12 So I said to myself...	Using stream of consciousness to indicate character	∗	W⇨1	A
13 Inside out	Body posture and movements can reveal inner feelings	∗∗	W⇨1	✓+A
14 Tom and Anne go swimming	Body language indicates feelings; writing thoughts to indicate feelings	∗∗∗	2⇨1	✓
15 Secret thoughts	People often behave differently from how they really feel	∗∗	W⇨1	
SPEECH AND DIALOGUE				
16 'I'll say it *my* way'	Characterisation through speech; people's speech is influenced by circumstances	∗∗	W⇨1⇨2	✓+A
17 I want ...	Developing awareness of the choices people make when speaking	∗∗	2⇨1	✓
18 Don't do that!	The same character may use different language and tone depending on their mood	∗∗	W⇨2	✓
19 Mornings	Characterisation through what characters say out loud and what they say to themselves	∗	W⇨1	
CHARACTER STUDY				
20 Schooldays remembered	Writing a character study	∗∗	1	
21 Character detective	Basing characters on people you know	∗∗∗	2⇨1	✓✓+A
THE MAN WHOSE MOTHER WAS A PIRATE				
22 Bedrooms	The environments people create can indicate character and vice versa	∗	4⇨1	A
23 Character change	Characters can change during a story	∗	W⇨1⇨4	✓
24 Wanted!	Characters can change as the story unfolds; changes can be shown in different ways	∗∗	W⇨2	✓
25 Ahoy m'hearties	Identifying styles of speech	∗∗	W⇨4	✓
26 Instant impressions	Creating a character sketch	∗∗	4⇨1	
27 Writing a character	Writers reveal character through various means	∗∗∗	4⇨2	
A LION AT BEDTIME				
28 Pesky child!	Characterisation through what others say	∗	W⇨1	
29 Who is this lion?	Characterisation through action and description	∗∗	2⇨4	✓
30 Fearful movements	Characterisation through action and movement	∗	W⇨2⇨1	✓
31 Character planning	Analysing a character; structuring a character study	∗∗	2⇨1	✓
32 Night-time fears	The things that make us afraid make us different	∗∗	4⇨1	
THE GUARD DOG				
33 His bark is worse than his bite	Using comparisons to describe sound	∗	W⇨1	
34 Writing a character study	Characterisation through action and speech	∗∗	1	
35 Give a dog a bad name	Proper names may establish character	∗	4	
36 Meeting outside the dogs' home	Speech reflects character	∗∗	W⇨1	✓
37 Good things come in small packages	A character's most important qualities lie beneath the surface	∗	1	✓
38 Epilogues and happy endings	Characters behaving consistently; writing an epilogue	∗∗	W⇨4⇨1	✓

A = anthology page
W = whole group

GUESS WHO?

Teaching content
Developing descriptive vocabulary.

What you need
Photocopiable page 50, writing materials, self-adhesive labels (such as Post-it notes).

What to do
Explain to the children that when describing a person there are certain outstanding features that must be detailed. Tell them that they are going to describe the physical appearance of a fairy-tale character so well that their partner will be able to guess who the character is.

First each child must decide, in secret, upon a fairy-tale character to describe. Then ask the children to look at photocopiable page 50 to select the main features that should be described to help a reader picture their character. Tell them to underline the words that would be most helpful in writing a description of their chosen character. The underlined vocabulary can now be used as the basis of sentences, to produce a paragraph of descriptive writing.

Character descriptions should be swapped and partners allowed to guess the fairy-tale identities. Display writing under the heading 'Guess who?' and let children or visitors stick their guesses on to the work using self-adhesive labels.

Development/homework task
• Children could use the same techniques to practise writing descriptions of well-known television characters.
• Pictures of people may be cut out of magazines, described and made into an interactive wall display, challenging people to link written descriptions to pictures.

IDENTITY PARADE

Teaching content
Detailed observation and physical description.

What you need
A photograph for each child of an adult family member who would not be recognised by others in the class, photocopiable anthology page 202, chalkboard, photocopiable page 50 (optional), writing materials.

What to do
Ask the children to bring in to school a photograph of an adult family member who would not be recognised by others in the class. They must keep the photograph carefully hidden as this is the first part of a class competition.

Give each child a copy of photocopiable anthology page 202 and read through the descriptions with them. Together list the details that are used to describe each character.

Now, ask the children to study their photograph closely and to write a description of the person shown in as much detail as possible, without describing the setting. The person will be well known to the child and this makes it even more important to scrutinise the photograph carefully. The better we know someone the less attention we tend to pay to the details of their physical features.

To help them focus their ideas before writing, brainstorm possible aspects for description and ways of describing them. Write these on the board as prompts. For example, *eyes*: deep-set, heavy-lidded, round...; *nose*: button, straight, freckled, and so on. (Photocopiable page 50 provides some useful vocabulary for this.)

Finished pieces of writing should be shuffled and then distributed around the class to be copied in another child's handwriting. Display and number each photograph. Display and letter each piece of writing. If there are more than 26 children in the class, use A1, B1, C1 and so on.

Over the course of a week, give the children time to study and match the descriptions to the photographs. Allow them to work in pairs if they wish and encourage them to use a sheet like the one illustrated to record their decisions.

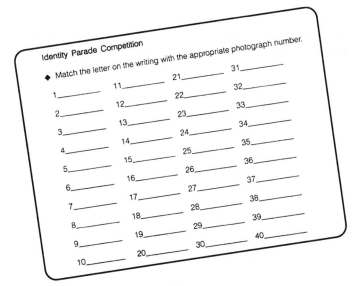

Identity Parade Competition
◆ Match the letter on the writing with the appropriate photograph number.

1____ 11____ 21____ 31____
2____ 12____ 22____ 32____
3____ 13____ 23____ 33____
4____ 14____ 24____ 34____
5____ 15____ 25____ 35____
6____ 16____ 26____ 36____
7____ 17____ 27____ 37____
8____ 18____ 28____ 38____
9____ 19____ 29____ 39____
10____ 20____ 30____ 40____

At the end of the week, the truth should be revealed. The child or pair who has correctly matched the most descriptions to photographs should receive the 'best reader' award/prize. The child with the most clearly detailed piece of writing should receive the 'best writer' award.

3

EYE SHADES

Teaching content
- Eyes can often distinguish characters.
- Writing similes.

What you need
Writing materials, chalkboard, mirrors, photocopiable page 51 (optional).

What to do
Eyes are one of the main features that distinguish us individually from one another. We automatically look into a person's eyes when we talk with them and often communicate merely by looking into eyes. Eyes move, can be filled with expression and contain a tremendous variety of colours.

Write the following list on the board and ask the children for ideas to finish off the comparisons, trying to think of something that is coloured exactly like the relevant shade of eye. If you wish, pick out examples from photocopiable page 51 to read to the children.
- Eyes as grey as...
- Eyes as brown as...
- Eyes as blue as...
- Eyes as black as...

- Eyes as green as...
- Eyes a mixture of yellow and brown
  Yellow like...
  Brown like...
- Eyes a mixture of black and blue
  Black like...
  Blue like...

Explain that writers use comparisons like these to help create an image in the reader's mind. If appropriate, tell the children that comparisons like these that use 'like' or 'as' are called similes.

Now ask the children to gaze closely into a mirror and to find the colour or colours in their own eyes. Ask them to write a list poem with a new simile on each line, attempting to capture the exact colours in their eyes through a variety of images.

Read out this poem by Ambreen Haindar (11 years) to illustrate what is required:

My eyes are dark brown
Brown as mud with the rain glistening and running through
Brown as the bare tree branches in winter
Brown as the outside walls of our garden shed
And dappled with black
Black as the wing of a raven
Black as Whitby jet.

Development/homework task
Play the Hansel and Gretel similes game with the children. Sit them in a circle and tell them to think about the witch in *Hansel and Gretel*. They are to find similes to describe each of her physical features in turn. Start them off with the phrase 'her eyes are as black as...' or 'her nails are as sharp as...' and ask each child to suggest a comparison to complete the phrase. Explain that if they cannot think of anything to contribute they should say 'pass'.

EYES – WINDOWS ON TO THE SOUL

Teaching content
Close description.

What you need
Photocopiable anthology page 203, writing materials, photocopiable page 51.

What to do
Often, people's eyes indicate their feelings, emotions and thoughts. To hide their true feelings on a subject, people may turn away or close their eyes. Menacing gangsters wear sunglasses to unsettle others and hide their thoughts and intentions. Read the extract from *Danny The Champion of the World* on photocopiable anthology page 203. Can the children think of other people who smile with their eyes as well as their mouth? Take some suggestions from the class and ask the children to look out for this, or for the converse – people who only smile with their mouths.

Writers say that eyes can be cold, warm, piercing, gentle, kind, merry, sparkling, laughing, dangerous or cruel. Photocopiable page 51 shows how descriptions of eyes are used not only to indicate appearance, but also to reflect infinite moods and personality.

Discuss the sort of person whose eyes could be described as cold, or warm. Can the children think of situations in which their own eyes could have been described in this way?

Often writers use comparisons to aid descriptions. Give examples from the photocopiable sheet (eg. 'eyes...like a cold fire', 'death-cold eyes', 'piggy eyes'). Ask them each to think of three comparisons using 'like' or 'as' to describe warm and cold eyes. Share these as a class and praise original ideas. Now, ask the children to imagine a situation in which they enter a room. The room could be full of friends invited for a surprise party, or a smugglers' den in which the child is an unwelcome intruder. The expression in the eyes of the occupants will be the focus of the writing.

Ask each child to choose a situation and to decide *the manner* in which the room was entered (did they walk in, fall in, creep in, bound in, were they pushed in?). Ask them each to begin a paragraph of writing with the words: 'The door swung open. I _____ in. They turned towards me. It was the eyes I noticed...' The rest of the paragraph should describe the eyes. Children could use some of the warm/cold similes discussed earlier and they may also find the ideas on photocopiable page 51 helpful.

Development/homework task
Ask the children to take this as the opening of a story and to write what happens next.

FAIRY-TALE APPEARANCES

Teaching content
• In some stories, such as fairy stories, appearance is used to indicate character.
• How stereotyping influences reader expectations of character.

What you need
Photocopiable page 52, writing and art materials, large sheets of paper, photocopiable anthology page 204.

What to do
Brainstorm with the class all the fairy stories they know. Include traditional and modern fairy stories and fairy stories from other cultures.

Give each child a copy of photocopiable page 52. Let them have about 10 minutes to cut out and sort the statements into three sets:
• Set 1: statements that generally apply to bad characters;
• Set 2: statements that generally apply to good characters;
• Set 3: statements that could apply to either.

Arrange the children in pairs to compare their decisions. Explain that there are no right or wrong answers: where individuals have classified statements differently, they should each explain why they made these decisions. Individuals may decide to change statements around as a result of this discussion, or may agree to differ.

Discuss the idea of stereotype and how this is used, particularly in fairy stories, to influence the reader's expectations of the characters. For instance, if the author describes a young, modestly-dressed, pretty girl, we expect her to be virtuous, honest, possibly a little naive and eventually to marry a handsome young man, preferably a prince.

Now ask the pairs to make a poster stating, and illustrating if appropriate, either the typical physical attributes of the good characters, or those of the bad characters in fairy tales. A smaller subheading should be added saying '*But this isn't always true...*' Here, the children can list characters whose appearance does *not* indicate their inner qualities.

Development/homework task

Explain that some modern stories give traditional tales an added twist by changing the appearance or personality of the main character. Give each child a copy of photocopiable anthology page 204 to illustrate this. Can the children think of any other examples? They may mention books such as *The Paper Bag Princess* by Robert Munsch or *Revolting Rhymes* by Roald Dahl. Which character would the children most like to change? Which aspect of the character's appearance or personality would they alter?

6

MONSTER MISTAKES
** † 50

Teaching content

• Using art to help create and describe a character.
• Physical appearance does not always reflect character.

What you need

Art materials (paint or collage), A3 paper, chalkboard, writing materials, photocopiable page 53, scissors, glue.

What to do

Many author/illustrators create their characters initially through art before they develop them through the written word. Ask the children to use paint or collage materials to create a frightening monster, at least A3 size.

Then ask them to imagine how someone would feel on meeting this terrifying monster. Write the following sentences on the board and give the children a few minutes to copy them down and complete them:

• The thing I immediately noticed was...
• Then I saw...
• When I looked closely...
• The monster moved like/by...
• When it saw me its expression changed to...

Now, give each child a copy of photocopiable page 53. Ask them to imagine that they are the monster and to complete the first half of the sheet. Tell them to cut this out and stick the words as a speech bubble coming from the monster's mouth.

Discuss the possibility that many characters in fiction look frightening or ugly, but are really kind and gentle, such as the Beast in *Beauty and the Beast* or the Giant at the end of Oscar Wilde's story *The Selfish Giant*. Suppose that everyone is wrong about these monsters and they are really honourable and good.

Ask the children to cut heart-shaped doors in the bodies of their monster characters, being careful to leave a reasonable joined part to fold back. Now, ask them to fill in the second part of photocopiable page 53 and to stick these behind the heart-shaped openings so that the words show through when the door is opened.

Display the monsters at a level where adults and children can open the doors to read the truth about these much maligned creatures.

Development/homework task

What sort of stories could arise from this situation, where the monster's appearance belies its true character? The following questions will help the children to plan and structure a story:
• Where does the monster live?
• How does he come into contact with the people who hold these views about him?
• What happens and what does the monster do to change their views?
• What happens in the end?

GENTLE GIANTS

＊＊ ▯ 👥 ⏱60

Teaching content

Using appearance to build reader expectations of a character.

What you need

Writing materials, photocopiable page 54.

What to do

Put the children into pairs and ask them to think of the ugliest giant they can imagine and to jot down 6–10 sentences or notes to describe what their giant would probably look like. Tell them to form these into a short paragraph of straight description.

Now, explain that writers sometimes build up expectations of a character and then shock the reader by showing that appearances can be deceptive. For example, the beast in *Beauty and the Beast* is kind and the beautiful queen in *The Snow Queen* is evil.

Ask the children to imagine that they have to visit this giant. Give each pair a copy of photocopiable page 54 and ask them to brainstorm ideas which show that their ugly giant is something quite different. Stress that each idea should be totally separate. Filling in this sheet will provide plenty of different options for how the character might surprise the reader and offer several choices for how the story may progress. When they have finished, ask some pairs to read their best ideas to the class.

Development/homework task

• The children can develop a story by linking their opening description to the passage at the top of the photocopiable page. Tell them to use the idea they like best from the photocopiable sheet as the turning point in the story and describe what happens next. This could be a short or extended piece of writing.

• The same idea can be applied to an apparently harmless character, who turns out to be much more menacing than he or she first appears. For example, children could describe an archetypal sweet old lady. After writing a short physical description, the children could use the same prompts from photocopiable page 54 to brainstorm ideas to show that this character is not all she seems.

HIDDEN PERSONALITIES

＊＊ ▯ 👥 ⏱30

Teaching content

Personality can be shown through what others say about a character and through what the character does.

What you need

Photocopiable page 55, magazines, scissors, glue, writing materials.

What to do

Put the children into pairs and let them look through some old magazines. Ask each pair to cut out a head and shoulders picture of *one* person they find interesting to look at. Use the first part of photocopiable page 55 to get the children to think about this character in more detail. The children should discuss and complete the first part of the sheet in their pairs.

Explain to the children that this character has a hidden vice or virtue, either some unpleasant personality trait (perhaps he is vain, spiteful, greedy, jealous, disloyal or a cheat) or a pleasant trait (perhaps he is generous, loyal, honest or brave). Ask the children to agree on their charcter's secret vice or virtue, and to record this in very small writing on the back of the photocopiable sheet.

Now, ask the children to describe *one* incident that happens that shows the character's hidden trait. Emphasise that it doesn't have to be a major incident and that it doesn't necessarily need to involve anyone else – it could be a situation in which the character is alone. The vice or virtue remains hidden to the outside world, but is demonstrated all too vividly to the reader.

9
HANDSOME IS AS HANDSOME DOES

Teaching content

• Appearance rarely provides an accurate indication of character.
• Writers often indicate personality through what a character does and says.

What you need
Chalkboard, writing materials.

What to do
In life, appearance does not always reflect what a person is like inside. 'Handsome is as handsome does' is an expression often used to warn people to be more impressed by what others do, rather than what they look like.

Show the children the following story opening written on the chalkboard:

Pete Brown strode along the High Street with a cheery grin on his handsome face. People passing by couldn't help but smile in return at seeing someone so obviously happy on this sunny morning. Pete ran his hand through his thick, shiny hair as he turned swiftly down Cottage Lane...

Explain that, up to this point, we know what Pete Brown looks like, but not what sort of person he is. The writer can indicate this by showing what Pete Brown does next. Read the following extract to the children:

'Can I help with that shopping?' he asked old Mrs Smith. As he lifted the bag, he noticed some of the items inside – small quantities of the cheapest quality foods. He made a mental note to drop off some strawberries from the garden for the old lady. 'I've just repaired an old shopping trolley, Mrs Smith. I dunno what to do with it. Could you make any use of it?' he asked.

Pete Brown, in this case, is obviously a thoroughly good and upright citizen – every mother's dream son!

Now, ask the children to write a different ending to the Pete Brown description, one that shows him to be a nasty, mean character. Ask the children to consider the following questions:
• What may such a character have done, or be going to do, to make him so happy?
• What might Pete Brown be thinking as he walks down Cottage Lane?
• What could Pete Brown do that indicates his meanness?

Development/homework task
Ask the children to write actions that would indicate a shy, self-centred or tactless person.

10
WHAT ARE THEY LIKE?

Teaching content
Describing a character through actions and thoughts rather than appearance.

What you need
Photocopiable anthology page 205, writing materials, chalkboard.

What to do
Give each pair a copy of photocopiable anthology page 205 and read the descriptions with the children. Point out that none of these descriptions actually states what the character looks like, but that when we read them we instantly start to imagine a particular person.

On a separate piece of paper, ask the children to write each of the characters' names as four different headings and to draw or write brief notes to show what they imagine each character would look like. Some children may find it useful to have prompts on the board such as:

- hair: colour, style...
- face: nose, eyes, chin...
- height
- build
- clothes
- age

Let the children share their answers, either in a class discussion or in groups of four.

Development/homework task

Ask the children to choose someone they know well and to write a short description of what sort of person they are, without saying what they look like.

RELUCTANT ARRIVALS

Teaching content

Body language can indicate attitudes.

What you need

Photocopiable page 56, writing materials.

What to do

We all have places that we don't like to visit. Make a list of these with the children. Discuss with the children how, when they go to those places, the way they move and hold their bodies can show how they are feeling. Photocopiable page 56 contains phrases to describe expressions, body posture and movement. Ask the children to work in pairs to sort these words and phrases and write them into the appropriate columns.

Now, ask the children to think of a place they hate to visit and to write a short description of going to this place. How do they walk? How do they hold their bodies? The vocabulary on the photocopiable sheet may help them. Some children may like to use a starter sentence, such as: 'As I left the house my shoulders were...'

Display the work along with charcoal drawings of the hunched unhappy figures.

Development/ homework task

This idea can also be applied to a happy journey.

SO I SAID TO MYSELF...

Teaching content

How to use a 'stream of consciousness' to indicate character.

What you need

Photocopiable anthology page 206, writing materials.

What to do

Explain that writers often use the things people say to themselves to indicate how a character feels. Such thoughts are often written as a list of, sometimes disjointed, phrases, words and sentences connected by sets of dots, or ellipses (...). This is called a 'stream of consciousness' and provides the reader with a window into the character's mind. For example, someone walking into the sea for a swim may be thinking:

'...this is going to be far too cold ... no, I can't bear it ... but the others will think I'm a coward ... my feet are numb already ... Jo Brown is in already, showing off splashing around ... I'll have to do it ... Arrgh...'

This person may be putting on a wonderful show of thoroughly enjoying the sea. Only the reader knows how she really feels.

Give each child a copy of photocopiable anthology page 206 which contains an extract from Anne Fine's *A Pack of Liars*, where the author uses both stream of consciousness and characters' actions to convey how the children feel and to move the story along. Ask the children to underline the sections that show what the characters are saying to themselves.

Now, ask the children to imagine themselves in one of the following scenarios and to write a suitable stream of consciousness for it. Depending on the experience, age or ability of the children, you may need to model an example on the board.

(a) You know that the teacher has discovered that you have copied your homework from someone else and you are on your way to school to face the music. What are you saying to yourself?

(b) You have foolishly told your friends in your new school that you can swim, but you can't. Now you have to go swimming with your class and soon all will be revealed. You are on your way to school. What are you saying to yourself?

(c) You are alone and see the neighbourhood bully standing in the distance with his friends. You will have to pass them. What are you saying to yourself?

(d) The puppy you have always longed for is waiting for you at home. This is your eagerly-awaited birthday present. You are rushing home from school. What are you saying to yourself?

(e) You are setting off for the holiday of a lifetime. What are you saying to yourself?

Development/homework task

This type of exercise should be repeated frequently. Children enjoy being released from more formal structures of language and they can produce insightful work connected with personal experiences of events such as 'buying new shoes', 'waking on a stormy night' or 'going to meet someone special'.

INSIDE OUT

Teaching content

Body posture and movements can show how we are feeling inside.

What you need

Photocopiable anthology page 207, photocopiable page 57, writing materials.

What to do

Give each child a copy of photocopiable anthology page 207 and read the poem 'Dumb insolence' with them. Discuss with the children the way in which our body posture and movements reflect how we are feeling. How might the person in the poem look? Ask the

children to describe some situations in which people are angry or joyful and how they might show this physically.

Now, ask the children to read the extract on photocopiable page 57. This is a child's stream of consciousness, showing the character's internal thoughts. Ask the children to jot down some answers to the questions on the photocopiable page.

Tell the children to write a paragraph describing how this character looks and moves. The character can be male or female as the writer wishes. Some children may find this opening sentence useful: 'He/She slammed the door and stormed towards the front gate...'

TOM AND ANNE GO SWIMMING

Teaching content
• Body language indicates feelings.
• Writing a character's thoughts to indicate feelings.

What you need
Photocopiable page 58, writing materials.

What to do
Read the extracts on photocopiable page 58 with the children and ask them to identify the attitudes towards swimming held by Tom and Anne. Point out that the writer has not stated explicitly what the difference in attitude is, and yet we can tell quite clearly how the two characters feel.

Arrange the children in pairs and give them a few minutes to underline those words that indicate how the characters feel. If appropriate, use the correct grammatical terminology, but take care not to turn the lesson into a session on adjectives and adverbs. Discuss with the class the other ways in which the writer has shown the swimmers' feelings.

Now ask each pair to write down some of the things that Tom or Anne might say to themselves as they walk along. They should write the thoughts in short phrases and try to find about four thoughts for each child.

Now ask the children to work individually to write a longer stream of consciousness for

either Anne or Tom. Explain that a stream of consciousness consists of several short phrases joined together, representing the internal thought processes of an individual character. The phrases can be disjointed or half-formed, and this is often shown by sets of dots or ellipses (...). The children may choose to use some, or all, of the thoughts from their joint brainstorm.

Development/homework task
The stream of consciousness can be added to the opening descriptions of Anne or Tom to form the first two paragraphs of a swimming story. Perhaps the story could be about Anne's success in the swimming gala or Tom's first swimming stroke.

SECRET THOUGHTS

Teaching content
People often behave differently from how they feel inside.

What you need
Chalkboard, writing materials, a thesaurus.

What to do

> Whenever I feel afraid,
> I hold my head erect
> And whistle a happy tune
> So no one will suspect
> I'm afraid.
> (from *The King and I* by
> Rogers and Hammerstein)

For different reasons, people sometimes put on acts to hide their true feelings. Writers may need to show characters behaving differently from how they truly feel.

Ask the children to give examples of times when they've done this or seen others do it. Try to steer away from the 'frightened appearing brave' scenario. Seek other examples, such as:
• pretending to be pleased when they are fed-up (at the end of a game they've lost?)
• acting gently or kindly when they don't feel it (when a young child has broken something important or scribbled on a favourite book?)

• being polite (to an unwelcome visitor? in order not to hurt someone's feelings?)
• acting the innocent (when they know more then they pretend?)

Ask the children to choose one occasion when they have pretended to be one sort of person on the outside, while feeling differently inside. The following list written on the chalkboard may help them to identify the emotions they feigned:

COURAGE   BRAVERY   PLEASURE
CONCERN   UNCONCERN   INNOCENCE
IGNORANCE FEAR   ENJOYMENT
RELAXATION CONFIDENCE ANGER

Now, ask them to describe what they did to hide their true feelings. The questions below will help them to focus on and describe exactly how they acted.
• What exactly did you do to indicate these feelings?
• What did you say to yourself? for others to hear? (and how did you speak?)
• Did you make any other noise? (singing? whistling?)
• Describe your outward facial expression, posture, movement.
• What did you do with your hands?

Now tell the children to complete the sentence: 'Inside, I was feeling...' Ask them to write a list of everything they said to themselves that reflected these true feelings. They should use a thesaurus for this, if necessary.

This work can be displayed effectively on a figure outline with the outward appearance described on one side and the private thoughts on the other.

16
'I'LL SAY IT MY WAY'

Teaching content
• Writers often create characterisation through speech and dialect.
• The way people speak and what they say is influenced by who they are, where they are and to whom they are talking.

What you need
Photocopiable anthology page 208, photocopiable page 59, writing materials.

What to do
Begin by giving each child a copy of photocopiable anthology page 208 and asking them to read (or reading with them) the extract from *The Battle for Badger's Wood* by Frederick Covins. Discuss how the author manages to convey the personality of each animal by reporting what they say and how they say it.

Give each child a copy of photocopiable page 59 and tell them to look at the character pictures and to read through the speech bubbles. Ask them to draw a line joining each character with what they would be most likely to say.

Now ask the children to join with a partner to look at the second half of the photocopiable page. Explain that, here, they should consider the different ways people speak and how this is influenced by where they are, whom they are speaking to and who may overhear them.

Ask the children to complete the photocopiable sheet and then, on a separate sheet of paper, to design their own situations in which people express similar sentiments in very different ways.

Development/homework task
This can make a good starting point for a drama lesson.

I WANT...

Teaching content

Developing awareness of the choices people make when speaking.

What you need

Chalkboard, photocopiable page 60, writing materials.

What to do

Divide the children into pairs. Ask them to imagine a young child who badly wants an ice-cream. The child may raise the subject and ask the parent for the ice-cream in a fairly oblique way at first: 'Those ice-creams look nice.' She will undoubtedly be very polite. Give the pairs a few minutes to discuss exactly what the child might say before recording suggestions on the board.

Now, tell the children to suppose that this gentle approach fails to work. Ask each pair to discuss how the child might ask again in a way that is more insistent and applies more pressure to the parent. As before, give the pairs a few minutes to discuss their ideas and then record suggestions on the board.

Finally, tell the children to imagine that this request also fails. How is the child's anger or frustration reflected in her final attempt to get an ice-cream? What does the child say, and how does she say it?

Now, give each child a copy of photocopiable page 60. They should choose one of the scenarios described at the top of the page and write down what a child might say on the first, second and then third attempt at asking.

Development/homework task

Ask the children to apply this same idea to an adult asking a child to do something several times. The child need not be themselves and the adult may be a parent, teacher or neighbour.

DON'T DO THAT!

Teaching content

The same character may use different language and a different tone, depending on their mood.

What you need

Photocopiable page 61, drawing and writing materials.

What to do

It is interesting to observe the very different ways in which people respond to exactly the same situation, depending on the mood they are in. Remind the children how they will wait until a parent is in a 'good mood' before asking for special favours.

Ask the children for examples of how their responses depend on their mood and point out

that people use different language as well as a different tone. In pairs, ask the children to consider photocopiable page 61 and to write what the mother would say in each situation.

Development/homework task
Ask the children each to imagine a situation at home in which an adult responds to the same event in a totally different way because of the 'mood' he is in. Ask them to produce a sheet similar to the completed photocopiable sheet to illustrate their imaginary situation.

MORNINGS

Teaching content
• What characters say aloud in a particular situation reveals their personality and mood.
• What characters say to themselves also shows what they are like.

What you need
Writing materials.

What to do
Ask the children to think about what happens in their households when they get up in the morning. Give them two minutes to list all the family members they see (including pets) in the morning before school.

Then, ask each child to list four or five things they say to other people as they get up. They can use their family list as a memory jogger. Can they remember the first thing they said to their mum this morning, for example? Stress that the children must write the *exact* words they say, rather than generally expressing the sentiments but in a summarised (or sanitised!) form. Remind them that what they say and how they speak will depend on who they are speaking to.

Next, ask the children to write a list of four or five things they say to themselves between waking up and leaving the house.

Ask individuals to read out some of their statements from either list and stress how easy it is to imagine them saying it.

Now ask the children to consider both lists and to choose five statements that best reflect how they think and speak at that time in the morning and to organise these into a list poem.

Development/homework task
Use the same structure for children to write poems about going out to play, arriving at school or going to bed at night.

SCHOOLDAYS REMEMBERED

Teaching content
Writing a character study.

What you need
Writing materials, chalkboard.

What to do
One good way to teach children how to observe others and to write and use character studies, is to ask them to write profiles of themselves and others they know well. Tell the children to use the questions listed below to generate a character profile of themselves. Show them how to string their answers together and to present the information as a character study from which it is relatively easy to draw conclusions.

Now ask the children if they have ever wondered what their parents were like at the age of eight. The children can use the same set of questions to find out what sort of character their mother or father was at school. They can write this up as a character study, including any further information they can find. Perhaps family photograph albums or grandparents could be consulted for additional details.

Ask the children to think about the information generated by this activity. Can they find ways in which they are similar to, or different from, their parent? If, by some trick of time, their parent joined their class, with whom would they be friendly? Why? What would the teacher think of them? What would the other children think and say about them?

Questions
• **Describe your physical appearance at the age of seven or eight.**
• **Describe your school clothes, and how they look on you.**
• **What do you enjoy or hate playing, and why?**
• **Which subject do you most like and which do you hate, and why?**
• **What do the teachers say about you?**
• **What do the other children say about you?**

CHARACTER DETECTIVE

Teaching content
Characters can be based on people you know.

What you need
Photocopiable anthology page 202, chalkboard, writing materials, photocopiable pages 62 and 63.

What to do
Give each pair of children a copy of photocopiable anthology page 202 and read through the character descriptions with them. Ask them what sort of details we are given about each person and list the main categories on the board. They will probably include such ideas as the characters' face and build, their clothing and how they move.

Now, explain that writers often base their characters on people they know. Careful study of the people in children's everyday lives can often provide 'raw data' for stories.

Choose an adult that the children know well, perhaps the head teacher or a dinner lady, and write on the board appropriate questions from photocopiable page 62. Ask the children to work in pairs to answer these questions, recalling as much detail as possible about the subject's appearance, mannerisms and speech. After a few minutes, ask the children to share some of their points. Now ask them to write a character study using their observations as a basis.

Explain that this has been a 'practice run'. They are now ready to begin their character study in earnest. Each child should choose an adult who is close to him and, over the next two days, observe the adult carefully. Give the children copies of photocopiable page 62 to record their observations. The adult 'in the frame' should not know they are being observed.

Keep reminding the children about the exercise and perhaps discuss some of their observations. After two days, the children should use their completed photocopiable sheets to write a character study of their chosen adult.

The final study should be presented to the adult along with the evaluation form on photocopiable page 63. The surprise element adds excitement to the exercise and the feedback from the adult is interesting for the children.

THE CHILDREN'S BOOKS

The Man Whose Mother Was a Pirate
The Man Whose Mother Was a Pirate by Margaret Mahy centres on two very different characters: Sam, a small, respectable, quietly spoken accountant and his mother, a larger-than-life, extrovert ex-pirate. The story describes their journey to see the sea and the liberating effect this has on Sam.

The book is beautifully written and illustrated and presents an excellent example of the writer's craft in developing and conveying characterisation. The story builds two rich and rounded main characters by describing their physical features and clothing, how they speak, what they say and what they do. The little man changes in gradual but clear ways to become Sailor Sam at the end of the story – truly his mother's son.

The storyline is simple, but offers sufficient depth and humour to appeal to children of all ages. The ease with which the story can be read and understood, allows children to have the necessary mastery and confidence to reflect on the writer's craft.

About the author
Margaret Mahy was born in New Zealand and began writing stories while still at school. This was not part of the curriculum in the early 1940s so she and her friends spent their time after school had finished writing for each other. A prolific and celebrated author, her titles include *The Haunting, Aliens in the Family* and *The Tricksters* as well as numerous contributions to short story anthologies.

How to use this book
Introduce the book by explaining that although this looks like a picture book for younger children, the story works on several levels.

Read, or choose a child to read, the entire book to the class or group before any of the activities are introduced. Ensure that all the children get an opportunity to view the pictures. Allow individual children to read the book if they wish.

Some activities require the children to re-read some or all of the story. This is shown under 'What you need' at the beginning of the activity and in the description of what to do.

22

BEDROOMS

Teaching content
The environments people create can indicate their characters and vice versa.

What you need
Photocopiable anthology page 209, *The Man Whose Mother Was a Pirate*, writing and drawing materials.

What to do
It is interesting to explore how people's personalities are reflected in their homes. Give each child a copy of photocopiable anthology page xxx. This contains a passage from Shirley Hughes' story *Charlie Moon and the Big Bonanza Bust Up*, where the children pay a visit to Uncle Owen. What can the group tell about Uncle Owen from the state of his room?

Now, ask the children to consider their bedrooms at home. What would a stranger be able to tell about each child? Are the girls' bedrooms different from the boys'? Why? How and why have the children's bedrooms altered as they have grown older? Clearly, some of the bedroom contents reflect the occupant's hobbies and interests, but the way in which they are organised (or not!) can also reflect character. Which children in the class jumble all their toys into a cupboard, and which have a place for everything and everything in its place?

Now read the first four pages of *The Man Whose Mother Was a Pirate*, giving the children time to study the pictures. Briefly discuss some of the differences in the way the little man and his mother's choice of clothes and breakfasts.

If the bedroom of each character reflects his or her interests and personality, how might the little man's bedroom differ from his mother's? In pairs, ask the children to consider how the following items might differ in the two bedrooms:
• books
• clothes
• bed
• chair
• table/desk/dressing table
• pictures and posters
• personal treasures
• things associated with hobbies

Ask the children to draw the bedroom of either the little man or his mother. Remind them to think about the character and to portray both the *contents* of the room and the *organisation*. Once completed, children can write a short description of the room. Finally, the children can swap descriptions and try to identify the best part of their partner's work. Is there anything the children would add to their partner's description?

Development/homework task
Ask the children to consider how the little man's bedroom might have changed by the end of the book. Drawings or written descriptions of this can be displayed beside the earlier work.

23

CHARACTER CHANGE

Teaching content
Characters can change during a story.

What you need
Photocopiable page 64, *The Man Whose Mother Was a Pirate*, writing materials.

What to do
Read the story to the children and ask them to think about the point at which the little man begins to change. How do they know?

Now give each child a copy of photocopiable page 64. Read and discuss the vocabulary at the top of the sheet to ensure the children understand all the words. They should then decide which words apply to the little man at the start of the story and which apply at the end. Are there any that apply at both times, or do not apply at all? Ask the children to sort the words individually and write them in the appropriate box. Then they should compare their decisions in groups of four and discuss their agreements and disagreements.

WANTED!

Teaching content
- Characters can change as the story unfolds.
- Changes can be indicated in different ways.

What you need
The Man Whose Mother Was a Pirate, photocopiable page 65, paper, writing and drawing materials.

What to do
Read the story to the class or group. Split the class into two halves and divide each half of the class into pairs. Give each pair of children a copy of photocopiable page 65. One half of the class must imagine that they are best friends with the little man before he sets off to see the sea. He then goes missing. The police are looking for him and ask the questions on the photocopiable sheet. Tell each pair to answer the questions using their imagination, but basing their answers on the type of person the little man is as he is described on the first four pages of the book.

The other half of the class must imagine that they met the little man only after the end of the story, and became friendly with Sailor Sam, knowing nothing of his past. The police are trying to track down a pirate who looks like him and ask the questions on the photocopiable sheet. Tell the children to answer the questions in pairs, basing their answers on what the little man is like at the end of the story.

Each pair should then use their answers to make 'WANTED! HAVE YOU SEEN THIS MAN?' posters which can be displayed around the school.

AHOY M' HEARTIES

Teaching content
Capturing styles of speech.

What you need
The Man Whose Mother Was a Pirate, photocopiable page 66, scissors, adhesive, paper.

What to do
Read the book to the children. The little man and his mother have quite distinct styles of speech. Ask the children what they can remember about how each character speaks. Can they give examples of the sort of things the mother says? What about the little man?

Divide the class into small groups and give each group a copy of photocopiable page 66. This contains several statements which might be made by either the little man or his mother. Ask the children to cut out the figures at the bottom of the page, sticking each into the middle of a plain sheet of A4 paper. Then tell them to read the statements carefully and to sort them into those they think might be said by the mother and those that might be said by the little man. Once all decisions have been agreed, the children should arrange and stick the speech bubbles around the appropriate figure.

Ask the children to make up two further speech bubbles to add to each character.

Development/homework task
Ask the children to imagine that the pirate mother and the little man have each been invited to school to talk about their life. What would each one say:
- to ask for directions to the school?
- on meeting the headteacher?
- to introduce themselves to the class?
- to a child who isn't listening?
- to bid farewell?

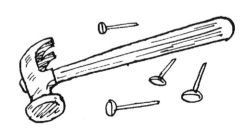

26

INSTANT IMPRESSIONS

Teaching content

Creating a character sketch.

What you need

The Man Whose Mother Was a Pirate, paper, drawing and writing materials.

What to do

Read the book to a small group of children, ensuring that all get a good look at the pictures. Then, remove the book from view. Ask the children to close their eyes and try to recapture an image of the pirate mother. Explain that the next two parts of the activity will be timed. They will not have time to do anything other than scribble quickly. You do not expect perfect work, but are looking for initial impressions.

Give the children four minutes to jot down individually all they remember about the mother's appearance, both physical features and typical facial expressions. Then give them four minutes to sketch a rough picture of her.

Ask the children to use their sketches and their brainstorms to write a short description of the mother. They should be given as long as they require to complete this part of the activity.

Finally, let the children re-examine the original story. An interesting display can be made from the brainstorms, quick drawings and the final, more considered, descriptions.

Development/homework task

Use the same tasks to create a description of the little man one year after the book has finished.

27

WRITING A CHARACTER

Teaching content

Writers reveal character through several means.

What you need

The Man Whose Mother Was a Pirate, chalkboard, paper, writing materials, adhesive.

What to do

Read the story to the children. Ask them to think about the character of the little man for the first seven pages of the story. What sort of person is he? They may say that he is shy, quiet, boring or methodical. Record the children's descriptions as a list on the board. Then ask, 'How do we know he is like this?' Ask the children to listen to the first part of the story again and to note evidence for each of the character statements listed. Direct them to consider different sources of evidence such as the illustrations, what the little man says, his job, how he speaks and what he does.

Ask the children, in pairs, to choose one of the statements and to write this as a heading on a sheet of paper. Then ask them to list the evidence from the text and illustrations that supports this view. They could use the following as sub-headings:

- illustrations;
- what he says;
- how he speaks;
- his actions;
- his job.

These pieces of writing could be stuck on to a large poster and discussed. They serve as a reminder of some of the ways in which writers indicate character.

A Lion at Bedtime

A Lion at Bedtime, by Debi Gliori, tells the story of a boy's night-time fears and how he learns to deal with them. The story is obviously written for much younger children, but the characterisation techniques used to portray the boy and the lion, and the personification of fear as a lion, make this an excellent book for older children to study the writer's craft. It also gives children an opportunity to explore and confront their own fears and a model of how to use these as a basis for story writing.

About the author
Debi Gliori, half Italian and half Scottish, grew up in Glasgow. She took a degree in illustration at Edinburgh Art College, then spent time in Milan before becoming a full-time illustrator in 1984. Titles she has illustrated include *Dulcie Dando Disco Dancer, Margery Mo* and *Margery Mo's Magic Island,* and her solo title, *Snow Lambs,* is published in 1995. Debi now lives near Edinburgh with her sons and daughter.

How to use this book
It is suggested that you – or one of the children – read this book to the group, showing the pictures clearly, before the children try any of the activities. Put the book on display in the book corner or library area so that the children may browse through it as they wish. Although it is not necessary for the children to consult the book during any of these activities, they may wish to do so to refresh their memories or to verify things they have written.

28
PESKY CHILD!

Teaching content
Characterisation through what others say about the character.

What you need
Drawing and writing materials, three large pieces of paper, marker pen.

What to do
The first thing the reader learns about Ben in *A Lion at Bedtime* is what everyone else thinks about him:

"Fearless," said his father.
"Courageous," said his mother.
"Pushy," said the cows.

What do these statements indicate about the boy and his relationship with the speakers. Can all the statements be true? Might any of them be partly true?

Now ask each child to draw three people who might make those same statements about them. This work can make an interesting display if you draw big speech bubbles on large pieces of paper and write the statements inside. The children's drawings could then be placed beside the statement to which they apply. Give the display a title, such as, 'Who thinks this about us?'

Ask the children to think about what the following people might say about them. Stress that the statements should be short and snappy.

- parent or carer
- little brother or sister
- grandparent
- neighbour
- best friend
- teacher

If the children need more support, give them a general list of statements that could apply and ask them to select the one that is most appropriate for each person. You could include some of the following:

an angel	horrifying
little devil	energetic
lazy	mischievous
cheeky	friendly
quiet and sweet	quick-witted
thoughtful	reckless

Make the children's work into a class book entitled: 'The real us'.

Development/homework task

In pairs, ask the children to decide what each of the people listed might say about their partner. They should then compare their ideas.

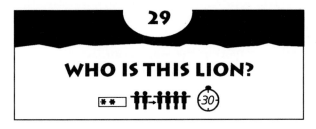

WHO IS THIS LION?

Teaching content

Characterisation through action and description.

What you need

Photocopiable page 67, writing materials.

What to do

Arrange the children in pairs and give each pair a copy of photocopiable page 67. This lists several statements made about the lion in the book. Ask the children to work in pairs and to describe what each statement in turn implies about the lion.

Then ask the pairs to join with another pair to form a group of four to compare and discuss their answers. Ask them to identify, as a group, the *two* statements that they think best capture Ben's fear of the lion, and why. Tell them to put a tick beside these statements. Now ask them to identify the one statement that they think best captures how Ben feels about the lion by the end of the story. They should put an asterisk by that statement.

Hold a class discussion about which statements the children chose and why.

FEARFUL MOVEMENTS

Teaching content

Characterisation through action and movement.

What you need

A Lion at Bedtime, chalkboard, photocopiable page 68, writing materials.

What to do

Re-read the story with the children and ask them to suggest what the lion does and the different ways in which he moves. List the children's suggestions on the board. They may mention some or all of the following: sneaked into the house; paddy-pawed his way upstairs; clackety-clawed; smiled, and so on.

Now go down the list with the class and identify whether each movement is described in a frightening or non-threatening way, recording the children's decisions beside each. Point out that most of the frightening movements are at the beginning of the book, before Ben has got to know the lion well. Why do they think this is?

Now, ask the children to work in pairs and give each pair a copy of photocopiable page 68. Ask them to consider the list of animals and to think of frightening and non-frightening ways to describe how each animal might move. They could begin by imagining that they are scared of each animal in turn. How would they describe what that animal does? Then ask them to imagine that each animal is friendly or appealing. How might they describe what it does now? Ask the children to share some of their answers with the class.

Finally, ask each child to identify an animal they would use to personify fear. It may be someone's pet, an animal they have seen in a book or on television, or an imaginary animal. They should write a short passage describing what it looks like, how it moves and the sound it makes so that others can understand their fear. Display these under the heading 'Fear personified'.

CHARACTER PLANNING

Teaching content
- Analysing a character.
- Structuring a character study.

What you need
Photocopiable page 69, writing materials, photographs of each of the children (optional).

What to do
Tell the children that writers often think out a clear picture of their main character before they write their stories. Divide the class into pairs and give each pair a copy of photocopiable page 69. Debi Gliori may have used a planning sheet like this to build a picture of Ben in *A Lion at Bedtime*.

Explain that now they have read or heard the book, the children know the character of Ben well. What do they think Debi Gliori wrote on her planning sheet? Ask the children to complete the photocopiable page in pairs, then discuss the answers with the whole class. The last box will require a great deal of discussion, as some children may not have understood the resolution of the story.

Then, ask each child to take the information in order from the numbered boxes and write their rough notes into a paragraph describing Ben. Tell the children that this is called a character sketch or a character study.

Development/homework task
Give each child a copy of photocopiable page 69 and ask them to fill it in, imagining that they, themselves, are to be characters featuring in a story. They should then write a personal character study. These could be displayed along with the photographs of the children.

NIGHT-TIME FEARS

Teaching content
The things that make us afraid make us different.

What you need
Large sheets of paper, marker pens, writing materials.

What to do
A big part of the character of the little boy is shown through the things that make him afraid. Everyone is afraid of different things and these differences reflect the individual imaginations and experiences we all have. People with no imagination have never been afraid. Sometimes the things that frighten us are not actual objects, but noises or imaginary people or animals.

Arrange the children in groups of four and give each group a sheet of paper and a marker pen. Ask the children to brainstorm all the things that could frighten them at night – sounds, movements, sights (real and imaginary). Give them 10 minutes for this, then display all the brainstorms on the wall. Ask one member of each group to read their ideas to the class.

Now tell the children to each select the six things, from *any* brainstorm, that most frighten them. Tell them to write a short phrase about each fear to make it into a line of poetry, such as: 'Night-time, dark shadows grabbing and sneaking'. Finally, they should sequence these into a list poem, which can then be illustrated and displayed in the classroom.

The Guard Dog
The Guard Dog by Dick King-Smith tells the story of a small, but very loud, dog whose small fluffy appearance belies his terrifying bark. Unfortunately, his bark is so repugnant that he almost finds himself being put down, but is rescued at the last minute by a deaf man for whom he proves to be the ideal pet.

This book provides excellent opportunities for studying characterisation because of the rich and engaging nature of the main character. Other characters are more sketchy and, in fact, it is through their attitudes to the guard-dog that we come to know them and also know more about this funny, and brave, little dog.

About the author

Dick King-Smith was born in 1922 in Gloucestershire and has firmly rooted himself in that part of the country. He served in the Grenadier Guards from 1941 to 1946, but returned to Gloucestershire to spend the next 20 years farming before taking a chance and retraining as a teacher at the age of fifty.

His first story, *The Fox Busters*, was published in 1978. In 1984 he won the Guardian Award for Children's Fiction for *The Sheep-Pig*.

How to use this book

Read up to page 18 and then do the first activity with the children. After this, it is a good idea to read to the end of the story with the whole group. Children will not need to study the text closely in order to carry out any of the activities, but will probably want access to it or to re-visit it in order to refresh their memories.

The audio cassette contains an interview in which Dick King-Smith talks about his work and reads from the book.

HIS BARK IS WORSE THAN HIS BITE

Teaching content
Use of comparisons to describe sound.

What you need
The Guard Dog, writing materials.

What to do
The noise made by the guard-dog is one of his most important characteristics and ultimately crucial to the meaning of the story. It is valuable, therefore, to allow children time to consider this in order to prepare them for its significance. Read the story up to and including the sentence at the beginning of page 18: 'Then, out of his hairy little mouth came the most awful noise you can possibly imagine.'

Next, ask the class what are the most awful sounds they have ever heard. There will be an instant response but allow only one or two examples per person, as it is important to engage every child's imagination in this task. Ask the children to write a list of the worst sounds they have ever heard, then ask them to

choose their own personal 'worst' from the list and to share their ideas with the rest of the class. Children may now amend their lists so that they have approximately six lines with one idea per line. These can be copied out as list poems.

Lastly, read the description of the guard-dog's bark on pages 18–19 and see how many of these ideas have been used by the children. It is possible that every idea here will appear in the children's poetry. Explain that the best way for the author to give us a clear idea of the sound made by the guard-dog is to compare it to other dreadful noises.

Development/homework task
Similar list poems may be produced listing the most beautiful sounds to be heard in the world.

WRITING A CHARACTER STUDY

Teaching content
Action and speech reflect character.

What you need
Chalkboard, writing materials.

What to do
When creating characters in a story, writers often show what they are like through the things they do and say and the way they look. Gradually a picture of the character grows in the reader's mind until we feel we know them well and either like or dislike them. Ask the children to think about what they know of the character of the guard-dog. List the following characteristics on the board.

BRAVE   NOISY
DETERMINED   CHEERFUL
HARDWORKING   HONEST

Ask the children to write these down and then describe an event in the book which illustrates how each of these characteristics fits the guard-dog. Then ask the children to think of another characteristic and add it to the list.

Next, the children should rearrange their lists in order of priority, starting with the main and most noticeable characteristic, and ending with the least important in their opinion.

Finally, ask the children to use these notes to write a character study of the guard-dog, beginning with a physical description, followed by a character account which should be illustrated by events in the book.

Development/homework task

Use the notes from this task to devise a 'For Sale' notice advertising the guard-dog, stressing characteristics irresistible to the buyer.

35
GIVE A DOG A BAD NAME

Teaching content

Proper names may establish character.

What you need

The Guard Dog, reference books about dogs, drawing and writing materials, large sheets of paper, scissors, glue.

What to do

Writers are very careful about the names they give their characters. Names can be used to establish a type of character. None of the animals in this novel is given a proper name, because their characters are indicated so clearly by their speech and the way they are described.

In groups of four, ask the children to draw pictures of the dogs in the following list, by looking at the novel and at reference books.

• small guard-dog
• pug
• poodle
• Labrador
• Old English sheepdog
• springer spaniel
• sad dog
• terrier

Each child in the group should be responsible for drawing two dogs. Discuss which dogs will not be found in a factual book about animals.

When they have finished, the children should choose appropriate names for the dogs they have drawn. In group discussion these names may be changed until everyone is satisfied. The pictures should be cut out and displayed on a large poster along with the character names.

36
MEETING OUTSIDE THE DOGS' HOME

Teaching content

Dialogue reflects character.

What you need

The Guard Dog, photocopiable page 70, writing materials, felt-tipped pens.

What to do

Ask the children to remember the boastful way in which the puppies in the pet shop speak about themselves and how they scoff at the small, scruffy dog. Re-read pages 11–16 to refresh their memories.

Explain that writers often show what characters are like through the language the characters use and the things they say. Tell the children that, on the day they were all sold, the puppies agreed to meet outside the dogs' home one week later to catch up on the news. Of course, when they meet, who do they see in the home but the little guard-dog. Discuss with the class what the dogs might say to each other. Younger children will take more time to grasp the fact that each dog must speak in character and it might be valuable to have them act out the scene in groups before writing. Part of what is said by the animals should be a boastful statement about how successful they are in their new lives. The other part should be some sneering statement about the guard-dog.

Give each child a copy of photocopiable page 70 and explain that they should fill in the speech bubbles to show what each dog would say. After writing, the children may like to colour the dogs, possibly adding bows to the poodle and the pug!

37

GOOD THINGS COME IN SMALL PACKAGES

Teaching content

A character's most important qualities lie below the surface.

What you need

Photocopiable page 71, writing materials, a class list, slips of blank paper, envelopes.

What to do

The guard-dog is a character who recognises his own best qualities. Other characters in the book judge him by his appearance and see him merely as a small, sweet, almost pathetic creature, which is how they want him to behave. When he lets them down by showing his dreadful bark, they turn from him. He is brave and loyal but that doesn't interest people.

Give each child a copy of photocopiable page 71, and ask them to look at the list of five characters who meet the guard-dog. In the first column they should write what each character thought of the guard-dog before it barked, and in the second column they should write what they thought after the dog barked.

Development/homework task

Ask the children to think about people in their class and to consider the qualities that make them special. This should help them realise that important qualities have nothing to do with the way people look.

Photocopy a class list twice, cut up individual names from the three lists and place them in a hat. Each child must take three different names from the hat and, for each of those people, write on a slip of paper one good quality that they have. Give an envelope to each child and ask them to write their name on it, then display all the envelopes on the notice-board. The children should then place their slips of paper into the appropriate envelopes. In this way every child will have three positive statements to read about himself. Every part of this activity should be kept secret. Make sure that the children work with a serious and responsible attitude and warn them, before statements are written, that other children may be hurt if anyone makes fun of the activity.

38

EPILOGUES AND HAPPY ENDINGS

Teaching content

* Characters behaving consistently.
* Writing epilogues.

What you need

Photocopiable page 72, writing materials.

What to do

Explain to the children that sometimes writers add an epilogue to a story in order to tell what happens to the main characters and tie up any loose ends. It is usually quite short and doesn't go into great detail. The final chapter of *The Guard Dog* ends with two interesting characters walking away to begin a new life together. The book ends on a tantalising cliff-hanger leaving us to wonder if the old man ever finds out that he is the owner of a champion guard-dog.

Tell the children that they are going to write an epilogue to *The Guard Dog*. Firstly, in groups of four, they must answer, in order, the questions on photocopiable page 72. Having decided on the answers to these questions, the children should then individually write the epilogue. This should be no longer than one side of writing and should sum up the events decided by the group. The final sentence should make it clear that the old man and the guard-dog live together happily ever after.

GUESS WHO?

◆ Underline the words that best describe your character.
If none of the words is suitable, write your own.

Height

tall   lofty   tiny   small   short   average

Build

bulky   heavy   slim   massive   light   dainty   petite

well-built   filled out

Lips

curving   full   thin   cruel   turned down   wide   smiling

cracked   lined   pink   rosebud   bloodless

Teeth

even   broken   pearly   blackened   protruding   rotten

yellowed   jagged

Skin

smooth   glowing   wrinkled   dry and flaking   yellowed

pink   oyster   weathered   pitted   scarred

Eyes

close-set   wide   large   tiny   piggy   popping   velvet brown

squinting   dreamy   sapphire blue   piercing   cruel   kind

lined   tired

Hair

flowing   scraped back   bald   curling   poker straight   wavy

blonde   dark   golden   chestnut   shining   matted   tangled

greasy   fiery red   jet black

EYES – WINDOWS ON TO THE SOUL

'...tiny, piggy eyes staring straight ahead...'
(*Danny, Champion of the World*, Roald Dahl)

'...unnaturally bright eyes...'
(*The Silver Sword*, Ian Serraillier)

'...the man's eyes were small, repulsive, light in colour, their expression never changing...'
(*I am David*, Anne Holm)

'...deep set, dark eyes with the light behind them like a cold fire that never went out...'
(*Green Witch*, Susan Cooper)

'...he felt the chilling influence of the death-cold eyes...'
(*A Christmas Carol*, Charles Dickens)

'...black bead eyes glittered at them...'
(*Green Witch*, Susan Cooper)

'...eyes the colour of the blue mountain flowers which grew in Spring...'
(*Farthest-away Mountain*, Lynne Reid Banks)

'...pale disinterested eyes...dark serious eyes...'
(*Farthest-away Mountain*, Lynne Reid Banks)

'...eyes which seemed to flicker through the dark glasses...'
(*Farthest-away Mountain*, Lynne Reid Banks)

'...the mischievous glint in Tanya's eyes...'
(*The Patchwork Quilt*, Valerie Flournoy)

'A spark of anger lit up Davie's eye...'
(*The Desperate Journey*, Kathleen Fidler)

'...adoring eyes...'
(*Charlotte's Web*, E.B. White)

'...eyes red with crying...'
(*Charlotte's Web*, E.B. White)

FAIRY-TALE APPEARANCES

◆ Cut out and sort these statements into 3 sets:

Set 1 – statements that generally apply to bad characters;
Set 2 – statements that generally apply to good characters;
Set 3 – statements that could apply to either.

has warts on face	moves gracefully
has beautiful hands and nails	has black, rotten teeth
wears dirty clothes	has a long thin beard
has small, neat features	is tall
wears a crown	has piercing eyes
has knotted, untidy hair	wears expensive bejewelled clothes
has long, flowing hair	dresses in dark colours
wears lots of make-up	has a slim waist

MONSTER MISTAKES

This is what the monster is saying:

People think that...

If I met a lost child I would

_____

If I saw someone crying I would say

_____

If I saw a baby drop its ice-cream I would

_____

If I knew it was your birthday I would

_____

...but really I am kind and I am good...

If I met a lost child I would

_____

If I saw someone crying I would say

_____

If I saw a baby drop its ice-cream I would

_____

If I knew it was your birthday I would

_____

_____

GENTLE GIANTS

'I had never visited the giant's home before! I crept into what appeared to be the sitting room. I was terrified until...'

◆ At this point you get an indication that this is not the ferocious giant he has always appeared. With your partner, fill in every one of these possibilities of what *might* happen next. This is a brainstorm and your ideas should be separate and unconnected.

...the giant said

1.'_____'

2.'_____'

3.'_____'

...I noticed

1._____

2._____

3._____

... , from the next room, I heard

1._____

2._____

3._____

...I saw what the giant was doing

1._____

2._____

3._____

...until my nostrils filled with the smell of

1._____

2._____

3._____

HIDDEN PERSONALITIES

Everyone thought _____ was a wonderful/terrible person.

This is because _____ did things at home like:

This is because _____ did things for strangers like:

People said wonderful/terrible things about _____.

The family said:

The neighbours said:

Friends said:

BUT...

_____ had a secret vice/virtue. It was:

One incident that showed this clearly was...

NAME

RELUCTANT ARRIVALS

frightened eyes   dull, lifeless eyes   head held high

sure feet   dreary expression   wide eyed

smiling eyes   shining eyes   head bent   turned down mouth

skipping   hooded eyes   hunched shoulders

dragging feet   swinging arms

◆ Some of the phrases above describe a person who is eager to go somewhere and some describe a person who is reluctant to go somewhere. Write each of the phrases under the heading you think fits them best.

Wanting to go	Not wanting to go

Scholastic
IMAGINATIVE WRITING
Workshop

INSIDE OUT

'Slamming the door might teach them a good lesson ...and I'll slam the gate too ...how dare they stop my pocket money ...and for a month ...I was going to buy that new CD this weekend ...I would have had enough saved by then ...I hate them because they never understand me ...they don't care about how I feel ...I'll show them though ...I'll just go away and never come back ...they'll be sorry when it gets late and I'm not home ...they'll wish they'd believed me then...'

◆ The above passage is a stream of consciousness showing the inner thoughts of a character. Use the questions below to jot down a few ideas about what someone in this sort of mood may look like. What would they do to the stones on the path?

What would they do with their hands?

What speed would they move at?

What would their shoulders be like?

What would their lips look like? (Think of the shape.)

What would their eyes look like?

Would they stop at any point? When? For what purpose?

Would their expression change towards the end of the paragraph? If so, how would it alter?

TOM AND ANNE GO SWIMMING

Tom's head was bent dejectedly, his face buried deep inside the turned-up collar of his coat His shoulders were hunched and hands were lost in large pockets. His body shuffled forward with heavy reluctant feet hardly lifting from the ground. A tense elbow held the trunks and rolled towel tightly to his body. He was going swimming.

Anne was going swimming. Her hair bounced joyfully around her shoulders as she strode towards the pool. A large swimming bag swung from one hand as her arms propelled her swiftly and busily along.

◆ Write down four things that Tom and Anne might be thinking on their way to the swimming pool

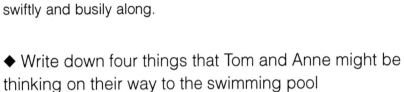

Tom	Anne

I'LL SAY IT MY WAY

◆ Join each speech bubble to the appropriate character. In the blank box draw an appropriate character for the speech bubble that is left.

Each of these characters is expressing the idea 'I don't like this food'.

◆ Write what you think each would say in the speech bubble.

I WANT...

...to stay up late   ...to watch ... on T.V.   ...to wear this....

...some more pocket money   ...to play out late with ...

...to go to a party   ...to buy this ...

First attempt:

Second attempt:

Third attempt:

DON'T DO THAT!

◆ How would the mother say 'Don't do that! Come with me,' in each of these situations? Write what you think she would say in the speech bubbles.

CHARACTER DETECTIVE

◆ Write down two things that this person often says:

1._____

2._____

◆ Write down two things that make this person smile or laugh:

1._____

2._____

◆ Write down two things that show this person is angry or unhappy:

1._____

2._____

◆ What clothes does this person wear:

1. around the house? _____

2. when going shopping? _____

◆ What does this person say when he or she meets you:

1. in the morning? _____

2. out in the street? _____

◆ What does this person say if you have done something wrong?

_____

◆ What does this person say if he or she is pleased with you?

_____

◆ Write down three typical mannerisms of this person:

1._____

2._____

3._____

NAME

CHARACTER DETECTIVE – EVALUATION

◆ Read the character study and answer the following questions.
Do you recognise the person in this character study?

Write down one point about yourself that you already knew.

Write down one point about yourself that you didn't already know.

Imagine that your character is going to appear in a television drama or play.
Which actor would you like to play your part?

Which actor do you think would play your part?

Please give this character study a grade:

| A - Excellent | B - Generally good | C - Okay, good in parts | D - Not very good | E - Awful |

- ✂ - - - - - -

NAME

CHARACTER DETECTIVE – EVALUATION

◆ Read the character study and answer the following questions.
Do you recognise the person in this character study?

Write down one point about yourself that you already knew.

Write down one point about yourself that you didn't already know.

Imagine that your character is going to appear in a television drama or play.
Which actor would you like to play your part?

Which actor do you think would play your part?

Please give this character study a grade:

| A - Excellent | B - Generally good | C - Okay, good in parts | D - Not very good | E - Awful |

CHARACTER CHANGE

careful	joyous	carefree
controlled	liking routine	unadventurous
adventurous	obedient	worried
dull	boring	good fun
happy	bored	negative
concerned	careless	carefree
clean	competitive	shy

◆ Some of the words shown above may describe the little man in *The Man Whose Mother Was a Pirate*. Sort them into their appropriate sets.

Set 1 - words that apply to the little man at the start of the story:

Set 2 - words that apply to the little man at the end of the story:

Set 3 - words that apply to the little man at the start and the end of the story:

Set 4 - words that do not apply to the little man at all:

WANTED!

Does the little man have a daily routine? What is it?

What sort of things give the little man most pleasure?

What worries him?

What hobbies does he have?

What television programmes does he like to watch?

What is his favourite sort of music?

What do the neighbours say about him?

AHOY M' HEARTIES

I'm so hungry I could eat ten sharks and a cabin boy.

Excuse me, but I think you've dropped your hanky.

We need provisions - I'll paddle off to the shops.

I am feeling rather peckish, now I think about it.

I must hurry now, I don't like to be late.

C'mon let's party and hear the fish sing shanties.

Ahoy m' hearties, that frothing ale will drown m' thirst.

Do you think you could be just a little quieter, please?

Would you mind if I closed the door?

Settle down, midshipman. You'd deafen seagulls in a storm.

Yes, sir. Right away, sir. Sorry about that, sir.

Batten down the hatch, it feels like a force 10 gale through here.

Oh dear, oh dear, there's mud on my shirt.

WHO IS THIS LION?

◆ Read the following statements about the lion in *A Lion at Bedtime*.
What does each one imply about the character of the lion?

That smelly lion is here again.

The lion sneaked into the house in the dead of night.

The lion clackety-clawed its way up the stairs.

The lion paddy-pawed its way along the corridor.

The lion's paws were frozen stiff from walking in the snow
    and he really needed to get warm.

The lion was huge and freezing and smelly.

The lion was furry and breathing very loudly.

The lion smiled toothily at Ben.

The lion looked with huge yellow eyes.

The lion's breath stank.

The lion was shivering.

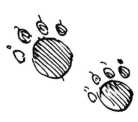

The lion was smiling a dazzlingly white, minty smile.

The lion carried Ben into the bathroom on his back.

◆ Which two statements do you think best capture Ben's fear of the lion?
Put a tick by these.
Why have you chosen these?

◆ Which statement do you feel best captures how Ben feels about
the lion by the end of the story? Put a star by this.
Why have you chosen this?

FEARFUL MOVEMENTS

◆ Think of frightening and non-frightening ways to describe how each of these animals moves. Write your descriptions in the appropriate column.

Animal	Fearful	Not fearful
cat		
rabbit		
worm		
horse		
hamster		
whale		
eagle		

CHARACTER PLANNING

❷ What does this character look like?

Hair:

Eyes:

Build:

Height:

Skin colour:

❸ Who does this person love or like?

❹ What does this person like to do?

❶ Name: _____

Age: _____

Where this character lives:

_____

❺ What frightens this character?

❻ What does this person do when frightened?

❼ Does this person learn to face up to his or her fears? Can you explain how this happens?

MEETING OUTSIDE THE DOGS' HOME

◆ Write in the speech bubbles what you think each dog is saying.

GOOD THINGS COME IN SMALL PACKAGES

◆ Write in the appropriate column brief
notes about what each of these characters
thought about the guard-dog before and
after hearing him bark.

Character	What the character thought before hearing the bark	What the character thought and did after hearing the bark
Spoiled child who bought him		
One of the other puppies in the pet shop		
Kennelmaid		
One of the people who came to the dogs' home		
Old man		

EPILOGUES AND HAPPY ENDINGS

◆ Consider possible answers to these questions. They will form the plan for an epilogue to the story of *The Guard Dog*.

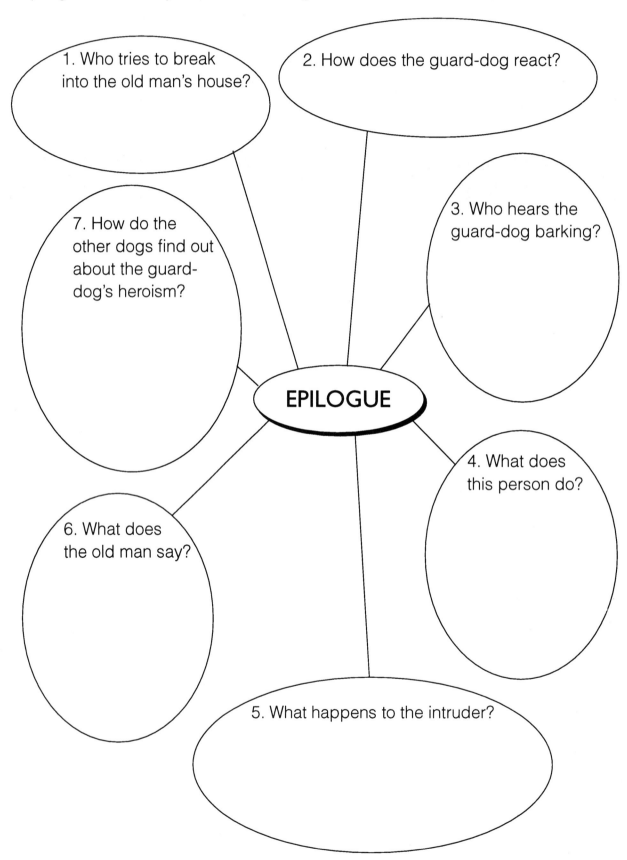

1. Who tries to break into the old man's house?

2. How does the guard-dog react?

7. How do the other dogs find out about the guard-dog's heroism?

3. Who hears the guard-dog barking?

EPILOGUE

4. What does this person do?

6. What does the old man say?

5. What happens to the intruder?

Scholastic WRITING Workshop

Chapter Four

SETTING THE SCENE

INTRODUCTION

The importance of setting

When writers describe the setting for a story, they provide a backdrop that helps the reader understand the action and events that take place. Establishing the context of time and place provides the canvas on which the rest of the story is painted. However, the description of a place, setting or scene frequently does more than this. Writers use it to evoke a particular mood which colours the reader's expectations and emotions. When this happens, the setting of a story not only provides a canvas for the reader's imagination, but also determines the palette to be used as the story unfolds in the reader's head.

What do children know about 'setting the scene'?

Children know, from the stories they have enjoyed, that readers need some sense of a setting – *where* the story happens. They recognise that it is easier to visualise the action and understand the sequence of events when the reader has some idea of the physical backdrop. However, children are slower to understand that descriptions of a place or setting are not neutral, that a setting can be described in different ways to evoke different moods. Appreciation of this is necessary because, as writers, they need to make decisions about how the scene is to be imagined and make appropriate linguistic choices. Unless children are encouraged to reflect on how and why writers describe scenes in particular ways they will be unable to use the techniques and skills that allow writers to capture and portray scenes evocatively.

What do children need to learn?

Children need help with the different aspects of creating, describing and using place, settings and scenes within the stories they write. They need to appreciate the importance of inventing a full and detailed context, even if much of this detail is not, eventually, to be shared with the reader. They need to learn how to structure and focus a description and to experiment with the consequences of revealing different amounts of detail. They need to know that good writers set the scene effectively but economically and

use place, setting and scenes to affect the reader's emotions and thereby move the story forward.

To underpin all this, children need to have developed a sense of place. They need to move through the landscapes of their lives with the keen eye of the writer, observing detail, noting the unusual but also thinking of new ways to frame the familiar. They need to be confident in using all their senses to describe the essence of a place and they need to recognise and use particular linguistic devices, such as similes, that sometimes help writers do this.

What do children find difficult?

When children build their own contexts for writing, they often need help to think through all the small details to create a firm image in the mind. When this is done the child becomes the expert on the place and the setting and, as its creator, knows far more about it than the teacher. The difficulty then becomes deciding what to tell the reader, and how. Often, particularly when the context is well established in the child's mind, he forgets that the reader does not share this knowledge and omits important details from the story. Other children are themselves vague about the context, and this lack of depth and detail in the mind of its creator leads to a story that appears flat and one-dimensional to the reader.

How can teachers help?

Teachers can help in the way they structure lessons and respond to children's work, as well as through specific teaching inputs which give children reading and writing experiences that

develop awareness and skills. The teacher's task, therefore, is three-fold. First, teachers must help children create the story setting. Often this can be done by asking appropriate questions, or by identifying/listing specific aspects for children to think about. Secondly, teachers can help by playing the part of the 'naive listener', pointing up what the reader needs to know. Thirdly, children need to be encouraged to read with the eye of a writer, to notice effective writing that captures the essence of a scene and, because they have experimented and practised specific techniques themselves, be able to recognise and appreciate how other writers use these.

Helping children to link experiences in reading and writing can become a powerful teaching technique. When children begin to read with the eyes of writers they recognise the function of particular story settings and begin to be able to identify how particular linguistic devices create particular effects. In this way, children will learn from fellow writers and learn to use their experience as readers to inform their own writing.

CONTENTS AND ORGANISATION

This chapter provides activities which aim to raise children's awareness of place, setting and scenes and encourage them to think about these in greater depth. It also provides activities that focus attention on how writers use descriptions to manipulate the reader's emotions and activities to highlight and develop some specific skills and techniques that writers use.

The following aspects are covered through activities in which children invent and describe places and scenes and through activities that draw on the anthology extracts to reflect on the craft of published writers:

Straight descriptions of place

These activities help children to observe places or scenes and to structure their descriptions to help the reader imagine it also. Children need to know that it is not long descriptions with lots of adjectives that make a story effective. In fact, long descriptions are often counterproductive because they interrupt the storyline and slow the pace, losing the reader's attention. The skill

often lies in capturing the essence of a place in as few words as possible. However, children need to write longer descriptions before they are able to recognise how to focus and which parts capture the essence. How such children edit their work, and what they say about why, can provide crucial evidence of their thinking in this respect. The writing cannot be divorced from the writer and teachers need to consider both when assessing future needs.

Emotive descriptions of place

These activities have been designed to raise children's awareness of why and how writers use descriptions of place and setting to predispose the reader towards a particular emotional response. The activities target children's understanding of this technique through making them aware of their own experiences as readers and by encouraging them to experiment with different ways of portraying a scene.

Language selection and use

These activities target how writers choose words and make use of specific devices such as similes and personification. Children need to feel the power of words and images and need their attention drawn to how subtle differences in word choice can exert powerful effects. Activities in this section introduce these ideas to children and encourage them to experiment and to discuss their own, and others', work.

The children's books

The three children's books chosen for this chapter are Ann Grifalconi's *The Village of Round and Square Houses*, Bernard Ashley's *Dinner Ladies Don't Count* and *Fair's Fair* by Leon Garfield.

The *Village of Round and Square Houses* is presented as a nostalgic memory of childhood. Descriptions of the people and their lifestyles and customs combine with descriptions of the houses, fields and mountains to create a setting in which the story of an ancient myth can be told. The sense of a place that is warm, orderly and secure persists long after the story has finished.

Bernard Ashley's story 'Dinner Ladies Don't Count' is, in contrast, a very realistic and immediate story of a lonely and unhappy boy, whose school life is nearly destroyed but saved at the last minute by an unexpected friend. The story springs from the author's experiences of everyday life in a primary school. Children can recognise the evocative details of the classroom and playground settings and this story helps them to realise that rich stories can emerge from familiar surroundings.

'Dinner Ladies Don't Count' is one story in a book of the same name. The other story, 'Linda's Lie', also has a familiar school setting and, although it is not used as the basis for any of the activities, children may like to read it anyway to further their experience of this very popular children's author. The children may like to listen to the interview with Bernard Ashley on the audio cassette, where he talks about his work and reads from the book.

The third of the children's books used in this chapter, Leon Garfield's *Fair's Fair*, is a superb story set in Edwardian London. The storyline is straightforward and strongly anchored to descriptions of atmosphere and place. The descriptions of the scenes and the settings drive the story just as much as do the mysterious events. Most children will find the story easy to read and the sequence of events easy to follow, freeing them to appreciate the skill with which it is written.

The activities linked to these stories encourage children to read as writers and provide a way to introduce or develop a range of writing skills for describing place, settings and scenes within an integrated context. The books also provide examples of the writer's craft upon which the children are asked to focus.

Helping children with setting the scene

Teachers can help children develop their understanding by:
• helping them create complete pictures in their imaginations to work from as they write;
• encouraging them to note and think about ways to capture the atmosphere and feel of places as well as straight descriptions of the physical aspects;
• encouraging them to read the work of other authors in an informed and analytical way;
• encouraging them to consider the emotional reaction they want their readers to have and to write with this in mind.

The following are some useful points to bear in mind when talking to children about their writing.
• Respond to writing in a way that highlights what the reader needs to know rather than by explaining what the child needs to alter. Through this, children retain ownership of their work and learn to become more analytical about writing.
• Rather than offering your own ideas and images, try to find out about the pictures in the child's mind and ask questions that help her to elaborate, focus or select from these.
• Don't assume that greater use of adjectives and adverbs improves the quality of writing; it often compensates for a weak noun or verb.
• Teach children about specific techniques and strategies and use informal situations to encourage them to look out for these techniques in their own work, in the work of fellow writers in the class and in published authors.

Activity		Teaching content	Star rating	Group size	Photo copiable
STRAIGHT DESCRIPTIONS					
1	Picture poem	Describing from a picture stimulus	*	2	✓+A
2	Tell me about...	Paying close attention to detail	*	Ⓦ⇨2	
3	The view from my window	Building up accurate descriptions	*	Ⓦ⇨2	
4	The street where I live	Building and structuring a description	*	1	A
5	Capture the essence	Sharpening an image	**	1⇨2	✓
6	Preparations	A place can contribute to atmosphere of story	**	Ⓦ⇨1	A
7	Fresh eyes on familiar places	Writing clear and accurate descriptions	***	1⇨2	✓✓+A
8	Through the keyhole	Describing an imaginary scene	**	Ⓦ⇨2⇨1	
9	The play park	Writing detailed description; same place appears different at different times	***	3	A
EMOTIVE DESCRIPTIONS					
10	Rooms: cold or comforting?	Selecting images and language to evoke reader's emotions	**	2⇨1	✓
11	Music mood writing	Creating a mood and setting using music as stimulus	**	Ⓦ⇨1	✓
12	Playground perspectives	Describing a scene from different points of view	**	Ⓦ⇨4⇨1	✓
13	Miss Rickets and Miss Racket	Writing descriptions to evoke positive/negative feelings	**	2	✓
14	A place to play	Structuring emotive descriptions; different point of view	***	1⇨2	✓
LANGUAGE USE					
15	The sun has got his hat on	Using personification	*	Ⓦ⇨2	A
16	Who am I?	Personification	**	2⇨1	✓+A
17	Similes	Recognising similes	*	1⇨2	✓
18	The sea	Writing similes; writing poetry	**	1/2	✓
19	Trees: weird and wonderful	Making careful word choices; using a thesaurus	**	2⇨Ⓦ	✓
20	Dangerous waters	Selection of strong/weak verbs	*⇨***	1⇨4	✓
THE VILLAGE OF ROUND AND SQUARE HOUSES					
21	Home of my heart	Visualising and drawing from an evocative description	*	Ⓦ⇨1	
22	The arrivals	Setting the scene by describing people and their actions	*	2	✓
23	Thunderstorm fights	Using personification to describe a thunderstorm	**	Ⓦ⇨4⇨2	
24	Horrible visitors	Writing emotive descriptions of settings	**	Ⓦ⇨2⇨6	✓
25	Childhood places	Describing a place from memory	*	1	
26	Angry world	Understanding and conveying the close relationship between setting and characters	***	4⇨2⇨1	
DINNER LADIES DON'T COUNT					
27	Places I know	Successful writers draw on their own experience	*	4	✓
28	Book Corner	Concise descriptions of a place	*	Ⓦ⇨1	
29	Violent verbs	Creating atmosphere in descriptions of place	**	Ⓦ⇨2	
30	Danger alert	Creating atmosphere through descriptions of objects	**	Ⓦ⇨2	✓
31	Our class	Setting the scene by describing activity	**	Ⓦ⇨4⇨1	
FAIR'S FAIR					
32	The worst street	Visualising and researching setting; creating impressions rather than detailed descriptions	*	Ⓦ⇨1	
33	An unexpected turn of events	Sometimes writers describe scenes to build expectations and then surprise the reader	**	Ⓦ⇨1⇨2	
34	Straight from the horse's mouth	Actions and comments of incidental characters can quickly create impression of a scene	**	5	
35	The homecoming	Using a scene to establish mood	***	4⇨1	
36	Snow	Describing a scene through the eyes of a character	***	4	A
37	Dumb animals?	Using animals to add to atmosphere of a scene	**	Ⓦ⇨1	✓

A = anthology page
Ⓦ = whole group

PICTURE POEM

Teaching content
Straight description.

What you need
Photocopiable page 102, writing materials, photocopiable anthology page 210.

What to do
Give each pair a copy of photocopiable page 102. Ask the children each to look at the picture and to write down:
• *five* words or phrases to describe what the picture shows;
• *four* things the snow or the picture makes them think of;
• *three* words to describe sounds they may hear in the picture;
• *two* images of what the snow would feel like on their skin;
• *one* emotion the picture makes them feel.

Now ask the children to share their answers with their partner. Ask them to put their answers where they can both refer to them for the next part of the activity.

Tell the children to think carefully about the picture and about what they have written. Ask them to make a list poem by selecting, combining and sequencing appropriate phrases, drawing from both brainstorms. The children may work individually or in pairs to do this.

Finally, give each child a copy of the snow poem on photocopiable anthology page 210. Ask them to comment on it in the light of their experience of writing a snow poem. Which parts do they particularly like? Why do they think they are effective? Does reading this poem make them think any differently about parts of their own work?

TELL ME ABOUT...

Teaching content
Encouraging children to pay attention to detail.

What you need
No special requirements.

What to do
This is an oral language game to develop children's descriptive ability. It is best introduced to the whole class, either as part of a language lesson or as a drama warm-up activity.

Begin with a demonstration in front of the class. Select one child to be the speaker and take the part of the listener yourself. Ask the speaker to imagine a table laid out for a birthday party. What is on it? Once the speaker has begun to describe the things they see, the listener may interrupt at any point and request more detail about a particular item the speaker has mentioned, or to ask the speaker to stop describing an item. The listener may only use the two commands: 'Tell me about...' and 'Okay, what else can you see?' The listener cannot backtrack or introduce a new subject or item. The speaker must try to ensure that all descriptions are fluent and provide as much detail as the listener requests.

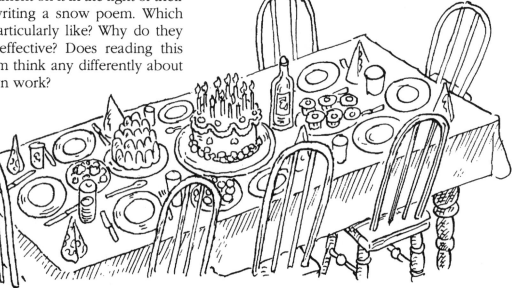

The game may sound something like this:

In the middle of the table there are big plates of food...

Tell me about the food.

Well, there is a plate of sausages and some bowls of crisps...

Tell me about the bowls.

They are small and dark blue on the outside and a creamy colour on the inside, about the same colour as the crisps, really...

Tell me about the colour of the crisps.

Well, the tomato and ham flavoured ones have a slightly reddish glow compared to the salt and vinegar. If you look closely you can tell the difference.

Okay, what else can you see?

I can see plates of biscuits...

Once finished, ask each individual to list the five most important things on their party table and to write their own description of each, starting with the item that is most striking. Encourage the children to swap their descriptions with a partner and to compare this description with their own imaginary table.

Development/homework task

This approach can easily be adapted to a variety of contexts and subjects, and children improve with practice, becoming more fluent and precise. You may like to generate descriptions of the table *after* the party.

THE VIEW FROM MY WINDOW

Teaching content

Building up a description.

What you need

Chalkboard, a window that you can see out of (or a poster depicting a view).

What to do

Ask the children to tell you five things they can see from the window of the classroom (or on the poster) and list these down the centre of the board. They may offer things like: buildings; tree; playground; sky; climbing frame. Take the first item and ask the children for two or three words to describe it (use the term 'adjective' if you feel it is appropriate). Choose two from those suggested and write them *in front of* the word, for example 'Tall, grey buildings'. Now do the same for each of the words on the board, producing five descriptive phrases of things that can be seen from the classroom window.

Now, read the first phrase to the class and ask the children to suggest possible ways to finish it off. If the response is slow, ask 'Tell me about it. What is it doing?' Do this with each of the descriptive phrases in turn. If several alternatives are suggested, ask which the children prefer, for example 'Tall, grey buildings full of people working' or 'Tall, grey buildings blocking out the sun'.

Finally, explain that the children can present this writing either as a poem or as a descriptive paragraph (in which case they will have to devise ways of linking the phrases as full sentences to make the description flow). In either case, the children should work in pairs to consider each of the phrases and how to sequence them. They may make any deletions, additions or changes they deem necessary.

The final work should be displayed within a window frame, or behind windows that open in the appropriate manner to reveal the writing. On the front of the windows the children should paint or draw the scene that has been described.

Development/homework task

Ask the children to use this formula to write a description or poem about the view from their bedroom window.

THE STREET WHERE I LIVE

Teaching content
Building a description.

What you need
Photocopiable anthology page 211, chalkboard, writing materials.

What to do
Give each child a copy of photocopiable anthology page 211, which contains Gareth Owen's poem 'Salford Road'. Explain that the author is trying to convey an affectionate description of the neighbourhood he grew up in and the people he remembers from his childhood.

Write the following prompts on the board and ask the children to think of the street where they live and to write brief answers to each of them:
• the name of the flats, street or house;
• what the entrance looks like (front gate, garden, front door...);
• one place in their street, house or flat where they play;
• what this is like;
• one set of neighbours whom they particularly like;
• one thing that makes their neighbours' house or flat different;
• one thing they like about their street.

Explain that you do not want the children to write a poem, but you would like them to produce paragraph containing an affectionate and personal description of their own neighbourhood. It is not necessary for them to use all the answers to all the questions, and they can use their answers in whatever order they think appropriate.

When completed, the work should be mounted and displayed either on the wall or in a class book. Encourage any children who live in the same street or in nearby streets to read and comment on each other's descriptions.

Development/homework task
Use this same technique to get the children to write an affectionate description of a place where they play or somewhere they would like to play.

CAPTURE THE ESSENCE

Teaching content
Sharpening an image.

What you need
Photocopiable page 103, writing materials.

What to do
Ask the children to read the extract on photocopiable page 103 and to edit this in order to capture the essence of the description in just three or four sentences. Explain that by editing, you mean that the children should change individual words, delete, re-write or change the order of sentences as they see fit. Encourage them to be as adventurous as possible. Once finished, ask the children to compare their edited results with a partner and to explain the changes they made and why. In what ways are the two pieces of work similar or different?

After this discussion, ask the children which edited result they prefer and why. Explain that maybe they like both pieces, but for different reasons. In this case, the children should explain why they like each piece.

PREPARATIONS

Teaching content
• Structuring a description.
• Describing a scene to establish the atmosphere of a story.

What you need
Photocopiable anthology page 212, A4 card, paper, art materials, scissors, writing materials, adhesive.

What to do
Begin this activity by reading aloud the extract on photocopiable anthology page 212, describing the bustle and excitement in the Cratchits' house on Christmas Day.

Ask the children to think about a school classroom on a winter's afternoon. It is dark outside and the class is preparing for a celebration. Ask them to imagine and describe the scene from the viewpoint of someone looking in through the window. The children may put themselves into the scene as characters in the room if they choose.

The following prompts will help them to organise their ideas.
• what is the class doing?
• what can you hear (music? singing? talking?)
• do you notice any children/group in particular? who?
• what do they look like?
• what are they doing?

Some children may find a starter sentence helpful, such as: 'Gazing into the window I saw...'

Present this work on a sheet of A4 card folded in half like a greetings card. Ask the children to draw the window of the room from the outside on the 'front' of the card, and to stick the written description on the inside so that it is revealed when the window opens.

Development/homework task

Ask the children to describe the scene in the classroom just after something really serious has happened. The class is waiting in silence for the headteacher to arrive.

FRESH EYES ON FAMILIAR PLACES
★★★ 👕-👕👕 ⏱

Teaching content

Writing clear and accurate descriptions.

What you need

Photocopiable anthology page 213, photocopiable page 104, photocopiable page 105 (optional), writing materials.

What to do

Give each child a copy of photocopiable anthology page 213 which contains an extract from *I'll Take You to Mrs Cole* by Nigel Gray and Michael Foreman. Read through the passage with the children and ask if there are any parts of the description that they find particularly

vivid and why. Then give each child a copy of photocopiable page 104 which contains a series of specific questions about a room. Tell the children that tomorrow they will write a description of either their own living room or kitchen, whichever they think is most interesting. Explain that they have one evening in which to gather detailed evidence for this writing and should use photocopiable page 104 to help them do this.

The following day, ask the children to read their completed questionnaires to a partner, who should ask questions to elicit any important details that have been omitted. Once this has been done, tell the children to use this information as the basis for a descriptive paragraph about the room. They must decide how they are going to begin their descriptions and in what sequence they will use the observations on their sheet.

Once the descriptions have been completed, ask the children to re-read photocopiable anthology page 213. Some children may want to alter parts of their own descriptions as a consequence of re-reading this extract, and they should be allowed to do so.

Development/homework task

The children could take their descriptions home and work with their parents to complete photocopiable page 105. It is interesting to display this writing alongside a photograph of the room.

8

THROUGH THE KEYHOLE

Teaching content
Describing an imaginary scene.

What you need
Keyhole-shaped paper, writing materials, rough paper.

What to do
Writers use descriptions of people's houses to set the scene or create a mood for the action in a story, or to tell the reader about a character.

Remind the children of the story of *Sleeping Beauty* and how the twelfth fairy took revenge for not being invited to the christening of the little princess by putting a terrible curse on the innocent baby.

Tell the children they are going to describe a glimpse through the keyhole of the living room door of the twelfth fairy. As a class, brainstorm some of the things that might be seen through her keyhole. The following questions may help to stimulate ideas:
• What does the wallpaper and furniture look like?
• What objects are displayed on the mantelpiece?
• What books are lying on the table?
• What evidence is there of pets and other creatures?
• What pictures are hanging on the walls?
• What evidence is there of hobbies, or of jobs unfinished or waiting to be started?

Give each child a copy of the keyhole-shaped paper and ask them to sketch what they can see. Explain that they will be given the opportunity to elaborate on these drawings later. Now, ask the children to work with a partner and, taking each item in turn, discuss what it might look like and list four or five words or phrases to describe it. This will help to ensure that each has a broad basis of ideas and vocabulary for individual writing

Now ask the children to write a paragraph describing their glimpse through the wicked fairy's keyhole.

When the writing is complete, give the children an opportunity to finish their pictures. The writing can then be mounted on to a second keyhole shape and attached to the drawing with a paper fastener as illustrated.

9

THE PLAY PARK

Teaching content
• Structuring a description.
• Accurate description of a familiar place in unusual conditions.

What you need
A3 paper, marker pens, a thesaurus, photocopiable anthology page 214.

What to do
Explain that, working in groups of three, the children are going to write a collaborative description of the local play park as it might

appear at one of the following times:
- at *night;*
- in the *fog;*
- in the *rain.*

Ask each group to choose a different situation and to write the keyword (italicised above) in the middle of their sheet of paper. Then, ask the children to sit facing each other and explain that they are going to play a word association game to help them write accurate and evocative descriptions.

The children should consider the word(s) on their sheet and each, in turn, write one additional word associated with this keyword. For example, the *night* group might suggest 'dark', 'stars', 'shadows', 'cats', 'eerie shapes', 'silence', 'bushes quietly rustling', 'owls', 'something scuttling in the bushes...' Those who cannot think of a new word should say 'pass' and miss a go. The group should continue until everyone has 'passed' and no one can think of any more words. You may like to encourage the children to use a thesaurus at this point.

Now, give each group a copy of photocopiable anthology page 214 and tell the children to read the passage that refers to the particular weather conditions they are writing about. They should underline any words or phrases that they find powerful or evocative, adding these to their A3 sheets where necessary.

If possible, take the children to the local play park, but if not, ask them to imagine it. Ask each child in the group to write a short descriptive paragraph of *one* of the following aspects, drawing on the words and phrases elicited earlier:
- the ground;
- the sky/trees/skyline;
- the rides.

Once finished, each child should read their work to the rest of the group and the paragraphs should be combined into a coherent whole. Those groups who are not good at working collaboratively should do the following:
1. Decide on an order for the paragraphs.
2. Appoint a reader who should read the paragraphs aloud in the correct order.
3. Identify any parts that may need to be altered or re-written to make them fit better.
4. Try to work together to re-write these sections. If this leads to arguments, choose one person to re-write each part. A skilled group of collaborators may decide to interweave the paragraphs. This is to be encouraged, provided that the work of each child in the group is included in the final piece.

Development/homework task
The children can make evocative drawings to accompany their writing.

ROOMS: COLD OR COMFORTING?

Teaching content
The images selected, and the language used to describe them, can stimulate particular emotions in the reader.

What you need
Photocopiable page 106, scissors, writing materials, paper.

What to do
Sometimes writers describe a scene using emotive language to prepare the reader for what is to happen, or for the introduction of a particularly pleasant or unpleasant character. For example, the phrase 'comfortable slippers warming in the soft glow of the fire' gives a feeling of well-being. The use of such words as 'comfortable', 'warming', 'soft' and 'glow' evokes these feelings and the overall image is positive and reassuring.

Divide the class into pairs and give each pair a copy of photocopiable page 106. Ask them to cut out and sort the statements into two sets:
- set 1 – a room in which something joyful is going to happen;
- set 2 – a room in which something sad is going to happen.

Once the children have sorted the statements, ask them to circle those words with positive connotations that lead to the expectation of a joyful event, and those with negative connotations that lead to the expectation of a sad event.

Now, ask them to choose either the positive or the negative phrases and to form them into a description of a room. Children should add their own ideas to describe:
- the paintings on the walls;
- the cat sitting on one of the chairs;
- the flower arrangement on the table.

Remind the children that the mood must be reflected in these descriptions and that their choice of vocabulary is important in this respect.

MUSIC MOOD WRITING

Teaching content

Creating a mood in describing a setting using music as a stimulus.

What you need

Music cassette, a cassette player, writing materials, paper.

What to do

Explain that the different art forms – music, art and literature – all inspire and influence each other. Writers, musicians and artists all attempt to build scenes in their imaginations and present these in their work.

Tell the children that they are going to listen to a piece of music and they will then write a description of an imagined scene it suggests.

Choose a short evocative extract of music to play to the children: *The Lark Ascending* by Vaughan Williams, 'Morning' from Grieg's *Peer Gynt Suite*, 'Spring' or 'Winter' from Vivaldi's *Four Seasons* or 'Mars' from Holst's *Planets Suite* are all possible pieces. Ask the children to

close their eyes and to listen to the music without moving. Explain that they should simply allow images, ideas, scenes and situations, or even just colours and shapes to flow through their minds.

Play the music again and this time ask the children to focus on one scene or image that is particularly strong. They should jot down any details that occur to them. These may concern things they can see, smell or hear, or they may be about particular feelings or colours that arise.

Now, ask children to use these rough jottings to write a description of the scene or image in their imagination. Stress that this is not action writing, but a description of a place that may or may not have people in it.

Record the children reading their descriptions with the music playing quietly in the background. They should decide when to pause in their reading to allow the music to burst through for a few seconds before continuing.

Development/homework task

• The taped descriptions could be used as the opening of a play or story inspired by the music.

• Ask the children to choose their own music to use as a stimulus for writing.

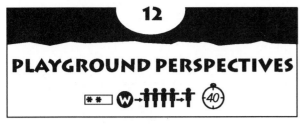

12

PLAYGROUND PERSPECTIVES

Teaching content

Describing a scene from different points of view.

What you need

Chalkboard, photocopiable page 107, character cards (as below), writing materials.

What to do

Discuss with the children how different characters can view the same scene but perceive it differently. For instance, a lost child in a strange, busy street will experience different emotions and focus on different features from a pickpocket, a policeman or a busy shopper on the first day of the sales.

Ask the children to imagine their own school playground on a drizzling winter's afternoon. They should brainstorm all the things that can be seen, heard, smelled and tasted. Write these on the board. Explain that these things will be viewed differently by different characters.

Divide the class into groups of four and give each group a copy of photocopiable page 107. Ask them to match the statements to the characters. This should give children a starting point for a passage of writing.

Now give each group a folded piece of paper with the name of one of the following characters:
• bully
• new pupil
• lost kitten
• child with toothache
• popular child
• headteacher
• inspector

The children must then work individually to describe the playground from this point of view, keeping their character secret from other groups. They should use the ideas on the board to decide on which aspects of the playground their descriptions should focus.

Display the finished descriptions for the children to read and let them guess from whose perspective each one is written.

Development/homework task

• Ask individuals to carry out this same task, choosing their own character viewpoints.

• Ask children to compare and combine descriptions from the work of several individuals in the class. They may choose several descriptions that reflect the same viewpoint, or they may select and integrate opposing observations and comments from two characters about the same features

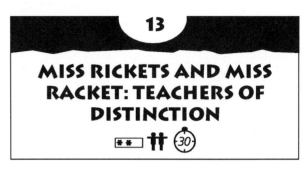

13

MISS RICKETS AND MISS RACKET: TEACHERS OF DISTINCTION

Teaching content

Descriptions can be written to evoke positive or negative feelings.

What you need

Photocopiable page 108, writing materials.

What to do

In stories, writers frequently choose to describe settings through the eyes of their characters. Such descriptions are coloured by the mood and intentions of the character and contribute to the emotional effect of the story. Descriptions can be made positive or negative by choosing to focus on particular features, and this is the point that needs to be made to most children of this age. However, you should also point out

that negative features can be fondly described to create a warm feeling in the reader, or pleasant features can be described in negative ways. Thus, a row of pictures can be described as 'carefully mounted' or 'regimented' and a gutter that needs painting can become 'softly peeling paint creating patterns' or 'tatty, rusted guttering'.

Give each pair of children one extract from photocopiable page 108. Each pair is to describe the entrance to their school as it might be seen through the eyes of the character in the extract. Allow the children a short time to read and briefly discuss their extract. Then, ask them to stand at the school gate looking at the scene they are going to describe. Those with extract A should list the unpleasant and ugly things and brainstorm all the negative descriptive phrases that come to mind. Those with extract B should list the positive things they see and brainstorm positive descriptive phrases. If necessary, remind the children that they will need to imagine that it has been raining, as in the original extracts. The questions at the bottom of the page provide a more structured approach to observation for those children who need it.

Pairs should use their notes to write a short descriptive paragraph, ending with the schoolgirl entering the school.

Development/homework task

Ask the children to find examples of positive and negative descriptions in any stories they have recently read.

14

A PLACE TO PLAY

★★★ 👥 ⏱40

Teaching content

- Structuring emotive descriptions.
- Different points of view.

What you need

Photocopiable page 109, writing materials.

What to do

Ask the children to think of a place in which they love, or have loved, to play. This may be indoors or outside and it can be a place in which they currently play, or a place they

remember from when they were younger. It can be a place in which they play alone or with others.

Ask the children to close their eyes and to concentrate on their play place. What time of year/day is it? What does it *really* look like? Ask the children to list on photocopiable page 109 five things that an adult in authority (maybe a parent or the headteacher?) would notice, were they suddenly to come across this place.

Next ask them to list things that may not be noticed by an adult or a casual observer but are particularly important to the children who actually play in it. These are the things that make it a special place. They may be particular physical objects or features of the place, or they may be other attributes, such as space, privacy, absence of adults, silence and so on. Ask the children to list as many as possible.

Now, ask the children to write two paragraphs about their place. The first should describe it through the eyes of a stranger and begin with the starter sentence 'This place has...' Their first list will contain many ideas to help them write this paragraph. Then ask the children to write a second paragraph describing all that is special about this play place, and explaining why it is special. This should begin with the starter sentence 'But the place where I play has...' The features identified on the children's second list will obviously provide a useful basis for this.

Explain that the two paragraphs will give different views of this place, and the second paragraph should particularly appeal to children. Once finished, ask the children to read their work to a partner or a small group. For each piece of work they hear, ask them to identify one thing they find particularly effective and, if they can, one thing that, were it their own work, they might change, explaining how and why. Emphasise, however, that it is only the author who can decide whether to take this peer advice on board and alter what has been written!

Development/homework task

Ask the children to think about what sort of illustration they would choose for their writing about their play place and why. Is there a particular illustrator they would commission for this work? Children can use the school library or books at home to look at different kinds of illustrations: watercolours, pen and ink, woodblock pictures, cartoons and so on. If possible, ask the children to illustrate their writing in their preferred style.

15

THE SUN HAS GOT HIS HAT ON

Teaching content

Personification.

What you need

Photocopiable anthology page 215, chalkboard, writing and illustration materials.

What to do

> The sun has got his hat on
> Hip hip hip hooray
> The sun has got his hat on
> And he's coming out to play

Personification is common in many children's stories, poems and songs. The song above describes the sun as a person who comes out to play. In *The Selfish Giant*, Oscar Wilde imagines the North Wind and Hail as people with thoughts and ideas who come to play in the Giant's garden. Explain the meaning of 'personification' and ask the children to suggest examples of it from books or songs.

Read the extract on photocopiable anthology page 215 to the children and ask them to imagine that the Sun comes to play in the Selfish Giant's garden. What would it do and how would the sunlight and warmth transform the garden?

Write the following questions on the board to help the children to focus their thinking:
• The North Wind came wrapped in furs. What would the Sun wear?
• The Hail wore grey. What colours would the Sun wear?
• The North Wind roared and the Hail rattled. What sounds would the Sun make?
• Is the Sun male or female?
• Is the Sun young or old?
• How would the Sun move?
• What six things could the Sun not resist touching in the garden?
• How would these things change after being touched by the Sun?

If appropriate, the children can begin their writing with the following sentence: 'Spring invited the Sun to visit the Giant's garden. He came wearing...'

Display this writing within beautiful sunbursts or alongside paintings or pictures of the children's personified suns.

16

WHO AM I?

Teaching content

Using personification.

What you need

Photocopiable anthology page 216, photocopiable page 110, writing materials.

What to do

Good description of place demands the ability to breathe life into inanimate objects. One way in which writers do this is by projecting human characteristics on to plants, landscapes, animals or the elements, often through the use of similes, but sometimes by giving the object or element a voice, allowing it to express human emotions directly to the reader. What the object says and how it speaks influences how the reader imagines the scene. Explain that attributing human characteristics such as speech to objects or animals is called personification. To give the children an example of this, give each pair a copy of photocopiable anthology page 216. This contains a poem by D.J. Enright entitled 'The Old Field', describing how lonely the field is once the children have gone home.

To introduce children to this mode of thought, encourage them to imagine they are, for example, a tree, the playground, a mountain or a stream and tell of life from this particular object's point of view. Give each pair a copy of photocopiable page 110 and let each child choose an object to personify in this way. They should then use the photocopiable sheet to help them generate and discuss ideas. Having worked on this sheet, the children should then work individually to organise their ideas into their preferred sequence and end by posing the question 'Who am I?' Others can read the writing and guess.

Teaching content
Recognising similes.

What you need
Photocopiable page 111, pencils.

What to do

Explain that a simile compares one thing with another. It can often be recognised because it is (or can be) prefixed by words such as *like* or *as*. Similes are most effective when they make the reader stop and think. This means that they have to capture the phenomenon accurately, but present it in a new and original way. When similes are over-used, they cease to have the same arresting effect on the reader. Similes such as 'as white as a sheet' are used so often that they do not make the reader think. The following similes are from Leon Garfield's novel *The Wedding Ghost*. They are successful because they surprise the reader by presenting familiar objects in an original and often surprising way.

Across the road he could just make out an elderly building, with a witch-like, gingerbread air. It seemed to have a broken back, and was leaning heavily on crutches...

There was a jeweller's shop nearby, with a clock hanging up outside, like an enormous biscuit-tin with hands...

Most mysteriously, a policeman was standing beside him, steaming gently, like a coffee-pot with buttons.

Give each child a copy of photocopiable page 111 and ask them to decide which of the similes listed they feel are over-used. They should cross these through lightly with a pencil. Then, ask each child to select three similes which they feel are particularly effective and to put a tick by them; then they should choose three that are particularly weak and put a cross by them. Tell them to share these with a partner and to try to agree on the three most effective and three weakest similes. Each pair should then share their list with another pair, explaining which similes they chose and why.

18

THE SEA

Teaching content

Writing similes.

What you need

Paper, writing materials, chalkboard.

What to do

Ask the children to imagine the sea on a stormy day. They may imagine all or any of the following:

wind	breakers	driftwood
seaweed	waves	stones
rocks	ship	

Ask the children to choose *at least* five things that they might see and hear on a stormy day at sea. They may select from the list above, or generate their own list individually or in groups.

Now, they should use the list below to identify verb phrases to describe how each of their chosen items sounds or moves during a storm at sea. The children will need to finish each verb phrase with a suitable simile before deciding on the best sequence of the lines to make a list poem.

Write the following verb phrases on the board for the children to use:

snarling like	gurgling like
roaring like	wild as
crashing like	straining like
snapping like	angry as
grinding like	punching like
rushing like	whipping like
heaving like	smashing like

19

TREES: WEIRD AND WONDERFUL

Teaching content

- Using a thesaurus.
- Selecting vocabulary carefully.

What you need

Photocopiable page 112, a thesaurus, writing materials, paper.

What to do

Writers need to pay careful attention to choosing words when setting a scene to create an atmosphere. Ask the children to work in pairs and to look at the three trees on photocopiable page 112. There are phrases written to describe parts of these very different trees. Tell them to look up the underlined vocabulary in the thesaurus and replace each underlined word with another that is better or equally good.

Next, ask the children to decide the time of day or night it would be best to describe these three trees in order to create a happy, a spooky or a peaceful atmosphere for a story. Ask them to list the very different wildlife (birds as well as animals) that could be described in each scene. Allow the children ten minutes to share their answers in groups before holding a class discussion.

Development/homework task

The children could now choose one tree and use the phrases and creatures to create an atmospheric description. Phrases may be copied or changed. Display the writing alongside pictures of trees drawn or painted by the children to form three interesting friezes, each depicting a different scene.

DANGEROUS WATERS

Teaching content
Selection of the best word.

What you need
Photocopiable page 113.

What to do
Photocopiable page 113 contains three short passages of varying levels of difficulty. Give each child a copy of the passage most suited to their ability and ask them to work individually to select the best word from each of the suggestions listed. Then arrange the children in groups of four according to the passage they have worked on and ask them to compare and discuss their choices. Did they all agree on all the words? Why did they choose each word in particular?

Development/homework task
Ask the children to assume that the paragraph on the photocopiable sheet is the beginning of a story and to write the missing part.

THE CHILDREN'S BOOKS

The Village of Round and Square Houses

This is a 'how it came to be' story based on a real place – the village of Tos in Cameroon – and what happens when the volcano, Naka, erupts. It is a tale within a tale that evokes the oral tradition from which the literature of creations, origins and beginnings grew. The central theme is the relationship between the people and the place in which they live.

It is written in a warm and nostalgic style, that uses descriptions of the people and their daily routines to paint a rich and rhythmic picture of village life. Ann Grifalconi uses personification of the landscape and descriptions of the people's physique, clothes, stories and customs to create an emotive and gentle image of a place where people have a fine sense of their own history and an understanding and acceptance of their environment.

How to use this book
Do the first activity before you read the book to the class. Then read the whole book to the children, making sure that they can see the pictures. Return to re-read particular descriptive passages when this is required by specific activities. Because all the revisited sections required by activities are short teachers may want, in some instances, to copy them on to a large sheet of paper, for all the children to read and study during the activity.

HOME OF MY HEART

Teaching content
Visualising and drawing from an evocative description.

What you need
The Village of Round and Square Houses, writing materials, paper, coloured chalks, chalkboard.

What to do
Explain that the story *The Village of Round and Square Houses* is set in a real place – the place where the author grew up and lived. The descriptions in the story are descriptions of a real place, as it was experienced and remembered by the author. Explain that, before you read the story, you want the children to develop a sense of the place in which it was set, and of the author's feelings about that place.

Read the story prologue to the children without showing them any pictures or discussing your own ideas. Ask the children to close their eyes and imagine that they are in this place. What does it look like? Ask them to imagine silently what they can see, hear and smell. What time of day is it? What is the weather like? What are the dominant colours and objects in the scene? Who is working nearby and what are they doing? What general mood does the scene convey? Write these up on the board as headings, along with the prologue, for the children to refer to during the activity. Ask the children to jot down a maximum of three points under each heading.

Now ask the children to use the chalk to draw the scene they imagined. You may have to remind them of the different effects they can achieve with the chalk (hard lines, blocked colour, misty colour and lines, colours smudged into each other, and so on) and of the importance of experimenting on spare paper and of working cleanly.

Once finished, they should use their notes to write a short paragraph of description to accompany their chalk drawings.

Shortly after this activity, introduce and read the whole story of *The Village of Round and Square Houses* to the class.

Development/homework task

• Ask the children to think about the environments in which they are growing up. What are they like? Ask them to draw a picture at home that captures the mood, weather, the important landmarks and the pastimes of the people in their lives. At school, help them to write an evocative description that could serve as a prologue to a story about their own childhood.

• Ask the children to find out about the place in which their parents grew up. How do their parents remember it? Ask them to work with their parents to produce a description or drawing that effectively captures its mood and features.

THE ARRIVALS

Teaching content
Setting the scene by describing people and their actions.

What you need
The Village of Round and Square Houses, photocopiable page 114, scissors, drawing materials.

What to do
Explain that writers often describe what people are doing to set a scene. Illustrate this by reading to the children pages 2–4 of the story of *The Village of Round and Square Houses*.

Give each pair a copy of photocopiable page 114. Explain that this contains a series of statements describing relatives coming for a meal. Tell each pair to read the statements and sequence them into a logical order. They should leave any statements they are not sure about and discuss them at the end.

Finally, ask the children to draw a picture to illustrate the scene.

Development/homework task
Tell the children to think of a time when they have had relatives to visit and describe this to their partner. Then, ask each child to write about five or six sentences to describe what happened and how. The sentences they have sorted may give them some good ideas.

23

THUNDERSTORM FIGHTS

Teaching content

Using personification to describe a thunderstorm.

What you need

The Village of Round and Square Houses, A3 sheets of paper, marker pens, writing materials.

What to do

Read to the children Gran'ma Tika's description of the volcanic eruption from pages 13–19 of the story of *The Village of Round and Square Houses*. Stop when you reach the point at which the people realise that 'NAKA HAD SPARED THEM.' Explain that what you have just read is an example of personification – giving human characteristics to an object. Ask the children: What has been given human characteristics? (a mountain) What has been described? (a volcanic eruption has been described as an angry person).

Tell the children they are going to see if they can make the description of a thunderstorm come alive by imagining the thunder and lightning as people who are having an argument.

Divide the class in half and put the children into groups of four. Ensure that there are equal numbers of children in each half. Ask one half of the class to imagine that they are the thunder. Tell the groups to brainstorm both what the thunder might say and words to describe how it would speak. Tell the other half to do the

same, but to imagine that they are the lightning. They should use the marker pens to write their ideas on the A3 sheets. When each group has written down five or six ideas, they should appoint one person to read out their work and display the sheets so that everyone can see them.

Now ask the children to form pairs so that each pair has one person from a thunder and one from a lightning group. Each pair should produce a piece of writing to describe the thunderstorm and, if they wish, its aftermath. Remind the children to use the group brainstorms to help them.

Allow each pair to mount and display their own work – either on the wall, or in a class book.

24

HORRIBLE VISITORS

Teaching content

Writing emotive descriptions of settings.

What you need

The Village of Round and Square Houses, chalkboard, photocopiable page 115, writing materials.

What to do

Read to the children pages 3–4 of the story of *The Village of Round and Square Houses*. Ask the children for words to describe the feelings evoked by this description, and record these on the board.

Ask the children to consider how the same event might be described to create a negative scene. Give each pair a copy of photocopiable page 115 and ask them to note down what might be different about the scene: would they change actions, names, people, how actions were described? Explain that they may identify sentences, phrases or individual words to change, by circling or crossing out and writing alternatives.

Now ask each pair to write a negative description of the scene. Arrange the children in groups of six and ask them to read their work to the rest of the group and explain what they changed and why.

CHILDHOOD PLACES

Teaching content
Describing a place from memory.

What you need
Chalkboard, writing materials.

What to do
The Village of Round and Square Houses is based on a woman's memory of the place in which she was born and grew up. Explain to the children that any place can be described in this way. Ask them to think about the house or neighbourhood in which they currently live. How will they describe it when they are old and are writing a book about their childhood?

Write the following questions and starter sentence on the board to help the children structure their response:
• I grew up in...
• What kind of activities take place there?
• What kind of things do the adults and children do?
• Is it a good or a bad place to grow up in? Why?

ANGRY WORLD

Teaching content
Understanding and conveying the close relationship between setting and characters.

What you need
Large sheets of paper, writing materials.

What to do
Discuss with the children how the people in Ann Grifalconi's story feel themselves to be a part of the land upon which they live. Because the mountain was a part of their lives, when it erupted, the people were convinced that it was angry with them for some reason and asked 'What have we done to anger you so?' (page 15).

If the earth, hills, plains, trees, seashore or riverside where the children live were to become angry, how do they think this anger might manifest itself? Organise the class into groups of four and ask the children to write on a large sheet of paper:
(a) Which aspect of the landscape they are considering.
(b) What the people might be doing to make it angry.
(c) How this anger could manifest itself.
(d) What the people would do and say during this.
(e) What they would do and say to appease it.

Ask each group to brainstorm more detailed words and phrases to describe what could happen in (c) and (d). Then, ask the children to work in pairs and to write two short passages: one to describe the angry landscape and one to describe what the people do and say. Then let each pair share their work in their original groups of four.

Finally, ask the children to work individually to:

• Write one sentence to introduce the landscape feature.
• Write one sentence to explain what the people do to anger it.
• Use the two passages to write a short description of the anger and the people's response. They may use the passage verbatim, or adapt parts of it.
• Write a short piece (about two sentences) to describe what the people do and say to appease the anger and whether they alter their behaviour in the future.

Dinner Ladies Don't Count

Dinner Ladies Don't Count contains two stories: 'Dinner Ladies Don't Count' and 'Linda's Lie'. The activities in this section are based on the first of these stories.

In his story 'Dinner Ladies Don't Count', Bernard Ashley writes about Jason, a small boy who comes to school with a smack instead of his breakfast. He storms around the school in a temper and then gets the blame for something he didn't do. Jason is enabled to come to terms with some of his problems through the sympathetic help of a dinner lady.

About the author

Bernard Ashley is the headteacher of a London primary school and he writes with sympathy and insight about the problems encountered by children. His stories often have their starting points in, or are worked out against, the background of school. He writes about the places that he knows well. It is for this reason that 'Dinner Ladies Don't Count' has been chosen as a story that illustrates the writer's craft in terms of place and setting. With a remarkable economy of language, Bernard Ashley deftly sums up the essence of a primary school.

How to use this book

Read the story to the children, preferably in one session. For the first activity children will need access to the first two chapters. They could either re-read this themselves in groups, or you might prefer to re-read the first two chapters to the whole group, having first set the task. The other four activities require access to only a few paragraphs or sentences that may be read by you or a group member, although the children may like to refresh their memories by skimming or re-reading the whole story. There is an interview with Bernard Ashley on the audio cassette, which the children will find interesting.

27

PLACES I KNOW

Teaching content
Successful writers draw on their own experience.

What you need
Dinner Ladies Don't Count, photocopiable page 116, writing materials.

What to do
Arrange the children in groups of four and explain that 'Dinner Ladies Don't Count' is one of many stories by Bernard Ashley. He writes about the things that can happen to an ordinary person. We want to read to the end of his stories because we care about the characters and recognise, and often identify with, their problems.

Explain that Bernard Ashley writes school stories because he is a headteacher and knows the world of school intimately. Writers who write about unfamiliar places, or who write about historical times, need to do a great deal of research before they can begin to think of stories. This is one of the reasons why many writers choose to set their stories in a world that is familiar to them.

Re-read, or ask one of the children to re-read, the first two chapters of the story. Give each group a copy of photocopiable page 116 and ask them to consider the details in 'Dinner Ladies Don't Count' that indicate that the author knows about schools and the people who work in them.

Finally, ask the children to consider the places and organisations they know well, such as their home, a shopping centre, a sports club or dancing class. Do they think these places would form a good background setting for their own stories?

BOOK CORNER

Teaching content
Concise descriptions of place.

What you need
Dinner Ladies Don't Count, writing and drawing materials.

What to do
In 'Dinner Ladies Don't Count' the essence of the class book corner is summed up in just a few sentences. Read the children the description on pages 11–12, from 'He could smell the dust...' to '...but the floor and the books were too hard.' School carpeting is fairly uniform and the children will probably recognise immediately the ridged, scratchy library carpet. Its dustiness is also evocative. You can almost smell the dust and feel the hardness of that corner of the classroom.

Explain that short descriptions often capture the atmosphere of a place more effectively than longer ones. However, the words used to describe the main features must be clear and precise.

Ask the children to think of a small area in the school that they either like or dislike. Tell them to write a list of eight features that are central to

that place. They should think of smells, textures, colours and objects. Next, ask them to use this list to write four sentences that convey the essence of this place. Display these with an illustration of the place described.

Development/homework task
Ask the children to design and describe their ideal library corner.

VIOLENT VERBS

Teaching content
Creating atmosphere in descriptions of place.

What you need
Dinner Ladies Don't Count, chalkboard, writing materials.

What to do
Read the first two pages of 'Dinner Ladies Don't Count' (up to '...someone getting hurt.') to the group. Point out that, within a familiar setting filled with ordinary objects, Bernard Ashley has used particularly strong action words to evoke an atmosphere of violence. Explain to the children that action words are called verbs then re-read the first paragraph and ask them to list the violent verbs that they hear. They will probably note 'stormed', 'kicked', 'threw' and 'clanged'.

The second paragraph describes the classroom setting. Re-read the paragraph to the children, asking them to identify the phrase that describes the atmosphere before Jason enters ('...all love and kisses in her hands...') and what Jason does to spoil this atmosphere ('...knocking into chairs.'). Here Bernard Ashley again uses a violent verb alongside an ordinary classroom object to create atmosphere.

Arrange the children in pairs. Ask them to imagine a child who has left the house happily after a good breakfast and is on the way to school. Write the following questions on the board to help them.
• How might this child move along the street?
• In what way might the child greet school friends?
• What does the child do in the playground before school starts?

• In what manner does the child open the classroom door?

• What does the child do to the chairs in the classroom?

Ask each pair to brainstorm ideas for each of these points and then write, either individually or in pairs, an introductory paragraph that creates a very different atmosphere from that evoked in 'Dinner Ladies Don't Count'.

Development/homework task

Each child should write two very short accounts about coming to school in the morning: one describing coming in a good mood and the other in a bad mood. Then ask them to fold a sheet of paper in half like a card and write 'Coming to school' on the front cover. Inside, they should write or stick the good mood passage on one half and the bad mood passage on the other.

DANGER ALERT

Teaching content

Creating atmosphere through descriptions of objects.

What you need

Dinner Ladies Don't Count, photocopiable page 117, writing materials.

What to do

There is no doubt that the rubbish bin in the playground is dangerous. On page 35 Bernard Ashley tells us this in three sentences before he actually declares 'It was very dangerous, and against the school rules'.

In our minds, the idea of something being chained implies danger. Ask the children what sort of creatures or things are usually chained. Explain that writers make associations like this to alert the reader to coming danger. The second sentence introduces a second image of menace – a 'robot drinking from a giant mug'. The third sentence shows how the symbol of danger could be used to climb up the sides of the litter bin.

Arrange the children in pairs and give each pair a copy of photocopiable page 117. Ask them to look at the story openings and to decide which sentences are warning of danger to come and which are 'safe' beginnings. They should place a tick in the appropriate column. Then, ask the children to choose one sentence and to expand it into the opening paragraph of a story.

Development/homework task

The children could continue their stories from the opening paragraphs they have written.

31

OUR CLASS

Teaching content

Setting the scene by describing activity.

What you need

Writing materials.

What to do

Discuss with the children why a classroom is a strange and unfamiliar place to visit in the early morning or late evening. This is partly because the essence of a classroom is found in its bustle and business. The true character of a classroom is best summed up during a working day.

Several times in 'Dinner Ladies Don't Count' Bernard Ashley conveys the atmosphere of a classroom in a few deft phrases, for example:
• page 15 'With one half-closed eye...with the scraps.'
• page 26 'Already, friendly hands...in the fish tank, even.'

Arrange the children in groups of four and tell them to brainstorm phrases and words that describe the bustle of a classroom during an activity lesson. They could observe children in their own class or, if other teachers in the school would allow such observation, it would be useful if small groups of children could spend 20 minutes in a different class to watch the movement, listen to the sounds, note the smells and observe the relationships between the children.

Next, ask the children to work individually to write a paragraph describing the classroom they have observed, choosing the items that best sum up this place.

Finished descriptions could be mounted and made into a book to be presented to the host class entitled 'A snapshot of your classroom', 'A day in the life of...' or 'The secret life of...'

Fair's Fair

Fair's Fair tells the story of how Jackson, a lonely Edwardian street child, is led by a monstrous black dog to a grand, but deserted, house where he meets a similarly miserable girl, Lillipolly. The two are mysteriously given food, warmth and comfort, and take care of the dog and the house in return. They are finally rewarded for their kindness, bravery, patience,

honesty and generosity by being adopted by the owner of the house who has really been watching them all along. They will no longer be poor and homeless, but can live with him as his children.

The story is set in Edwardian London and descriptions of mean, freezing back alleyways contrast with the grand, sweeping avenues of the prosperous areas. The tiny starving orphans are poignantly placed in the sumptuous home of London's rich.

About the author

Leon Garfield himself made Highgate his home, the part of London that features in so many of his stories. He was born and educated in Brighton but had to break off his art studies because of the outbreak of the Second World War. During this time he served in the Medical Corps in England, Belgium and Germany, then afterwards worked as a biochemist before his writing career took off. Leon Garfield is one of the most widely acclaimed children's authors and has had screenplays made from several of his books. He has also received the first Guardian Award for *Devil-in-the-Fog*, the Carnegie Medal for *The God Beneath the Sea* and the Whitbread Award for *John Diamond*.

How to use this book

Read the book in its entirety to the children, showing the pictures as the story unfolds. Close examination of the actual text is only necessary for the first activity. The other four activities require only short extracts from the book, which may be read by the teacher or by one of the children. Make the book available for the children to read individually or in groups during the day. It may also be timetabled for reading at home.

THE WORST STREET

Teaching content

• Writers need a strong visual picture of the environment. This requires research into the period in which the story is set.

• Writers sometimes choose to convey an impression rather than a detailed description in a story.

What you need

Reference book(s) on Edwardians, *Fair's Fair*, art paper, charcoal.

What to do

Explain that any writer of a story set in the past must research the period carefully. This knowledge informs both the storyline and the story settings described in the book. In one sentence, Leon Garfield sums up the place where Jackson lives, giving a clear impression of the miserable place that Bluegate is.

He sat on the doorstep at the back of Paddy's Goose, which was at the worst end of the worst street in the worst part of town.

He also conveys the essence of the large and grand property at the other end of town.

There was a house surrounded by trees, bulging with chimneys and turrets and looking like three houses that had climbed on top of each other.

These descriptions create a strong impression, rather than a detailed description, of what these places are like. The reader is left to imagine the specific details of each scene. Can the children remember any other examples of Garfield capturing the essence, rather than the detail, of a place?

Explain that some writers draw or model the place in which the story is set to help them both capture the detail and reflect on the general atmosphere of the setting. To experience the effect of this, the children will research and draw the houses and streets mentioned in *Fair's Fair*. One half of the group will create Bluegate, 'the worst street in the worst part of town'. The other will create a street of grand and rich houses 'bulging with chimneys and turrets'.

First, the children must research the Edwardian period using both *Fair's Fair* and reference book(s). They must find out about the living conditions of the poorest or the richest in society and show this knowledge through their art work, each child producing one house. In Garfield's story, the only colours mentioned are black and white, so it would be effective to produce the art work using charcoal. The two rows of houses should be 'built' as a wall display. Appropriate street furniture and suitably clad pedestrians may be added to contrast the two streets further.

Then ask the children to do the opposite from Garfield and use the street drawings and their research knowledge to write a detailed description of the place. Emphasise that the miserable points should be exaggerated in the worst street and grand details must be highlighted in the rich area. This writing can be displayed, along with the earlier 'essence' quotes from *Fair's Fair*.

33

AN UNEXPECTED TURN OF EVENTS

■ ✱✱ ⬤W-✝-✝✝ (50)

Teaching content
Writers use scenes to build expectations and then surprise the reader.

What you need
Fair's Fair, writing materials.

What to do
Writers sometimes build readers' expectations and then surprise them with the unexpected. This keeps the readers involved and encourages them to question as they read. Ask the children to think of some specific examples of this from *Fair's Fair*. They might mention the following incidents:

• The description of the dog leads the reader to expect it to attack Jackson.

• The big house is first described as 'An old dead house with an old dead door, with an iron letter-box, as thin as a miser's mouth.' We are surprised by the lighted candles and the comforting smell of cooking inside.

• A grand and beautiful room is described with an imposing table, at the head of which is sitting '...a small thin, dirty, tattered, angry little girl'.

Let the children read the description of the big room again and ask half the class or group to describe the girl they might expect to find sitting at the head of this table eating this wonderful meal. They may find the following headings helpful:

• Hair: colour, length, style, condition
• Eyes: colour, expression
• Evidence of expression and mood
• What is she doing?

Ask the other half of the class or group to create a room that is the opposite of that described in the book, by writing an 'opposite' description for each of the following details Garfield describes:

• 'room...as long as a street, nearly, and tall and wide to match'
• 'candles in silver candlesticks'
• 'pictures in gold frames'
• 'china plates on a shining table'
• 'roast beef on a sideboard'
• 'a roaring fire in the grate'

Now, pair the children with a partner from the opposite 'half' of the class. Ask them to read each other's work and each to write a description of a shabby room with a beautifully dressed, rich girl sitting at the head of the table.

Development/homework task
Ask each pair to invent and write a story to explain how the rich girl got into this room and what happens next.

34

STRAIGHT FROM THE HORSE'S MOUTH

■ ✱✱ ✝✝✝✝✝ ⏱

Teaching content
The actions and comments of incidental characters can quickly create an impression of a scene.

What you need
Fair's Fair, large pen and sheet of paper per group

What to do
At the beginning of his book, Leon Garfield makes it clear that no one does anything about the plight of the homeless boy and no one misses him when he disappears from Bluegate for ever. Although we are given no details, we can imagine how other characters might behave toward Jackson to intensify the atmosphere of neglect and abandonment surrounding him.

Arrange the children in groups of five and ask them to imagine that they are each one of the following five characters leaving the Goose Pub at closing time:

• student out for a drink with friends
• rich and powerful business man or woman
• poor mother with six children at home
• sailor home on leave
• local policeman

Ask the children to decide and then mime how their character reacts to the boy, curled up on the step in the freezing snow. Do they notice the boy at all? Do they make fun of him, feel guilty, feel sorry for him or feel angry with him? Are they suspicious? Perhaps they feel threatened.

The rest of the group should watch each mime in turn, and together write a short description of how each character behaves, trying to make the characters' thoughts clear by describing their actions. If necessary, the writers may ask a character to repeat the mime several times.

Finally, allow the children *one* comment that exemplifies their character's feelings.

These descriptions should be displayed and discussed in the classroom, along with 'action replays' of the mimes.

THE HOMECOMING

Teaching content
Using a scene to establish a mood.

What you need
Fair's Fair, writing materials, paper.

What to do
Arriving home from school on a cold winter's afternoon can be a wonderful relief. Ask the children to work in small groups to brainstorm the first welcoming sensations that reach them as they open their front doors. The following questions may provide a few useful prompts.
• What do they see? On a dark winter afternoon the lights may be on. (In which rooms? Where does the light come from? What does it illuminate?)
• What do they hear (Voices talking? Who? The sound of the radio or television?)
• What do they smell (Cooking? The dog?)
Obviously for some children, homecoming will differ depending on family circumstances. The brainstorm must include all these very different experiences.

Explain how writers deliberately choose the smells, images and sounds that best convey the atmosphere they wish to create. Ask the children to re-read Garfield's description of Jackson first opening the door and entering the big mansion to find a warm and comforting scene (pages 22–25).

Now, ask the children to select the best words and phrases from their brainstorms to describe a warm and welcoming homecoming on a cold, bitter winter's evening. They may like to add imaginary smells, sights and sounds to increase the welcoming atmosphere. The children should then organise all these ideas into a paragraph of writing, and give their paragraph the title 'The homecoming'. A starter sentence such as the following may be useful for some children: 'Throwing open the door, I stamped my cold, wet feet on the mat. Inside...'

Development/homework task
An interesting way to present this writing is to stick it behind a close observation drawing of each child's own front door, cut out of A4 card so that the writing is revealed when the door opens.

SNOW

Teaching content
Describing a scene through the eyes of a character.

What you need
Fair's Fair, photocopiable anthology page 217, poster-sized sheets of paper, marker pens, writing materials.

What to do

Give the children a copy of photocopiable anthology page 217 and read the extract from *The Snow Spider* with them. Establish that this passage describes the snow as seen through the eyes of Gwyn, a nine-year-old boy who is trapped on a mountain. Ask the children to underline those parts in which the snow is described. What does this description tell the reader about how Gwyn feels about the snow? Ask each group to choose and explain one phrase or sentence that shows Gwyn's attitude towards the snow. Why do they think he feels like this? Ask them to list other people or animals who may see the snow as an enemy.

Now read the Dylan Thomas extract with the children. What is the attitude to snow here, and how do the children know that this is how the main character feels?

Ask each group to produce a large poster brainstorming all the things they love about snow. Display these so that all the ideas can be shared by the class.

Tell the children that they are going to write an epilogue for *Fair's Fair*. They will write a short description of Jackson and Lillypolly one year after the book's ending. It is Christmas Eve and the two children are looking out of a window of their home. What will they be wearing and how will they have changed? At the beginning of the story Jackson's attitude towards the snow is similar to Gwyn's. Will his feelings about the falling snow have changed now that he has a warm, comfortable home? Ask them to describe the view from the window through the eyes of either Lillypolly or Jackson. **NB:** Use the terms adjective, adverb, simile or metaphor appropriately when discussing the use of language, but only if this will not impair the children's understanding or enjoyment of the activity. It is vital, however, that this activity does not become a focus solely for teaching the meaning of these words.

37
DUMB ANIMALS?

Teaching content
Using animals to add to the atmosphere of a scene.

What you need
Fair's Fair, photocopiable page 118, writing materials.

What to do
The description of Growler and the way he communicates with the frightened boy adds to the terror of the scene at the beginning of the book. Leon Garfield chooses to emphasise the dog's size and blackness. Read the description of Growler meeting Jackson (pages 9–12). The mention of 'heaven' immediately before the dog's arrival causes the reader to think of hell when the 'black dog' appears. Even the snowflakes 'fry' on its great nose. Ask the children to listen or read carefully and to identify other aspects of language use that create the dog's menacing presence.

When writers describe animals, they have to observe real animals very closely in order to be convincing. Those children with animals at home will be able to cite examples of how they communicate in their own ways, using not just sounds, but their ears, tails, eyes, hair, bodies, whiskers, noses and mouths. Leon Garfield's dog communicates soundlessly:

' Liar!' says the dog; not in words but with its terrible eyes and rattling teeth...

'And I'm froze and hungry' says the dog; not in words but with its lean sides and smoking breath.

Give each child a copy of photocopiable page 118. Ask them to complete each of the 'speeches', adding a description of what each animal does to communicate its thoughts. Remind the children to describe the animal very carefully and perhaps emphasise certain points about its appearance, depending on whether they want the reader to trust or fear the animal.

PICTURE POEM

CAPTURE THE ESSENCE

◆ This description is too long. Try to edit it down to about four or five sentences only. You may edit it by: changing words, deleting sentences, re-writing sentences and changing the order of sentences.

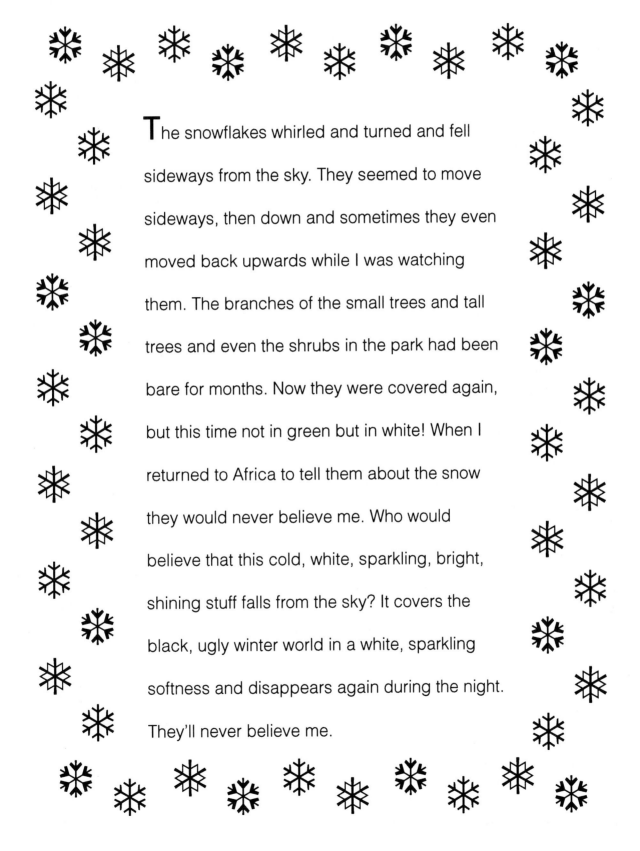

The snowflakes whirled and turned and fell sideways from the sky. They seemed to move sideways, then down and sometimes they even moved back upwards while I was watching them. The branches of the small trees and tall trees and even the shrubs in the park had been bare for months. Now they were covered again, but this time not in green but in white! When I returned to Africa to tell them about the snow they would never believe me. Who would believe that this cold, white, sparkling, bright, shining stuff falls from the sky? It covers the black, ugly winter world in a white, sparkling softness and disappears again during the night. They'll never believe me.

NAME

FRESH EYES ON FAMILIAR PLACES

◆ Describe the first object to catch your eye when you walk into the room.

◆ Where does the main source of light come from?
(window? central light? side lights? lamps?)

◆ Can you describe the quality of light in the room?

◆ Describe pieces of furniture that are important to the look of the room.

◆ Where does the light fall? Are there any particular objects that catch or reflect the light?

◆ Describe one small object that looks particularly good in this room.

◆ Imagine a family member who looks 'just right' in the room. Who is it? Where are they? What are they doing?

◆ Describe other important features that give a pleasant feel to this room.

FRESH EYES ON FAMILIAR PLACES: ASSESSMENT

Does this writing accurately reflect the room in question? In what ways?

Is there anything important that the writer has left out?

◆ Please use the questions on the accompanying photocopiable page to write a short description of your child's bedroom. Your child will do likewise. *DO NOT DISCUSS THIS TASK UNTIL BOTH PIECES OF WRITING ARE COMPLETE.*

◆ When both pieces have been finished, please swap your writing with your child and each answer the two questions above.

ROOMS: COLD OR COMFORTING?

◆ Cut out and sort the statements into two sets:
Set 1 – a room in which something joyful is going to happen.
Set 2 – a room in which something sad is going to happen.
Then circle the words in each statement that helped you to make your decision.

Flames leaping and dancing up the chimney

Logs crackling cheerfully in the hearth

Black burnt-out coals lying dead in the grate

Comfortable slippers warming by the radiant glow of the fire

Old cobwebs hanging in grey and dusty corners

Grimy mirrors shadowing the grey winter scene

Shiny brasses shimmering in the soft lamplight

Polished mirror reflecting flickering candle light

Dank smell of damp and neglect

Delicious smell of freshly baked bread

An abandoned meal mouldering on a plate

Musical sound of a clock ticking on the mantlepiece

Grating sound of a rat scraping in the corner

PLAYGROUND PERSPECTIVES

◆ Cut out these characters and match them to the correct statement.

The light from the classroom window shone warmly through the grey afternoon gloom, inviting me back inside.

I stood in a deserted corner of the playground, pretending that I liked to be alone.

I lifted my face to the welcome freshness of the light drizzle and kicked the ball with all my might down the wet pitch.

All around me, the feet and legs pounded and splashed in the puddles, soaking me as I cowered beneath the hut.

I stuck my hands in my pockets and whistled happily. I wanted crisps and I noticed that young Peter Brown had the flavour I liked best.

MISS RICKETS AND MISS RACKET

Extract A

Judith dragged her feet, dangling her schoolbag low over the puddles. She thought of Miss Rickets waiting in the classroom. She pictured the angular silhouette standing by the board, the skinny goat legs poking out from their thick, scratchy skirt. She imagined the hard, thin lips forming a cruel smile as the sharp little eyes searched the silent class, choosing their next victim.

   Judith rounded the corner and turned into the school gate...

Extract B

Jennifer skipped along, swinging her schoolbag low over the puddles. She thought of Miss Racket waiting in the classroom. She pictured her standing by the door, her tall frame bending to attend to the children spilling busily around her. She thought of her calm face and her good-humoured smile as she called the tumbling class to order.

   Jennifer's pace quickened as she rounded the corner and turned into the school gate...

What words would this character use to describe the following:
• the gate?

• the ground between the gate and the school building?

• the door/entrance to the school?

• any windows that can be seen?

• the roof?

• the sky?

A PLACE TO PLAY

The place I love to play is _____

Five things an adult would probably notice are:

1.

2.

3.

4.

5.

Things that are particularly special to me are:

Describe this place through the eyes of a stranger.

This place has...

Now describe what is special about your play place.

But the place where I play has...

WHO AM I?

Circle the object you will breathe life into:

tree   playground   stream   mountain

road   puddle   block of flats

house   school   storm cloud

◆ Write three sentences or phrases to describe yourself.
Think of your colour, height, width, texture, posture, shape and form.

1. _____

2. _____

3. _____

How long have you been here?

_____

Which season of the year do you like best and why?

_____

Which people do you like best and why?

_____

What are your dislikes?

_____

Circle the words that describe you and how you speak. Add others if you can.

grumble   whine   boom   squeak   chuckle

laugh   mumble   chime   soft   harsh   creaky

slow   lazy   gossipy   determined   wise   sneaky

playful   harsh   sing-song   clipped

SIMILES

◆ Read this list of similes. Lighty cross out those you think are over-used.

◆ Choose three that you think are particularly effective and put tick by them.

◆ Now choose three that you think are particularly weak and put a cross next to them.

The rain fell as softly as a child's tears

Black, bare, twisted branches clutching and catching like a witch's gnarled fingers

It was as black as night

Sunshine streamed like ribbons

The day was as dull as ditchwater

The fog was as thick as smoke

The mountain stood like a giant above the valley

Leaves flew like confetti in the wind

White-capped waves like sea horse's manes

The wind howled like a wolf

The sea was as green as an emerald

Stars shone like diamonds in the sky

Fields lay below like a patchwork quilt

Thunder roared like a lion

◆ Compare your decisions with a partner and try to agree on the three strongest and the three weakest similes.

TREES: WEIRD AND WONDERFUL

◆ Replace each underlined word with another that is better or equally good. Then decide what time of day or night it would be best to describe each of these trees to create a spooky, peaceful or happy atmosphere respectively. Finally, list the different animals that could be found in each scene.

Enchanted wood

strange silver branches, stretching into the clouds

the wind sleeps in the still boughs

roots hidden in the undergrowth

tall trunk

Time of day:

Animals:

Peaceful meadow

the wind laughs through the fresh green leaves

leaves flutter in the warm sun

boughs heavy with blossom

majestic trunk

old roots

Time of day:

Animals:

Graveyard

The sad wind cries through dead leaves.

bare boughs

branches that seem to clutch

twisted roots

thin trunk

R.I.P.

Time of day:

Animals:

DANGEROUS WATERS

Denny (loved/liked) his new bike. Every (day/morning), he got up early so that he could ride it before going to school. The (steep/long) road outside his house led down past the pond and Denny had been (warned/told) not to ride down the hill. One morning Denny (noticed/saw) that his mother had stopped watching him. He decided to take his bike outside the gate for just a minute. (Jumping/Getting) up on the saddle, Denny enjoyed the feeling of speed as the bike began to (race/move) downhill. Denny could not stop the bike. The (cold/dangerous) pond seemed to be speeding towards him...

Vicky (skipped/ran) happily over the wet sand. She was (glad/pleased) that she had (escaped/got up) before the rest of the family had woken up. Vicky had never (raced/walked) over a deserted beach before. (Looking/Glancing) swiftly back over her shoulder, she could see her footprints (marking/breaking) the smooth sand. The (curling/crashing) friendly waves seemed to beckon her in for a swim. (Forgetting/Ignoring) the warnings she had been given, Vicky dropped the towel from round her shoulders and (waded/plunged) into the sea...

Pete (held/clutched) the low hanging branch. This was his (best/only) hope. Down river, he could hear the (thunder/sound) of 'Death Falls'. He had been told stories since he was a boy of the unlucky few who had (dropped/fallen/plunged) to their deaths in these waterfalls. The rapids (pulled/heaved) at his helpless body. Perhaps Meg had seen the boat capsize and was (racing/running) to get help. Pete's hands were fast becoming (numb/frozen/cold). He couldn't hold on for much longer.

As the branch (cracked/broke) he heard a desperate (yell/scream/shout) rip from his own throat and mingle with the (spray/swirl/stream) of the (raging/racing/fast-moving) current...

THE ARRIVALS

◆ Cut out the following statements and arrange them in the correct order.

First through the door was Auntie, loaded with mysteriously shaped parcels and grumbling as usual about the long journey and Uncle's driving.

'First things first,' teased Auntie, still firmly clutching the parcels. 'A hot cup of tea will do nicely.'

Uncle followed – at a safe distance – with his arms outstretched ready to snatch up the little one and swing him into the air.

Mum quickly dried her hands, blew a wisp of stray hair off her face and hurried to the front door.

'They're here!' squealed the children, as the doorbell chimes confirmed the arrival.

'Hello! Hello!' they all chorused excitedly to each other, even before the door was open.

'Come in and take your coats off,' urged the older two, eyeing the parcels eagerly.

'Well, you've done some growing since I last saw you!' he groaned good-naturedly.

HORRIBLE VISITORS

◆ The following passage from *The Village of Round and Square Houses* describes a very positive scene of happy family life. Rewrite it so that it conveys a very negative, unhappy atmosphere. You may change sentences, phrases and individual words.

Every evening, after a day of work in the fields, Uncle Domo and Gran'pa Oma came to our round house for supper. We children would hurry to put out the low, wooden stool for Gran'pa Oma (for he was the eldest, and closer to the ancestor spirits).

Then we would unroll the grass mat for Uncle Domo, the next oldest, as was only proper and respectful.

And there they would sit proudly in their bright robes – Gran'pa Oma above, seated on his stool, hands on knees – and Uncle Domo below.

Then they would ask to see the children!

One by one we would come forward from the narrow doorway... and one by one we would be lifted to sit upon those high and bony knees, and Gran'pa would ask each one of us, 'What have you learned today?'

PLACES I KNOW

◆ Only someone who is very familiar with school life would know or notice some of the things that Bernard Ashley knows. Re-read the first two chapters of 'Dinner Ladies Don't Count' and note down three details for each of the following categories.

What classrooms look like

Things teachers say

Things children do when someone is in trouble

Things children do when the teacher is not looking

DANGER ALERT

◆ Look at the following story openings and decide whether each one conveys an atmosphere of danger or of safety. Tick the appropriate column.

Story opening	Danger	Safety
The chasm gaped wide like the jaws of an angry lion...		
The road led gently down to the sleepy village...		
Looking over the edge, he felt dizzy when he saw the people as small as ants below...		
The balmy summer breeze rustled through the golden corn...		
The hurricane howled like a wild ravenous beast...		
The deserted crows' nest high in the gnarled and twisted branches invited her to climb higher...		
The fresh green leaves shone in the bright sun, carefully shielding the tree house from strangers...		

◆ Now choose one sentence and expand it into the opening paragraph for a story. Use the back of this sheet for your rough draft.

DUMB ANIMALS?

◆ Complete each of the starter sentences listed below by writing a description of what the particular animal does to communicate its thoughts.

'I like you,' says the dog, not in words but with its...

_____

'I hate you,' says the cat, not in words but with its...

_____

'I'm hungry,' says the cat, not in words but with its...

_____

'Take me for a walk,' says the dog, not in words but with its

_____

'There's someone coming up the path,' says the dog, not in words but with its...

_____

'Don't take a step further,' says the dog, not in words but with its...

_____

'I'm comfortable here,' says the cat, not in words but with its...

_____

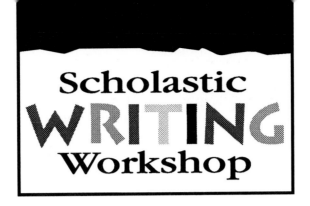

Chapter Five

STORY STRUCTURE

INTRODUCTION

Why is structure important?

The narrative structure of a story is like the framework of a building or the skeleton of a living being. The bare bones are fleshed out with detail and intricate designs, devices and colour but the original structure has shaped and strengthened the finished creation.

Unlike the framework of a house, however, which must remain unchanged throughout the building process, some aspects of story structure may be changed as the story is written. Although it is impossible to create a story without making decisions about structure, it is usual for writers to change and develop structures as characters and ideas unfold.

How children use story structure

Structuring a story involves children in making decisions about:
• the sequence in which the story will be told to the readers;
• the point of view from which the story will be told;
• how the story will be laid out and segmented for the reader – page layouts, chapters, chapter headings and titles.

When children first come to write their own stories, their planning process often consists of telling their story to themselves, telling it to someone else, or talking or drawing pictures about parts of their story. These activities all help the child to resolve structural aspects of the story without consciously thinking about it because they encourage the child to identify and sequence the main events and to clarify the storyline and the point of view from which the story is told.

Teaching story structure

It is important for children to be aware of how and why they make decisions regarding structure and of the effects of these decisions. Planning activities that prompt rigid structural decisions too early are not helpful. Teachers must constantly balance the need for children to be aware of, and experiment with different structures against the children's urgent desire to tell the story in the way that seems most obvious. Too much emphasis on structure produces writing that is stilted and stale.

Many professional writers have great success in re-working well-known stories. The thousands of versions of fairy stories, myths, legends and folk tales currently in print are proof of this. *3 Billy Goats Gruff* by Ted Dewan and *The Village of Round and Square Houses* by Ann Grifalconi, both of which are included in this workshop, are excellent examples. Re-writing well-loved and well-known stories can provide a valuable opportunity for children to play with the structural aspects of the story. They are removed from the task of having to create a story and are freed to concentrate on other story-telling skills. It is important that the purpose of such re-writing activities is understood by the children, otherwise this can be a soul-destroying and tedious task. Interesting publishing ideas for this work can further encourage reflection.

Adult writers, particularly modern writers, experiment with aspects of structure: playing with the sequence, finding new starting points, open endings and different points of view. They are constantly trying to create new effects by using new and different structures. Many children are familiar with some of these structures through their reading and television viewing.

However, before experimenting with such structures, children must first be able to tell a story chronologically from a beginning, through a middle, to an end and they must learn to tell the story consistently from one point of view, be it one of the characters or that of a narrator. The activities in this chapter are designed to help children do this, as well as exploring other aspects of structure.

CONTENTS AND ORGANISATION

The activities in this chapter seek to:
• raise children's awareness of how the narrative structure can shape and give character to a finished story.
• suggest how children may be encouraged to create and build a structure, to reflect on it and to alter it as they compose the story.

The activities in this chapter focus on four different aspects of structure: plot and sequence; beginnings and endings; point of view and use of dialogue; and divisions, layout and titles.

Plot and sequence

The easiest way to tell a story is to begin at the beginning and continue, in chronological order, until you reach the end. This is the narrative format with which children are most familiar and, if pushed, many children will state that stories have a beginning, a middle and an end.

The beginning of a story generally introduces the main characters, the place and the situation. The story takes off, however, when something happens to change normal circumstances – it may be an event, a surprise or a problem that arises. The story is about what happens – how the surprise is handled or the problem resolved.

Personal experience provides a valuable seam of story ideas that many professional writers mine effectively. Children should also be encouraged to do this. However, children often find it difficult to structure and organise their own experiences into story ideas that are exciting for others to read.

The activities in this section encourage children to focus upon planning formats, story sequence, and the place and nature of possible turning points in a narrative.

Beginnings and endings

The opening sentences of a story lure the reader over the threshold of the real world into the imagined world of the writer. They become an invitation into the world that the writer has created. No one accepts a boring invitation, and children can often cite times when they have read the beginning of a book and no further. Thus children know that the opening sentences are crucial to the success of the writing; they can make the reader decide to put a book aside or to read on.

Children also know from their experience as readers that stories can open in different ways. For example, they can begin with:

• a description of the main setting for the story:

When Chas awakened, the air raid shelter was silent. Grey winter light was creeping round the door curtain. It could have been any time. His mother was gone...
(From *The Machine Gunners* by Robert Westall)

• a conversation:

'Christmas won't be Christmas without any presents,' grumbled Jo, lying on the rug.
'It's so dreadful to be poor!' sighed Meg, looking down at her old dress.
(From *Little Women* by Louisa May Alcott)

• a statement of what the book will be about:

This is the story of a Polish family, and of what happened to them during the Second World War and immediately afterwards.
(From *The Silver Sword* by Ian Serraillier)

• a description of a character:

All of the Grimms were grim, except perhaps for Martin. He lived with his Great Aunt at No 1, Climion Street, Kensington. Great Aunt Grimm was certainly grim. She was wizened and cold and tough, like a winter onion.
(From *Grimm Grange* by W. Browning)

• a character in extreme jeopardy:

It was a dull autumn day and Jill Pole was crying behind the gym.
She was crying because they had been bullying her.
(From *The Silver Chair* by C.S. Lewis)

• the reflective thought of the narrator or character.

The first place I can well remember was a large pleasant meadow with a pond of clear water in it.
(From *Black Beauty* by Anna Sewell)

However, even when children realise the importance of a good beginning, and are aware of some of the possibilities, it is not always easy to write. Often, particularly when children have done a great deal of planning before they write, they are so familiar with the story and characters that they cannot re-cast their minds and identify where the story must start and what is needed in the opening sentences.

Endings can be equally problematic and children need to know that for the ending to be emotionally satisfying, all the problems need to be resolved, either happily or sadly. The reader's questions – 'Who did it?', 'How was it done?', 'What will happen?' or 'How will it end?' – must be answered.

Although modern writers often employ open endings to stories, suggesting that life moves on and that all situations contain unresolved problems, young writers need to explore how to close a story to the satisfaction of the reader before they experiment. Consideration of their own expectations of a good ending helps children to become more aware of how to end their own stories well.

The activities in this section help children to realise that for the readers, the story begins with the opening sentence, and that when it ends there must be a feeling of satisfaction. They raise children's awareness of the different ways in which stories can begin and end, and encourage them to use their experience as readers to make decisions about their own stories. When children have focused their attention on story beginnings and endings they are better equipped to make informed choices in their own writing.

Point of view and use of dialogue

All writers need to decide the point of view from which the story will be told – will events be seen through the eyes of one of the characters or by an unbiased narrator? Children often find it difficult to keep this consistent throughout a story and may switch from, for example, a first-person to third-person narration half way through. This is particularly the case when the story is based on a personal experience, where children often need help to write from the viewpoint of an objective narrator.

Teachers need to recognise that problems of inconsistency often arise when children have not considered their point of view before beginning to write, or when they have set themselves the difficult task of writing from the perspective of one of the characters. The activities in this section will help children to recognise that there are choices to be made, that different viewpoints may alter dramatically where the reader's sympathies lie within the story and that it is important to be consistent.

The use of dialogue in writing can also present problems for a young writer. Children often find it difficult to balance narrative and dialogue and to recognise that dialogue, if used sparingly, can draw the reader further into the story, change the pace of the story and make situations more real by helping to bring the characters to life.

The difficulties children find in using dialogue may arise for several reasons. Often, children cannot identify when dialogue will be effective. A few children, once into dialogue, find it difficult to escape, even to the point of writing whole stories in the form of a conversation, because they are either unable or unaware of the need to return to a narrative form. Teachers can help children by encouraging them to read their stories aloud during the composing process, to tell their stories to each other and to work with others. It is only when children are forced to respond as readers to their own writing that they will realise how problematic too much dialogue can be.

Obviously, if children are going to use dialogue, they need to know the conventions of punctuation and layout and they need to recognise when it is necessary to identify the speaker. They should consider how and why writers incorporate dialogue, and be able to use, if necessary, a variety of terms to avoid tediously repeating the word 'said'.

Divisions, layout and titles

A story is split into parts to make it easier and more enjoyable to read. Dividing the story into chapters can build suspense or allow the reader to take a break, to reflect briefly upon what has gone before and guess at what is to come. In doing this, the reader becomes emotionally involved and is further drawn into the story.

Writers, therefore, make important decisions when they split a story into chapters and decide on chapter headings. They need to know where to break the storyline to best effect – often at a turning point, or where the reader has unanswered questions, and is desperate to move on and find out what happens next.

The way the text is arranged on the page influences the way the reader reads. Layout can indicate tone of voice, pace and so on, and this can be used to great effect by an author.

Children need to explore how chapter headings may contribute to the story and they should be aware of the forms that chapter headings can take. Sometimes simple numbers are used, but sometimes the headings contribute to, or elaborate on, the storyline. They can be tantalisingly brief, building suspense by indicating what may happen, or they can be extremely full, providing brief summaries that lure the reader onwards, like a trailer for a film.

It is important to recognise that children will plan in different ways, depending on the story they are writing. Where children are working with a fixed storyline, they may well be able to plan their writing in chunks, or chapters. However, not all stories can be planned in this way. Sometimes, children will need to write the story first, and then split it into chapters.

Both ways of working have advantages and offer learning opportunities. Where children have written the story as one long sequence, re-reading in order to split it into sections encourages them to distance themselves from the story and see it through the eyes of a reader, rather than the writer. They begin to realise

Scholastic
IMAGINATIVE WRITING
Workshop

what the reader will feel and need at different points, and will often re-draft sections to make them more effective. Where children are more familiar with the storyline and have been able to identify chapters, or to 'chunk' it in some way at the planning stage, they are often better able to pace and plan their writing. The chapters provide a logical place to stop, either to take a break or to re-read, edit, re-draft or re-focus the story. Writing in chapters can also contribute to the writer's sense of achievement, giving a way to monitor progress and review what has been done in the light of what has yet to be written.

Much of the thinking that underpins the selection of chapter headings also applies to the selection of titles. The title is the reader's first point of contact with the story and should focus sharply upon its essence. For this reason, children are advised to choose the title for their story only after they have written it. They should be encouraged to jot down any ideas for titles that occur to them during the writing, but only to reach a final decision once the story is finished. After all, the essence of the story may change as it is written and a title chosen at an early stage may become inappropriate.

Children need to be made aware of how story titles are chosen: they may be drawn from the main character or place; they may indicate a central theme or they may be mysterious and suggest a certain mood, setting or atmosphere.

The children's books

The books used in this chapter are Ted Dewan's *3 Billy Goats Gruff*, Terence Blacker and Frank Rodgers' *Nice/Nasty Neighbours*, and *Matthew and the Sea Singer* by Jill Paton Walsh.

Ted Dewan's modern re-working of *3 Billy Goats Gruff* reflects the rhythms and rhymes and repeated refrains of the traditional tale. It is told in modern language, making great use of a mix of layouts and typographies to give the story immediacy and pace. The lively illustrations also help to bring this story right up to date.

Nice/Nasty Neighbours is a Flipper book which describes the same events in the lives of two very different families. The two stories told from each family's point of view converge in the centre of the book. Both stories give children the opportunity to study the structure of a story with a strong beginning, fast-moving plot and an unexpected, satisfying ending. The symmetrical structure and construction of the stories is physically reflected in the format of the book – the stories begin from opposite ends of the book and meet in the middle.

Matthew and the Sea Singer is the mystical story of an orphan boy with a beautiful voice who is stolen by the mermaids to sing in the sea caves. The story of how he is finally found and returned to the land is told through a series of chapters which end on tantalising clues. The reader is propelled firmly forward to a satisfying ending in which all questions are answered.

The accompanying audio cassette contains interviews with Frank Rodgers and Jill Paton Walsh who talk about their work and read extracts from their books.

HELPING CHILDREN WITH ASPECTS OF STORY STRUCTURE

The following are some ideas to help children develop their understanding of story structure:
• Don't ask children to think about the beginning, middle and the end of their story until you are sure that they have decided the characters, the setting and the problem and what will happen.
• Be prepared to use any knowledge and experience of story structure that children may have gained from watching television and films.
• Accept the need for a variety of planning formats and methodologies.
• Encourage children to use story plans to make decisions about structure and to reflect on the decisions made.
• Discuss alternative ways to begin a story.
• Discuss what the children believe makes a good ending and why.
• Make children aware of the ways in which authors use chapter divisions, titles and how and why authors alter the pace of a story.
• Encourage children to make conscious decisions about the point of view from which the story will be told.
• Encourage children to think about when, why and how authors use dialogue.
• Don't assume that greater use of adjectives and adverbs improves the quality of writing; it merely alters the pace.
• Direct teaching is useful, but remember the power of discussion and collaborative writing to motivate, personalise and deepen children's understanding of complex ideas.

Activity	Teaching Content	Star rating	Group size	Photo copiable
PLOT AND SEQUENCE				
1 Going for a dip	Simple story structure	★	(W)➪1	✓+A
2 The end of the holiday	Turning points	★★	2➪1	✓✓
3 The finding	Turning points and planning format	★	(W)➪4➪1	✓
4 A serial story	Story structure - beginning, middle, end	★★★	3	✓
5 The end of the rainbow	Turning points	★	1	✓
6 A race against time	Structuring a beginning, middle and end	★★	(W)➪2	✓
BEGINNINGS AND ENDINGS				
7 It's a cracking beginning	Ingredients of a good beginning; awareness of audience	★	1➪4	✓
8 New beginnings	Beginnings	★★	2➪1	✓+A
9 Spotlight on...	Beginnings; identifying turning points and authors' ideas	★★	2➪(W)	✓
10 A hand on your shoulder	Starting points	★★★	4➪1	✓
11 They all lived happily ever after	Components of a good ending	★	(W)➪1	✓
12 The end	Different styles of ending	★★	(W)➪2	✓+A
POINT OF VIEW AND USE OF DIALOGUE				
13 The lost kitten	Voice	★	2	✓
14 Inside a bear's skin	Point of view	★	(W)➪1	A
15 The voice of the teller: story swaps	Viewpoint	★★★	2	
16 Perspectives on a place	Describing a place from the point of view of a particular character	★★	(W)➪1	✓
17 Stop!	Dialogue as part of a story	★★	3➪(W)	
18 'Save my puppy!'	Conventions of direct speech in stories	★★	1	✓
19 A story in the life of ...	Creating stories from real life experiences	★★	(W)➪1	
DIVISIONS, LAYOUT AND TITLES				
20 Pause for breath!	Text divisions; chapter headings	★★	(W)➪2	
21 A publisher drops the pages	Sequencing and dividing into chapters	★	3	✓
22 How would you say it?	How layout affects the way the reader reads	★★	2➪(W)	AAA
23 Titles to make you read on	What makes a good title	★	2	✓
24 Favourite titles	Devising titles	★	1➪(W)	
3 BILLY GOATS GRUFF				
25 Who said that?	Writing dialogue; alternatives to 'said'	★	1➪4	
26 'STOMP STOMP STOMPITY-STOMP!'	Describing actions in ways that speed up or slow down the pace of the story	★★	(W)➪1	
27 'Billy Goat footsteps...'	Refrains	★	(W)➪2	✓
28 Layout and lettering	How layout and print affects the way the reader reads	★★★	(W)➪1➪2	
29 Fairy-tale endings	Elements of a satisfying ending	★★★	4➪2	
NICE/NASTY NEIGHBOURS				
30 Doors into new worlds	Beginnings; prediction	★	(W)➪2➪1	✓
31 Editors in action	The symmetrical structure of a flipper book; devising chapter headings	★★	6➪(W)	✓
32 More flipper stories	Presenting a situation from two viewpoints	★★★	(W)➪1	
33 Lou the footballer and William McNastikov, ballet dancer	Identifying turning points; writing direct speech	★★	(W)➪4➪2	
34 Supermarket mayhem	Different characters use different styles of speech	★	(W)➪2	✓
MATTHEW AND THE SEA SINGER				
35 Endings and beginnings	Cliff-hanging endings and beginnings that make you want to read on	★★	(W)➪4	✓
36 Word detective	Opening sentences give clues to the nature of the story	★★	4➪(W)	✓
37 Happy thoughts	Creating images of happiness; exploring turning points	★★★	(W)➪2	
38 The dry side of the water's edge	Conveying contrast	★★★	4	✓
39 Writing trailers	Identifying main events	★★★	(W)➪7	
40 Finding the title	What makes a good title	★	(W)➪1	

A = anthology page
(W) = whole group

Scholastic
IMAGINATIVE WRITING
Workshop

GOING FOR A DIP

Teaching content
Structuring a simple story.

What you need
Photocopiable anthology page 218, photocopiable page 148, scissors, drawing and writing materials, adhesive, prepared zigzag books.

What to do
Stories and story poems depend on characters who encounter problems or events. Children can only make decisions about how to structure the telling of a story once the basic ingredients – the characters, setting and events – have been identified. This activity highlights some of the decisions authors have to make when they reach this point.

Give each child a copy of photocopiable anthology page 218 which contains the poem 'Daddy Fell into the Pond' by Alfred Noyes. Read the poem aloud with the children. Draw the children's attention to the pictures that illustrate each section of the poem. Point out that the first section describes a scene, the second is very short and simply states what happened and the third describes the same scene immediately afterwards, highlighting the reactions of the different characters.

Next, give each child a copy of photocopiable page 148 which contains three pictures. Ask the children to cut out the pictures and arrange them in the correct sequence to tell a story. Explain that the faces on the last drawing have been left blank for the children to decide how each character will react and to draw in the most appropriate expression. Does the character find it funny? Perhaps it makes them angry or worried. If the children wish, they may add speech bubbles to indicate what particular characters say.

Now, ask the children to write the story of what happens in three parts, describing what is happening in each picture. Explain that it may be written as a story or a non-rhyming three-verse poem. It is not to be long but must be well written; the children must think carefully about what to say about each picture.

Finally, let the children decorate and mount the pictures and their writing on to a zigzag book or a wall display.

THE END OF THE HOLIDAY

Teaching content
Turning points.

What you need
Photocopiable pages 149 and 150, writing materials.

What to do
From their experience as story readers and listeners, children know that the beginning of a story introduces the characters and place. For a story to develop, however, something has to happen.

Ask the children in pairs to read the story introduction on photocopiable page 149. Explain that a surprise or problem must be introduced to propel the action forward. The photocopiable sheet suggests four possible types of turning point, leaving the fifth open for the children's own ideas. Ask each pair to brainstorm the possibilities, making it clear that each box should indicate a totally new way forward for the plot. They can decide later which ideas they prefer.

Having discussed and jotted down an idea for each box, the children should each select their preferred idea and produce an outline plan for a story, using photocopiable page 150 if they wish. (This is a generic planning sheet and could be used to plan any story.)

Development/homework task
• The outline plan can form the starting point for a drama lesson.
• The children can flesh out one part of the story or write the whole story using the plan they have produced.

THE FINDING

Teaching content
Turning points and planning format.

What you need
Photocopiable page 151, chalkboard, writing materials.

What to do
Read the introductory paragraph on photocopiable page 151 to the children and ask them what we know about the story of John and Ambreen so far. As children supply information, write this on the board and explain that most stories begin by introducing the main characters and setting them in a particular place. However, something has to happen for the story to take off.

Ask the children to decide what sort of thing John is pointing to. Brainstorm ideas with the class. The brainstorm should only be used to get ideas flowing. Then ask the children in groups of three or four to fill in the boxes on the photocopiable sheet.

Explain to the children that they are going to finish writing the story individually, each choosing one idea from the brainstorm that they think will lead to an exciting story. Children may stick a copy of the photocopiable introduction on to a sheet of paper and then continue the story underneath, or you may prefer them to copy out the introduction in order to move into the style of the story telling before continuing with their own middles and endings.

A SERIAL STORY

Teaching content
Story structure – beginning/middle/end.

What you need
Photocopiable page 152, scissors, writing materials, paper-clips.

What to do
Arrange the children in groups of three and explain that each member of the group is going to write a beginning, a middle and an ending for three different stories.

Give each group a copy of photocopiable page 152 and ask them to look at the three story lines. Each child in the group should choose a different story and the page should be cut into three strips and distributed.

Now, ask each child to write an opening paragraph based on the picture at the top of their strip. They should describe the setting and the mood of the scene, lastly describing the mysteriously abandoned object at the centre of the picture. The story strips should then be fixed to the writing with a paper-clip and passed on to the person on the right.

Ask the children to read carefully the work they have been given before deciding what will happen to spark this into a 'story'. They should then look at the prompts on the story strip and write part two of the story, ending on a cliff-hanger. Finally, ask the children once again to pass their work round to the right and invent a suitable ending for the work they have been given. This ending should tie up all the loose ends and answer all the questions logically and sensibly.

This activity asks children to make a critical evaluation of two other people's writing which, in turn, helps them to reflect upon their own skills. The focus upon a structure for story writing helps to establish a framework within which young writers can work confidently.

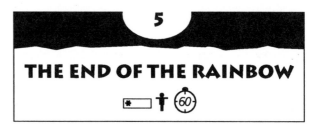

THE END OF THE RAINBOW

Teaching content
Turning points.

What you need
Photocopiable page 153, art and writing materials, scissors, glue.

What to do
Give each child a copy of photocopiable page 153. This contains the opening paragraph of a story and then lists three possible turning points. Some characters are introduced, but not

described in any detail. Explain that writers often leave a little mystery in the introduction to stories, as this makes the reader want to continue reading.

Ask the children to read the opening paragraph and then to choose the turning point that they feel will lead to the most exciting story middle and ending. They should cut out the beginning of the story and stick it at the top of a large sheet of paper. Then they should imagine what the travellers may look like and, underneath the story opening, illustrate their arrival on Earth. Next, the children should stick in the turning point of their choice.

Now, encourage the writers to read through the first two parts of the story and to write a suitable ending which will answer all questions satisfactorily.

The finished stories should be shared. It will be interesting to compare different solutions that writers have devised.

6

A RACE AGAINST TIME

Teaching content
Structuring a beginning, middle and end.

What you need
Photocopiable page 154, writing materials, scissors, glue.

What to do
Give each child a copy of photocopiable page 154 and ask them to read the paragraph at the top of the page. This introduces two characters obviously in a desperate situation. Next, ask the children to read the two alternative endings to this story and to choose the one they find more interesting. Arrange the children in pairs according to their chosen endings and ask them to brainstorm ideas for the middle part of the story. They may like to draw up a list of events that happen during the desperate journey. Remind them that their writing should be in the same style as the paragraph on the sheet. The pairs should either copy the paragraph or cut it out and stick it on a separate piece of paper, then write the middle of the story, and finally stick in their chosen ending.

Share and compare the finished work.

7

IT'S A CRACKING BEGINNING

Teaching content
• Recognising the ingredients of a good beginning.
• Awareness of audience.

What you need
Photocopiable anthology page 219, writing materials.

What to do
Give each child a copy of photocopiable anthology page 219 and ask them to look at the story beginnings. They should each select two that they think are particularly good for a story aimed at their own age group and one they think would be good for a younger child.

Arrange the children in groups of four and ask them to share their choices and explain the reasons for them. Finally, ask each group to produce a short statement about what makes a good beginning for readers such as themselves and what makes a good beginning for younger readers.

Share these with the class. If possible, mount all the statements and display them in the classroom with appropriate headings.

NEW BEGINNINGS

Teaching content

Beginnings.

What you need

Photocopiable anthology page 219 (optional), photocopiable page 155, writing materials, chalkboard.

What to do

Explain that when story-tellers begin a story they often choose from several possible openings. Photocopiable anthology page 219 contains a wide variety of story openings and could provide a useful starting point for this activity. Put the children in pairs and ask them to look at photocopiable page 155 and consider the three sample beginnings of the story of *Cinderella*. Each pair should compose a suitable beginning for the story under the category 'Description of a character'. They will first have to decide which character from *Cinderella* they will describe to open the story. Then one child should write down their chosen opening and the other read it to the class. Invite comments on each contribution, focusing on the following points which may be written on the board.

• Was this a good choice of character?

• Was the character well described to set the mood for the story?

• How might this opening be improved?

Finally, having listened to all contributions, the children should individually write a finished version of the opening of *Cinderella* using a character description. They may use the one they have already composed or choose a totally different character.

The beginnings should be displayed in the classroom to be compared and discussed by the class.

Development/homework task

Ask the children to write the entire story or an opening paragraph from a preferred starter sentence.

SPOTLIGHT ON...

Teaching content

Awareness of beginnings, problems, authorship, getting and using ideas.

What you need

A collection of children's books, photocopiable page 156, writing materials.

What to do

Ask the children to brainstorm a list of authors or books that they have enjoyed reading. Ask them whether they can remember how any of these books opened. Tell each child to choose one book from the list to investigate in more detail.

To carry out the investigation, tell the children to do the following:

1. Re-read the first few pages.

2. Read the first few sentences and think about how the story begins. Does it begin with a place, a description of a character, some questions?

3. Think about what happens in the story. Try to identify *one* event that prompted the rest of the story (that is, had it *not* happened, the story would not have occurred).

If the children find this last task difficult, they should discuss it with a friend or parent who has also read the book. If they can find nobody who has read the book, tell them to describe the story to somebody else and see if, between the two of them, they can identify what prompted the rest of the story.

Ask the children to report their findings to the class, using photocopiable page 156 as proforma if necessary. It is interesting to see the similarities and the differences between books and to note the range of different strategies or ideas an individual author has. Children and adults can be surprised at how, when the turning points are identified, they are frequently quite small, almost unremarkable events. Moreover, it is this, along with the skill of the story-teller, that makes the story believable, interesting and exciting.

These reports can be bound together to form a class book which the children might like to use as an ideas bank for future reference in their writing work.

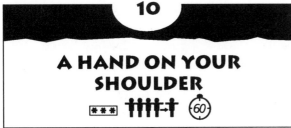

A HAND ON YOUR SHOULDER

Teaching content
Beginnings.

What you need
Photocopiable page 157, writing materials, chalkboard.

What to do
Explain to the children that the quality of writing in the opening of a story must be very high as it is at this point that readers decide whether to continue or discard a story. There are many points from which a story may begin and children must consider several before deciding on one when they come to write.

Arrange the class in groups of four and give each group a copy of photocopiable page 157. Write the bare bones of an adventure story on the board.
- Child out alone
- Place he or she has been warned not to go
- All is quiet and still
- Suddenly a firm hand on the shoulder
- Child runs and is chased

The groups should discuss and make decisions about the questions on the photocopiable sheet.

Next, ask each child in the group to choose a different starting point from the list on the photocopiable sheet and to write their name opposite their chosen starting point. They should then write the story from that starting point, incorporating the details discussed by the group.

When finished, the children should read their opening sentences to each other and then share them with the class. It will be interesting also to compare the very different stories that will have grown from similar bare bones.

THEY ALL LIVED HAPPILY EVER AFTER

Teaching content
Endings.

What you need
Photocopiable page 158, writing materials.

What to do
The essentials of what happens at the end of any well-known story remain constant, but details change with different story-tellers. This activity helps children to analyse the components of a good ending within the safe and familiar context of a well-known story.

Discuss how important it is when we read a story to have all our questions answered at the end. We want to know what has happened to all the main characters and we only consider an ending to be satisfactory if it can be sensibly explained and if it fits in with what has gone before.

Explain that the ending of the story of *Cinderella* varies from version to version: some end with the wedding of Cinderella and the Prince, while others go on to tell of what happened to the other characters. Tell the children that they are now going to write their own version of the end of the story from the point where Cinderella tries on the slipper. A starter sentence is given on photocopiable page 158. The children should complete a final paragraph, making sure that all the questions on the photocopiable sheet are answered and then re-written in a sensible sequence.

THE END

Teaching content
Recognising different styles of endings.

What you need
Photocopiable page 159, photocopiable anthology page 220, paper, scissors, adhesive.

What to do

Explain to the class that there are many ways of ending a story. Give each pair a copy of photocopiable page 159 and read through the different types of ending with them. Can they think of any stories which fit any of the categories listed?

Now, give each pair a copy of photocopiable anthology page 220 which contains seven story endings. The children should decide which ending fits which category. When they have decided they should cut out the individual endings and categories and stick them in two columns on a large sheet of paper headed 'Story endings'.

13

THE LOST KITTEN

Teaching content

Voice.

What you need

Photocopiable page 160, writing materials.

What to do

Explain to the children that writers choose who is to tell their stories before they begin to write. Some decide to write as story-tellers but others tell the stories from the point of view of a character in the story.

In pairs, ask the children to read the different beginnings to the story of the lost kitten on photocopiable page 160 and consider which character is relating each beginning. After comparing the answers, ask the children to choose one beginning, copy it and then write the rest of the short story using the same voice throughout. The children may write in pairs or individually

Publish the finished stories in a book shaped like the narrator and entitled 'The Star's Story', 'The Kitten's Story' and so on.

14

INSIDE A BEAR'S SKIN

Teaching content

Point of view.

What you need

A copy of the story of *Goldilocks and the Three Bears*, photocopiable anthology page 221, chalkboard, writing materials.

What to do

If any of the children in your class do not know the story of *Goldilocks and the Three Bears*, tell the story quickly or get those children who are familiar with the tale to tell it. It will be natural for you or the children to tell the tale as a narrator would. Next, explain that writers often choose to tell a story from the point of view of one of the characters. Give each child a copy of photocopiable anthology page 221 and ask them to read the two extracts shown. The first is an introduction to the story of the *Three Little Pigs* told by a narrator, while the second is an introduction to the same story told by the wolf. They will notice that the second passage is much more direct and personal in style.

Tell the children that they are going to use this technique to re-tell the story of *Goldilocks and the Three Bears*. Write the following list of characters on the board and ask the children to choose the one from whose point of view they will tell the story.

Characters	Sample starter sentences
Goldilocks	It all started when I was walking through the woods one day and the delicious smell of porridge made me follow my nose.
Baby Bear	I wanted to eat my breakfast first, but Mum and Dad decided to have a walk before we ate.
Mother Bear	When we arrived back home after the walk my little baby started to cry because someone had eaten his porridge.
Father Bear	I must say that I was very worried that morning when we realised that the house had been broken into while we were out walking.

In order to write successfully, the children will have to imagine what it is like to be inside the character's skin. Read out the sample starter sentences above (which the children may then use as a beginning if they wish). Ask them to write half a dozen lines of the beginning of the story as if they are the chosen character and explain that is called writing in the first person. Some children may find it helpful to act out the beginning and/or record it on to tape before writing it down.

Compare the children's beginnings and pick out some of those which show best how the different points of view from which a story can be told alter the start of the story completely.

Development/homework task
Either complete the story or begin again from another point of view.

THE VOICE OF THE TELLER: STORY SWAPS

Teaching content
Viewpoint.

What you need
Writing materials.

What to do
Children know from their reading, that stories can be told from different points of view. When the writer wants the reader to identify closely with the story, events are often related through the eyes of one of the main characters. Other types of stories, for example fairy stories, are usually told by a narrator who describes the story events as an outsider.

In pairs, ask the children to imagine the following scenario:

There is a child of about five or six years old, whose family has been playing host to a distant relative with a young toddler. Everyone, including the older child's parents, thinks that the toddler is wonderful and pays him or her a lot of attention. The toddler is constantly kept amused, bought presents and allowed to eat (or not eat) whatever he or she chooses. It doesn't seem fair and the older child is feeling left out.

Ask each pair to choose one situation from the list below and to decide what happens. They should give the various characters names and discuss what happens, what each character does and why. Each child should choose either the main adult, the older child or the role of a narrator and write the story from this point of view.

1. The toddler does something that the older child is not allowed to do (spills food, spoils a game, breaks something...). What does the older child do that causes trouble and why?

2. The toddler does something that everyone says is very clever. The older child does this thing all the time and is never congratulated. What does the older child do that causes trouble and why?

3. An adult is playing with the toddler and sends the older child away when he tries to join in. (What are they playing? What does the child do to try and join in? What does the child do when told to go away?)

When they have finished writing the children should swap stories with their partner and compare them. In what ways are they similar or different? Can either of them be said to be 'true'? Which viewpoint do they think is most effective and why?

Make the stories into class books based on the viewpoint of the story-teller.

PERSPECTIVES ON A PLACE

Teaching content
Point of view.

What you need
Photocopiable page 161, writing materials.

What to do
Explain to the children that writing about a place from unusual perspectives can often create exciting and original stories. A circus, for example, seen from the viewpoint of an old and tired elephant, an escaped prisoner or a young, talented and enthusiastic acrobat on the day of her first performance will yield very different but equally interesting stories. An unusual perspective on a familiar theme is something that all writers seek.

Introduce this activity by first building a description of a fairground from the point of view of an excited child. Ask the children to think of descriptions of sounds, smells, colours, shapes and objects and write these up on the board as phrases and sentences. Then ask the children to use these ideas to structure an account of a fairground visit told in the first person from the point of view of the child. Because of the amount of support provided, each child should produce a vibrant piece of writing. Ask a few individuals to read out their descriptions and point out how easy it is to hear the 'voice' of a happy young person visiting the fairground.

Now give each child a copy of photocopiable page 161 and ask them to choose one of the characters listed at the top of the page. They should then complete the photocopiable page from the point of view of their chosen character, before writing another description of the fairground in their character's voice.

At the end of this drama session, discuss how these one-minute scenes could be written as very short stories. Explain that when writers create stories they mix the actual words that are spoken by characters with narrative or story-telling by the author. A story that is written all in conversation might possibly be better written as a play.

Writers are also very careful only to use direct speech to show more about the characters or to move the action of the story forward. It is easy to bore the reader by having long conversations between characters that may be true to life but do nothing to progress the story.

Ask the groups to select from the scenes they acted out only the most important things that were said and write these down. The rest of the scene, when transferred into a short story, should be told by the narrator. Depending on your class, you may like to model this yourself at first, using one of the dialogues.

STOP!

Teaching content
Dialogue as part of a story.

What you need
Writing materials.

What to do
Arrange the children in groups of three and explain that each group is going to invent and act out a one-minute scene beginning with the word 'Stop!'

They will have to decide secretly what will happen in their scene. Who is saying 'Stop!'? Who are they speaking to and why? Having decided on a scenario, groups should then develop a short dialogue that lasts for no more than sixty seconds. Ask them to give their scene a title and to rehearse it ready to perform to the rest of the class.

When the groups are prepared, the scenes should be performed. Each group should jump up in turn, announce their title, act out their play, bow at the end and sit down. In this way, even large classes of children may all view the short scenes.

19

A STORY IN THE LIFE OF...

Teaching content
Creating stories from real life experience.

What you need
Writing materials, photographs (optional).

What to do
Explain that writers often use other people's real life experiences to create stories. Sometimes they will change the events and re-name characters in order to protect their sources.

Tell the children that they are going to ask an adult they know to share with them a good story of something that happened to them in the past. The adults may like to tell a story about their own childhood. If you feel that some children may have difficulty gaining help from an adult at home, then involve adults in the school and set up interviews for these children.

Give the children time to gather the stories (an evening or a weekend, say) and then let them tell the story to a partner in order to clarify the storyline. Next, children must change the names of the characters involved and then write the story of what happened.

Finished stories should be displayed, possibly alongside a photograph of the main protagonist. These stories create great interest on parents' evenings. Any activity that encourages people to read children's work is of great value.

18

'SAVE MY PUPPY!'

Teaching content
Conventions of direct speech in story writing.

What you need
Photocopiable page 162, writing materials, a collection of published novels.

What to do
Read the short dialogue on photocopiable page 162 and ask the children to re-write this into a very short story. Ask them first to underline the words that they think are essential to the storyline. Any other parts of the dialogue must be omitted from the story as they will only bore the readers.

Explain to the children that when characters' actual words are quoted in a story, then each new speaker begins a new paragraph. This is best demonstrated by examining published novels. It is a convention that children may not have noticed and yet it makes the reading of any story much easier. Encourage children to remember this when they are writing.

Also point out that constant repetition of the word 'said' in any story can become tiresome and it is a good idea to use some of the alternatives suggested on the photocopiable sheet. As this is being written as a narrative, descriptions of the characters and of the burning house may be added to give atmosphere.

Review the short stories and use successful pieces of work as models of good practice.

Development/homework task
Draw up lists of children's own alternatives to the word 'said' as wall posters or as helpful sheets for writing folders.

20

PAUSE FOR BREATH!

Teaching content
• Text divisions.
• Chapter headings.

What you need
A collection of novels, writing materials.

What to do
Splitting our writing up into small parts is a convention that makes reading easier. Discuss

with the children the different marks we use to show pauses in writing and write these on the board. Ask the children to order these marks from the smallest division to the largest. Your list may look something like this:

• words – pause indicated by comma;
• phrase – pause indicated by comma, semi-colon, colon;
• sentence – pause indicated by full stop, exclamation mark, question mark;
• paragraph – pause indicated by indentation;
• part or chapter – pause indicated by a variety of marks.

Ask the children to look through published novels to find the various conventions used to head chapters. Children should work in pairs and list the types of headings they find, along with the title and the author. The following list shows some of the conventions that the children may find.

• 1, 2, 3
• Chapter 1, Chapter 2
• I, II, III
• Each chapter has a new name which indicates something about its content.
• A very short summary of main events.
• Chapter One, Chapter Two

Development/homework task

When children write stories in the future, allow them to choose a method of marking 'chapters' in their work. At the earliest stage of writing, every paragraph will probably be termed a chapter, but as children write longer stories the difference between paragraphs and chapters becomes clearer. A useful homework task is to ask children to learn the first ten roman numerals.

A PUBLISHER DROPS THE PAGES

Teaching content
Sequencing and ordering into chapters.

What you need
Photocopiable page 163, scissors, paper, glue.

What to do
Arrange the children into groups of three and give each group a copy of photocopiable page 163. This contains a summary of the story of *Sleeping Beauty*, but the events are in the wrong order. Ask the children to imagine that they are publishers and they have dropped the pages of a manuscript. They have to put the story back in the correct sequence.

In their groups, ask the children to cut out the statements and to rearrange them into the correct story sequence on a blank sheet of paper. When completed, they should join with another group to compare and discuss their results. When they are satisfied that the statements are in the correct order, the children should stick them on to the paper.

Next, the publishers must decide where the chapter headings fit. In their original groups, ask the children to divide the story into three sections and appoint a spokesperson to explain the reasons behind their arrangement. This story is a prime example of how writers often

chunk their stories in time bands. Some groups may have organised the chapters differently and as long as they have good explanations for what they have done, their results will be acceptable.

Development/homework task
In their groups, the children should take a chapter each and write out the story of *Sleeping Beauty*. This may be illustrated and published for the school library.

HOW WOULD YOU SAY IT?

Teaching content
The way text is laid out and printed affects the way the reader reads it.

What you need
Photocopiable anthology pages 222–224, chalkboard, writing materials.

What to do
Give each pair a copy of photocopiable anthology pages 222 and 223 which contain a poetry extract from Michael Rosen's *Mind Your Own Business*. Discuss how the layout of the poem contributes to the reader's understanding of who is speaking and how they are saying the words.

Point out that where the speaker is speaking very quickly, the phrases follow one another on the same line. Where the speaker is speaking very distinctly and precisely, the words are arranged on to different lines. This makes the reader read them more distinctly and precisely.

Now write the text of 'Father says...' (from photocopiable anthology page 224) on the board, but run it on as a single paragraph. Do not, at this point, show the anthology page to the children. Ask the children, in pairs, to imagine how the father might be speaking and to read the poem in this way to each other. Then ask them to work together and to lay out the poem to encourage the reader to read it in this way. Remind them of what they have learned from the previous poem about putting phrases together or spacing them on separate lines, and the effect this has on the way the reader reads the poem.

Let the children share the decisions they made with the rest of the class. Finally, show them how Michael Rosen chose to lay out this poem, which is reproduced on photocopiable anthology page 224.

Development/homework task
Ask the children to listen carefully to the things their parents say to them and to try to record *one* conversation verbatim, taking care to lay it out in the most appropriate way.

TITLES TO MAKE YOU READ ON

Teaching content
Exploring ingredients of a good title.

What you need
Photocopiable page 164, writing materials.

What to do
Give each pair a copy of photocopiable page 164 and ask them to look at the book titles at the top of the page. They should classify these into two sets: strong titles that make them want to pick up the book and read it, and weak titles that do not capture their interest at all. They should then list each title under the relevant heading on the photocopiable page.

Development/homework task
Ask the children to see how many of these books they can find in their school library. Do they change their opinion when they see the cover design?

24

FAVOURITE TITLES

Teaching content
Devising titles.

What you need
Writing materials.

What to do
Ask each child to write down the name of their favourite novel. This may be a book that they have read themselves or one that you have read to them. Next, ask them to write one sentence to say why the author chose this particular title for the book. Children who are not accustomed to reading novels may choose the title of a television programme as these are chosen in a similar way for similar reasons.

Share these responses as a class. There should be a wide variety of titles and explanations. Draw up a list of reasons for title choices on the board. This list may include:
• Name of main character: *Tom Sawyer*
• Name of central location: *Treasure Island*
• A catch phrase: *Fair's Fair*
• Central theme: *The Homecoming*
• Important building: *The Phantom Tollbooth*
• Any combination of the above: *The Whitby Witches*
• A title conjuring up a mystery: *The Ring O'Bells Mystery*

Take the story of *Goldilocks and the Three Bears* and devise a new title from each of the categories on the board. Now, ask the children to choose either the story of *Cinderella* or *Sleeping Beauty* and make up a new title for one of these. Share these new ideas around the class.

Development/homework task
Children could make up a new title for a well-known fairy or folk tale and design a book cover for it.

THE CHILDREN'S BOOKS

3 Billy Goats Gruff
This is a modern version of a well-known traditional tale. The children's familiarity with the basic story will allow them to appreciate how Ted Dewan has changed some elements, whilst preserving the traditional structure and rhythms. It provides a classic illustration of how a writer can make economical use of clear and simple language – the complete story is told in just 51 sentences – and of how the layout and division of the text can make the reader read it in particular ways. Dialogue and onomatopoeic words are used effectively to control the pace and flow of the story. The up-to-date context and style of presentation encourages children to reflect on what writers can bring to stories and on the infinite possibilities of interpretation of traditional stories.

About the author
Ted Dewan has been an illustrator and cartoonist since 1988, having studied engineering at Brown University and taught physics at Milton Academy in his native Boston. He has illustrated two non-fiction children's books, *Inside Dinosaurs and Other Prehistoric Creatures* and *Inside the Whale and Other Animals*. The latter won him the Mother Goose Award in 1992 and was shortlisted for the TES information book award. His other children's work includes *Top Secret*.

He lives in north London and is married to children's author/illustrator, Helen Cooper.

How to use this book
Read the entire story to the group, ensuring that the children can see the pictures and text. Alternatively, ask one of the children to read it, giving practice in reading aloud. The creative typography provides excellent prompts for intonation and should enable a very dramatic telling of the story.

Close scrutiny of the text is not required for these activities, but the children will need to look at particular page layouts and text styles.

WHO SAID THAT?

⁕ 🔲 ꝺ·ꝺꝺꝺꝺ ⏱30

Teaching content

- Writing dialogue.
- Alternatives to 'said' and why they may be used.

What you need

Chalkboard, writing and art materials, large sheets of paper, scissors, glue.

What to do

When writing direct speech, authors do not always wish to use 'said' to show which character is speaking. They may want to add to the drama of the dialogue by indicating *how* words are spoken, eg. 'whispered the scared old man'. Alternatively they may wish to add to the characterisation or to avoid repeating 'said'.

The following list shows alternatives to the word 'said' used by Ted Dewan in *3 Billy Goats Gruff*. Write this on the board:

- squeaked
- asked
- grumbled
- boomed
- slobbered
- thundered
- piped

Tell the children to decide individually which character was speaking when the word was used. Then ask them to compare their answers in groups of four, discussing how they made their decisions and, if there are any areas of disagreement, the different reasons for this. Quickly go through the alternatives with the whole class, asking children to explain what they decided and why.

Then, from the list of fairy tales and key characters below, write on the board as many as you think appropriate.

Fairy tales	Characters
Cinderella	Cinderella; Ugly Sisters; Fairy Godmother; Prince
Jack and the Beanstalk	Jack; Giant; Jack's Mother
Three Little Pigs	Wolf; Pig's Mother; First Pig; Third Pig
Little Red Riding Hood	Red Riding Hood; Wolf; Grandmother; Woodcutter
Rumpelstiltskin	Miller; Miller's Daughter; Rumpelstiltskin; King
Gingerbread Man	Gingerbread Man; Old woman; Fox
Hansel and Gretel	Witch; Father; Hansel or Gretel
Sleeping Beauty	Good Fairy; Bad Fairy; Sleeping Beauty; Prince
The Elves and the Shoemaker	Shoemaker; Elves

Give each group of four a fairy tale to consider. Ask them to discuss each character in turn and find at least four different words that could be used as alternatives to 'said' when that character speaks. Offer a special prize to any group that finds more than four alternatives for each of their characters!

Now ask each group to make a poster showing the title of their fairy tale with drawings of each character. They should make speech bubbles indicating the alternatives to 'said' that they have identified and fix them on to the poster near to the appropriate character.

Development/homework task

Ask the children to each select a story by their favourite author and to make a list of some of the alternatives to 'said' that are used in it.

26

'STOMP STOMP STOMPITY-STOMP!'

Teaching content

Describing actions in ways that speed up or slow the pace of the story.

What you need

3 Billy Goats Gruff, chalkboard, writing and drawing materials.

What to do

When and how the pace in story-telling is varied is something that children often find hard to recognise, let alone understand. This activity has been designed to give children a feel for, rather than complete understanding of, how to change the pace of a story.

In *3 Billy Goats Gruff* Ted Dewan uses repetition and detail very effectively to slow down the pace of the story and, at other times, uses as few words as possible to speed up the rate at which the story is told. The repetition of 'nibbling' is used as the story opens to slow the rate at which the events happen, capturing succinctly the uneventful lives of the three billy goats. Similarly, he builds suspense before Big Billy Goat crosses the bridge by providing a great deal of detail about what the Troll did to prepare for his meal, thus delaying the moment when Big Billy Goat arrives.

When the action is all-important, Ted Dewan speeds up the pace of the story by using as few words as possible, representing the action instead with sounds and pictures: 'BUT... STOMP STOMP, STOMPITY-STOMP! / STOMPITY STOMPITY WHOP!'

Read the story to the children – or ask one of the children to read it aloud – and draw their attention to how Big Billy Goat's action is described in terms of sound and movement. Point out that Ted Dewan could have chosen to describe the action in words. An example is given below of a possible paragraph, describing the action.

The Big Billy Goat lowered his horns, snorted loudly, pawed the ground and charged at the Troll. He butted him and the Troll flew high up into the sky, higher than the birds, over the clouds, higher than the sun, and he never came down again.

Indeed, this would have been a more usual way of describing what happened. Ask the children which method of description they prefer and why.

List the following events and actions on the board, and ask the children to choose one of them to describe in two different ways – one in words and one by focusing on the sounds with pictures.

- a rocket blasting into space;
- drinking through a straw;
- water bursting through a bank;
- an electric kettle reaching boiling point and switching off;
- an archer aiming her bow and arrow at the target and hitting the bull's eye ;
- a runner winning a race;
- a plumber turning off a jammed tap.

Once finished, encourage the children to compare their descriptions with a partner. This work makes an effective wall display.

27

'BILLY GOAT FOOTSTEPS...'

Teaching content

Why and how stories use refrains.

What you need

Chalkboard, photocopiable page 165, writing materials.

What to do

Traditional stories use refrains (repeated phrases or lines, sometimes rhyming) for a number of reasons. Firstly, when stories had to be remembered and told orally, rather than read from books, refrains helped the story-teller remember the story and provided a few moments of relief from having to think what to say next. Refrains are also an effective way of involving the audience, allowing them the pleasure of both recognition and participation, and helping to highlight the symmetry in the story structure.

Begin by asking the children if they know any other versions of the rhyming refrains in the story of the *Three Billy Goats Gruff*. Record these on the board. Point out that, while there is variation in the exact wording, all versions of the tale have a repetitive refrain.

Ask the children to think about other stories that have repeated refrains. Sometimes the refrains are repeated exactly: sometime there is a little variation in what is said. Give each pair a copy of photocopiable page 165 which contains a number of different refrains. The children should work together to identify:
• which stories they come from;
• how many times they are repeated in each story, and when they occur;
• which rhyme and which do not.

Encourage the children to think about how these stories all have sequences of actions or events that are repeated with small variations in either the characters or the situations. They should also consider how the use of the refrain encourages the listener to recognise, participate and become involved in the story.

Development/homework task

An increasing number of modern tales use refrains. Can the children find any modern tales with refrains that are repeated in a similar way?

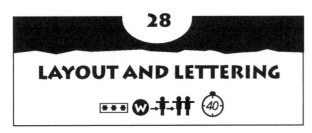

28

LAYOUT AND LETTERING

[***] W→†→†† (40)

Teaching content

The importance of typography and layout.

What you need

3 Billy Goats Gruff, photocopiable page 166, writing materials.

What to do

Show the children some pages from *3 Billy Goats Gruff*. Point out some of the different sizes and types of lettering. Particular examples that you may wish to focus their attention on are:
• ' "OOOOO! Now *that's* a treat!" squeaked Little Billy Goat Gruff'
• the Troll's rhymes
• Middle Billy Goat Gruff's conversation with the Troll: 'A BELLY-BURSTING BILLY GOAT...'

Why do the children think these different sizes and letterings were used? Ask them whether the way in which the words have been written affects the way the reader reads them.

Now, ask the children to think about how the words have been laid out on the page. Do they think that this could also make a difference to how the reader reads the story? Show the children:
• page 5 of the story ('Then, all of a sudden he stopped nibbling. His eyes popped open wide. Across the gorge lay the most dazzling sight he had ever seen.')
• page 10 ('Little Billy Goat Gruff trotted onto the Troll's bridge...')
Page 5 would obviously be read in quite a suspenseful way with long gaps between the sentences, whereas page 10 would be read in a much more straightforward narrative style.

Give each child a copy of photocopiable page 166 and ask them to read the passages. They should choose one to copy out and illustrate in any way they like, but before they do so, they should think carefully about:
• the size(s) of print;
• the type of print;
• the layout of the print;
• the style and layout of any pictures.

Ask the children to swap their finished work with a partner and give them an opportunity to read their partner's version aloud. Do they read it in a way that is different from how they read their own work? Is this how their partner intended it to be read?

29

FAIRY-TALE ENDINGS

⬛⬛⬛ 𝍱→𝍲 ④⓪

Teaching content
The elements of a satisfying ending.

What you need
Chalkboard, writing materials, large sheets of paper.

What to do
Ask the children to work in groups of four to consider the ending to Ted Dewan's story, *3 Billy Goats Gruff.* Can they remember how other versions of the same story ended? Some children will remember the Troll going splash into the river, some will recall him flying up into the air, but in both cases, the goats live happily ever after and the Troll is never seen again.

Discuss with the children how this satisfies the criteria for a good ending: it resolves the central issue or problem in the story and we know that it will not return; it indicates what happens to those characters that we have grown to like or sympathise with; it resolves what happens to the baddie in the story, who meets a suitably unpleasant end – evil is not rewarded.

Write the following list of traditional and fairy tales on the board.
* *Cinderella*
* *The Elves and the Shoemaker*
* *Sleeping Beauty*
* *The Princess and the Pea*
* *Rumpelstiltskin*
* *Hansel and Gretel*
* *The Three Little Pigs*
* *The Gingerbread Man*
* *Little Red Riding Hood*

Ask the children to work in groups to recall the endings of these tales. Ask them to discuss why the ending is emotionally satisfying for the reader by considering:
* what happens to the central 'good' character(s);
* what happens to the 'baddie';
* how the main problem presented in the story is solved.

Finally, arrange the children in pairs and ask them to choose one tale and to make a poster highlighting what happens in the end and why this is a good ending. If necessary, give them

some basic pointers to help them to structure their poster:
* Name of the tale
* What happens in the end? 'In the end...'
* This is a good ending because the baddie...
* The goodie...
* The problem can never return because...

These can form useful points of reference when the children come to write the endings to their own stories.

Nice/Nasty Neighbours
This book is fast-moving, amusing, wittily illustrated and written in language that speaks simply and directly to children in the middle and upper primary years. The book moves speedily through the standard structure of a story and then finds its reflection in the second story. Thus children are given the opportunity to focus on story structure twice over.

The symmetry of the two stories, moving from different points of view towards a resolution in the middle, makes an original and fascinating new story structure for children to enjoy and study.

About the author and illustrator
Terence Blacker worked in publishing before becoming a full-time writer in 1983. He writes for adults as well as children. His children's books include the successful Mr Wiz series. In 1994 he was the writer in residence at the University of East Anglia, where he lectured students, teachers, writers and publishers in the art of writing.

Frank Rogers is a popular children's author and illustrator. There is an interview with him on the accompanying audio cassette.

How to use this book
For the first activity, the children must have seen the introductory page of both stories only, as there is an element of prediction required by the activity. When they have completed this, read one of the stories to the children and then allow groups or individuals to read the second story over a short period.

It will be necessary for children to have access to the text in order to do the second activity. All other activities can be carried out without access to the actual text, although it is a good idea to keep it handy so that the children can re-read it if they wish.

There is an interview on the accompanying cassette with Frank Rodgers, who illustrated *Nice/Nasty Neighbours.*

DOORS INTO NEW WORLDS

Teaching content

- Beginnings.
- Predicting.

What you need

Nice/Nasty Neighbours, card, photocopiable page 167, writing and drawing materials.

What to do

Discuss with the children the fact that Terence Blacker and Frank Rodgers have chosen to begin their two Flipper stories with doors. The beginning of a book is often likened to the entrance to a new, imaginative and unknown world. A door therefore makes a very clever starting point for a story.

Ask the children to fold a piece of A4 card in half widthwise. On the front of this they will be drawing one of the doors at the beginning of the Flipper books. Arrange the children in pairs and ask them to choose opposite doors. The children may copy the doors shown in the book but should add their own personal ideas to the pictures.

The sentences on these first pages hint at what will be found inside the doors. Beginnings of books should set the scene for a story and tempt readers over the threshold. They should also allow readers to predict what lies ahead. The children's experience as readers will mean that they are aware of these facts about beginnings, although they may not have focused specifically on this area of story structure before. Discuss this with the children and then ask them, in pairs, to complete photocopiable page 167.

The children should now individually draw their very different hallways, using the details they have noted on the sheet. These drawings should be stuck on the inside page of the A4 folded card. Display these in pairs on the wall so that when the doors are opened, the pictures of the hallways are revealed. The contrast between the households will be evident.

EDITORS IN ACTION

Teaching content

- Examining the symmetrical structure of a Flipper book.
- Devising chapter headings.

What you need

Nice/Nasty Neighbours, photocopiable page 168, writing materials.

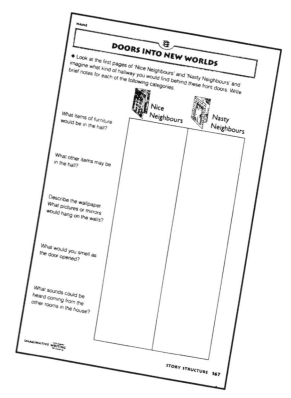

What to do

This task focuses attention on the symmetry of these two stories. The structures of the stories reflect and balance each other.

Many stories are separated into parts or chapters but the author of *Nice/Nasty Neighbours* has decided not to do this.

The two stories, however, clearly form distinct sections and on photocopiable page 168 they have been chunked into chapters. Arrange the children in groups of six and give each group a copy of photocopiable page 168. The children should study the text and decide what would make good titles for the chapters. Explain that this is a job that an editor might do to clarify or improve a story.

When all the groups have completed the photocopiable page, draw the class together again to compare chapter titles. Take this opportunity to highlight the symmetry between the two stories.

Finally, ask the children individually to list the ideas in order, from the best idea to the weakest. Then, discuss as a class the differing points of view for each situation and how easy they would be to contrast.

Development/homework task

Ask the children to choose the idea that they think is best and to write two versions of the story, one from each point of view.

32

MORE FLIPPER STORIES

Teaching content

Presenting a situation from two viewpoints.

What you need

Chalkboard, writing materials.

What to do

Explain to children that the Flipper book structure is a way of presenting a problem, situation or event from two opposite points of view. The two stories are balanced so that they meet in the middle of the book and both points of view are given equal weight. The end of each story leads back to the beginning of the other story. Any situation that is interesting and can be viewed from two standpoints may be produced as this kind of structure.

Write the following situations on the board and suggest that they would make good 'double-point-of-view' stories for a Flipper publication:
- a battle scene: soldiers on opposite sides;
- the play: performers preparing and members of the audience getting ready for a night out;
- the haunting: the ghosts and the haunted;
- first day back at school: pupil and teacher;
- the contest: the winner and the loser.

33

LOU THE FOOTBALLER AND WILLIAM MCNASTIKOV, BALLET DANCER

Teaching content
- Writing direct speech.
- Identifying turning points.

What you need

Nice/Nasty Neighbours, chalkboard, writing materials.

What to do

Explain to the children that they are going to concentrate on the parts of the stories where the turning points occur. Revise the idea of a turning point with the class – an initial situation has been set up, then something happens to propel the story in a new direction. Elicit from them that the turning point in 'Nasty Neighbours' is when Louise discovers she is a good footballer; the turning point in 'Nice Neighbours' is when Billy discovers he wants to be a ballet dancer. At these points in the book the author has chosen to tell the story largely through speech bubbles.

Arrange the children in groups of four, then ask one pair to concentrate on 'Nice Neighbours' and the other to concentrate on 'Nasty Neighbours'. Explain that each pair is going to re-write the speech from the bubbles as a passage of prose. Alternatively, the children could choose one speech bubble each to write as direct speech and then put them together to make a paragraph. Discuss with the children the conventions of writing direct speech, drawing upon their experience as readers. As suggestions are offered, clarify them and write them on the board. Make sure you cover all of the following.

• The actual words spoken sit inside speech marks. (Depending upon the ability of the group, decide whether to demonstrate speech marks as being in the shape of 6 at the beginning of speech and 9 at the end, or merely describe them as two commas.)

• When someone new speaks, the words they say are written on a new line as the beginning of a new paragraph. This makes reading easier.

• The first word inside the speech marks must be a capital letter.

• There must always be some mark of punctuation before the speech marks are closed at the end of the words that are spoken. This might be a question mark if a question has been asked, an exclamation mark, a comma or a full stop.

Explain to the children that when they write the spoken words as part of a narrative, there will be no pictures to show who has spoken and so the writing must say who is speaking. Writers do this by saying, 'said Billy' or 'exclaimed Billy' or 'asked Billy' or 'shouted Billy'. Write some examples on the board and stress that it is important to find alternatives to 'said' as this becomes repetitive and boring. At this point it will be helpful to compose the first part of the narrative orally so that every child is clear about what is required.

Next, the pairs should copy out the starter sentence from the top of the relevant page, as this will help them to move quickly into the required style of writing. The ends of the passages may also be copied from the book. When the children have completed a rough draft they should swap with the other pair in their group and make helpful comments. It is always easier to spot mistakes when reading someone else's work.

Display final copies of this work in pairs, showing the symmetry that exists between the two turning points in the stories.

SUPERMARKET MAYHEM

Teaching content
Different characters use different styles of speech.

What you need
Photocopiable page 169, scissors, glue, writing materials.

What to do
Ask the children to explain the ways in which the author has indicated that characters are speaking. In this book, all conversation is written either in speech bubbles or in inverted commas. What the characters say and how they speak is appropriate for who they are. Organise children into pairs and give them copies of photocopiable page 169. At the top of this page is a picture of the two fathers in the story saying the words we first 'hear' them speaking in the book. From their speech we immediately know what to expect from them in the future!

Explain that the McNastys and the O'Naices are talking as they walk down separate aisles of a supermarket. Ask the children to cut out the speech bubbles and to stick them into the correct aisle. The empty speech bubbles should be filled with extra appropriate comments, cut out and stuck in place.

Development/homework task

Children may choose two speech bubbles from either family and write a short dialogue, using speech marks as part of a passage of writing entitled 'The McNastys go shopping' or 'Shopping with the O'Naices'.

Matthew and the Sea Singer

This book is beautifully written by Jill Paton Walsh. The language is simple but its use is highly sophisticated and the story may be understood at many different levels. It has the resonance and the quality of the ancient folk- or fairy-tale genre.

The novel could be used as a short novel study. Characters are interesting, beautifully rounded and speak with individual voices. Scenes are vividly etched on our imagination and the abstract quality of some of the writing is closer to poetry than prose.

It is a well-constructed, highly-crafted novel providing a good illustration of each of the above categories.

About the author

Jill Paton Walsh graduated from St Anne's College Oxford to become a teacher of English at a London grammar school. She started writing at 26, when she was living at home with her new baby and missing the children she had been teaching. She has won many awards including the Book Festival Award in 1970 for *Fireweed* and the Whitbread Prize in 1974 for *The Emperor's Winding Sheet*. She was also a judge for the Whitbread Prize in 1984.

She now lives in Cambridge where she co-runs a small specialist publishers called Green Bay Publications.

How to use this book

The first activity should be done before the children read the book. Then you may like to read the story to the class or divide it into a number of instalments and ask individual children to read it aloud in turn. The story chapters provide ready-made breaks with cliff-hanging endings.

It will be useful to have the book available while the children are tackling the follow-up activities.

There is an interview with Jill Paton Walsh on the audio cassette which accompanies this workshop. The children will probably find this very interesting to listen to, either before they read the story or after reading the story, before starting the activities.

ENDINGS AND BEGINNINGS

Teaching content

Identifying cliff-hanging endings and beginnings that make you want to read on.

What you need

Photocopiable page 170, writing materials, *Matthew and the Sea Singer*.

What to do

Explain to the children that writers often split stories into chapters in order to create suspense and force the reader to read on. Chapters often end on a cliff-hanger and the chapter beginnings often introduce a new idea that arouses curiosity and invites the reader to make predictions. Well-written books are very difficult to put down because the reader is constantly tantalised to read on through the story.

Arrange the children in groups of four and give a copy of photocopiable page 170 to each child. Explain that each of the four passages on the sheet has been formed by taking sentences from the end of one chapter and the beginning of the next in *Matthew and the Sea Singer*.

Ask the children to take each group of sentences in turn and to decide, first individually, where the split lies, and then to discuss their ideas with the others in their group, trying to arrive at an agreed decision. This discussion is a very valuable part of the activity, where children can clarify their thinking and make decisions evaluating information from a variety of sources.

Finally, when each group has completed the sheet, a spokesperson should explain the reasons behind the group's decisions. You may then like to reveal how Jill Paton Walsh actually split the chapters. Alternatively, the groups could check this for themselves in the book.

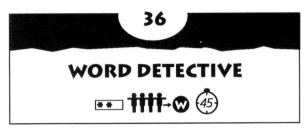

36

WORD DETECTIVE

** ╫╫╫→ⓦ ⒋⒌

Teaching content
Opening sentences can give clues to the nature of a story.

What you need
Matthew and the Sea Singer, photocopiable page 171, writing materials.

What to do
Remind the children that the first sentences in a story are intended to draw the reader right into the new world created by the writer.

Arrange the children in groups of four and ask them to appoint a spokesperson, a scribe, a chairperson and a timekeeper. Explain what each of these roles involves: the scribe records the group's findings; the spokesperson reports the group's work to the class; the chairperson reads the questions out one at a time and ensures that everyone gets an opportunity to speak and speaks quietly and appropriately; the timekeeper keeps an eye on the clock and ensures that everyone stays on task.

Tell the children that they are going to examine the opening sentences of *Matthew and the Sea Singer* to discover as much as possible about the world that has been created. They should think about and discuss the meanings of the words. In this way they will use the words as clues and can work like detectives to find out what sort of story this is going to be.

Give the children 15 minutes to read the introduction and to discuss and answer the questions on the worksheet. Then, draw the class together to share their findings. Encourage the children to comment on what other groups have said. In this way, they will see for themselves the importance of selecting words for specific effects. The atmosphere should be one of 'learning together in an environment of inquiry' rather than of finding correct answers.

The discussion may raise the following issues:
• 'Once' is a word that begins all fairy tales and is probably the one word that indicates the folk/magic story genre of this tale.
• The names of the characters are unusual, rural and slightly mysterious.
• The place and time is defined by the occupation of the characters and old money.

• The first sentence both establishes the mystery and shocks the reader.
• The differential amount of information about each character adds to the mystery, particularly the lack of information about the boy.

If the children are tempted to read on, you may like to end the lesson by reading chapters two and three in preparation for the next activity.

37

HAPPY THOUGHTS

*** ⓦ→╫ ⒍⒌

Teaching content
• Creating images of happiness.
• Exploring turning points.

What you need
Matthew and the Sea Singer, chalkboard, writing materials.

What to do
The story of Matthew progresses smoothly through to the point where he sings for the church congregation. When he sings, he creates a wonderful magic. Read pages 13–14 to the class.

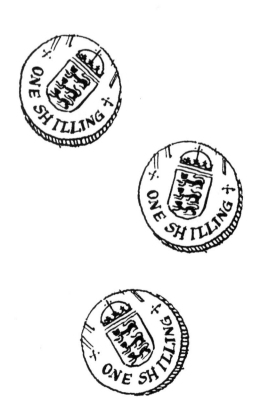

Write the following set of sentence starters on the board. Ask the children to work in pairs to add to the list of thoughts that people may have when they hear Matthew singing.

- He made prisoners think...
- He made the homeless think...
- He made teachers think...
- He made old women think...
- He made busy mothers think...
- He made children think...
- He made me think...
- He made me think...

Tell the children to write down the things they think would make these people especially happy. Encourage them to look at the poetic quality of the writing and to copy this style. The final two lines ask each partner in the pair to think of things that would give them most happiness.

Finished pieces of work should be given titles by the children and displayed as poems.

This activity should help children focus on the happy and comfortable nature of the story that has been built up. Thanks to Birdy's generosity in giving her precious money for this boy, a great happiness has been brought to the village. This mood is dashed by the short sentence at the beginning of page 16:

Then one day Matthew went missing.

This is the turning point in the story; it is the major problem that must be resolved. Read pages 16–17 to the children and compare the misery on these pages with the happiness of what went before. The sharp divide is marked by this one sentence. Remind the children that all stories need strong turning points in order to move the action forward and surprise the reader.

THE DRY SIDE OF THE WATER'S EDGE

Teaching content

Conveying contrast.

What you need

Matthew and the Sea Singer, photocopiable page 172, writing materials.

What to do

There are two distinct worlds presented in the story. There is the strange, unknown sea world and the familiar world of the land. Page 43 – 'Birdy brought Pagan to the dry side of the water's edge, and the seal-queen brought Matthew to the nearest rock ashore' – shows the characters meeting on the line between the two worlds.

Ask the children, in groups of four, to look at photocopiable page 172 and to fill in the names of the two main characters from each world. Ask them to find phrases that contrast the effect of Matthew's and of Pagan's singing. Page references are provided. The children should then look at the passage on page 44, and write the contrasting feelings evoked by the singing on to the appropriate side of the photocopiable sheet.

The end of any story should solve the problems that have been raised. Read the final paragraph of the story to the children. Ask them to think as you read and say which is the best sentence that shows the coming together of the two different worlds in a mysterious and beautiful way. This is, of course, the final sentence of the book.

39

WRITING TRAILERS

Teaching content

- Identifying main events.
- Writing chapter titles.

What you need

Matthew and the Sea Singer, writing and art materials, blank zigzag books, glue.

What to do

Ask the children to write down two reasons why writers split their writing into chapters. They may come up with some or all of the following:

- Parts can show the passage of time.
- When something quite new happens this divides into a new section.
- If the story moves into different places this can be indicated by new parts.
- Sometimes a new point of view can be found in new chapters.
- It is easier to read in short parts. The end of a part provides a natural stopping point.
- If writers have planned the story in parts, they can concentrate on perfecting one short part at a time before tackling the next piece of writing.

Now, examine the way in which Jill Paton Walsh has chosen to divide her story into seven chapters with numbered headings. Discuss with the children the different ways authors choose to indicate new chapters. Some books, for example, have chapter titles and even short summaries of the content of each chapter, which give tantalising glimpses of what is to come, rather like trailers for films.

Arrange the children in groups of seven, giving each child responsibility for one chapter in the book. Tell the children to read their allocated chapters and then to draw the picture that best illustrates the key event in that chapter. A few sentences summarising only the main events may be written on a second piece of paper. Finally, ask each person to think of a title for their chapter. Give each group a zigzag book and ask them to stick a chapter title, picture and summary on to each page. A group decision may be made about how to number chapters in a different way from the original book.

Compare the different presentations to let the children see how other groups analysed the main points.

How do the children think that Jill Paton Walsh planned the divisions in her storyline and why? Why do they think the chapters are numbered and not titled?

40

FINDING THE TITLE

Teaching content

Identifying what makes a good title.

What you need

Matthew and the Sea Singer, writing and art materials.

What to do

When writers create titles for their work, they often make long lists of possibilities in order to find the one that perfectly captures the essence of the story. *Matthew and the Sea Singer* is the title chosen by this author. Ask the children to think of two reasons why this is a good choice. Share these reasons, emphasising the fact that titles must:

- be interesting and intriguing enough to draw the reader on to open the book;
- focus on the main ideas within the story.

Now ask the children to invent two new titles for this story and to design a new cover for the book, illustrating what they think is the best title. Display these next to copies of the actual book.

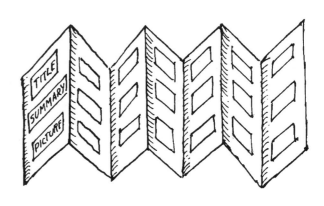

GOING FOR A DIP

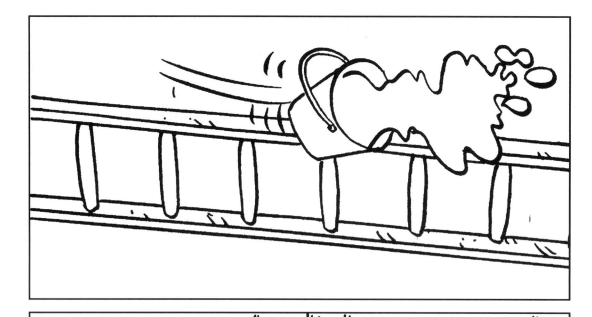

◆ Cut out the pictures and arrange them in the correct order to tell the story. Fill in the blank faces to show the people's reactions.

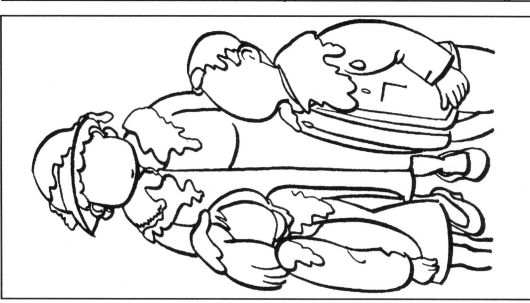

THE END OF THE HOLIDAY

◆ Read the following story opening, then write an idea for a turning point in each of the boxes. Four have categories already specified, but the fifth has been left open for your own idea.

This was to be their final visit to the ruined castle. Every lazy day of the holiday had been spent in this paradise. Dark, secret rooms and grassy open spaces between broken-down walls offered more adventure than any theme park. Tom, Pete and Claire climbed the hill with packed lunches strapped to their backs. The dog followed, falling behind while he snuffled amongst piles of rubble, then bounding ahead, effortlessly climbing the hill. The sun shone from a cloudless sky and the promise of the day filled their thoughts.

ARRIVAL OF A NEW CHARACTER

AN ACCIDENT

SOMETHING FOUND OR LOST

WEATHER CHANGES

SOMETHING ELSE

THE END OF THE HOLIDAY: PLANNING SHEET

◆ This is a planning sheet. It may be used for very brief notes on the content of the three main parts of a story.

Introduction/beginning

This may include information to describe:

- characters;

- place;

- setting;

- atmosphere.

Surprise/turning point

What is the problem or surprise that changes things?

The end/how the problem is solved

What happens at the end?

Make sure that all the problems have been resolved.

THE FINDING

Beginning

*Characters and setting
are introduced:*

Ambreen Haider and John Scott were next door neighbours.
They walked home from school together over the common.
On this particular afternoon, as they walked along the rough
path towards the pond, they had no idea that this was the
beginning of an adventure they would never forget.

'Look at that!' gasped John, pointing...

◆ What have Ambreen and John found? In groups, brainstorm the possibilities
and write them in the boxes.

Options for a turning point

Something very large
Something shiny
Something tiny
A message saying...
Something dangerous
Something magic
An animal
A person
Two other things

What happens next?

A SERIAL STORY

The abandoned bicycle

PART ONE

Describe the scene above as if you were there.

- What would you smell/hear?
- What colours would you see?
- Would you feel a pleasant breeze and the warm sun on your skin?

Describe the abandoned bicycle as the last part of this paragraph.

PART TWO

What happens to move the story along?

- Where is the owner of the bicycle?
- Has there been an accident?
- Is the bicycle stolen?
- Do searchers come on the scene?

Describe what happens and leave part two on a cliff-hanger.

PART THREE

Does this story have a happy ending?
How will you resolve the cliff-hanger?
Remember to tie up all the loose ends.

The empty rowing boat

PART ONE

Describe the scene above as if you were there.

- What would you see?
- What sounds would you hear?
- Do you feel the wind and wave spray?

Describe the deserted boat as the last part of this paragraph.

PART TWO

What happens to move the story along?

- A swimmer comes on the scene.
- Another boat appears.
- A desperate animal appears.
- Something else.

Describe what happens and leave part two on a cliff-hanger.

PART THREE

Does this story have a happy ending?
How will you resolve the cliff-hanger?
Remember to tie up all the loose ends.

The open rucksack

PART ONE

Describe the scene above as if you were there.

- What colours would you see?
- What sounds would you hear?
- Would you feel the biting, icy wind?

Describe the open rucksack as the final part of this paragraph.

PART TWO

What happens to move the story along?

- Where is the owner of the rucksack?
- Has there been an accident?
- Will there be a rescue?

Describe what happens and leave part two on a cliff-hanger.

PART THREE

Does this story have a happy ending?
How will you resolve the cliff-hanger?
Remember to tie up all the loose ends.

THE END OF THE RAINBOW

◆ Read this opening paragraph of a story.

They travelled to Earth on gigantic arcs of coloured light. Showers of glistening raindrops eased their path as they slid and shimmered through the morning air. To Earth people they were invisible. They could carry out their business undisturbed. They came to check their stores of treasure kept safely hidden within the planet.

◆ Now choose which turning point you feel would lead to the most exciting middle and ending.

❶ One day a savage storm cracked their rainbow of coloured light and terrified, they found they could not return.

OR

❷ Whilst happily admiring the wonderful treasure trove hidden beneath the cellars of an old school, the travellers were shocked to realise that they had been spied by a young Earthling.

OR

❸ After one of their long journeys, the travellers returned to their own star to discover that one of their younger beings had been left behind.

A RACE AGAINST TIME

◆ This is the middle section of a story

The boy stumbled, almost dropping his burden as he plunged headlong on through trees. Desperate gasps were wrung from his dry throat but he cared no longer about the noise he made. Cathy's body was now a limp dead weight in his arms. When they first began their desperate dash he had covered up his own terror, knowing it would only add to her fear. Now it didn't matter any more.

◆ These are two possible endings to this story. Which do you prefer?

Ending ❶
The gang who had kidnapped the Brown twins were quickly captured. The story of how Harry Brown escaped, carrying his wounded sister and probably saving her life, was in the news for weeks after.

Ending ❷
When he awoke in hospital the next day, Harry was embarrassed to discover that he was a national hero. Headlines in the papers told of a young boy's courage in rescuing a small child from an illegal animal trap. Doctors said that his presence of mind in calming the child, wrapping her in his coat and getting her swiftly to the hospital had saved her life. The story of his desperate journey from the forest to Stobhill hospital amazed everyone.

Scholastic
IMAGINATIVE WRITING
Workshop

NEW BEGINNINGS

◆ Read the following possible opening of the story of *Cinderella*.

Description of a place

The people of the city always paused at the beautiful palace as they passed by. This was the shining, sun-drenched palace of their Prince. On this day, the people whispered as they passed, wondering who would be the lucky ones to receive an invitation to the Grand Ball.

A statement or conversation

'Well, I know one person who won't be going to the Ball from this house,' muttered the uglier of the Ugly Sisters as she tore poor Cinderella's invitation into fragments.

A happening

The golden coach raced through the cobbled streets delivering invitations to the Grand Ball.

Traditional beginning

'Once upon a time...'

◆ Now write your own opening for the following category.

Description of a character

SPOTLIGHT ON ...

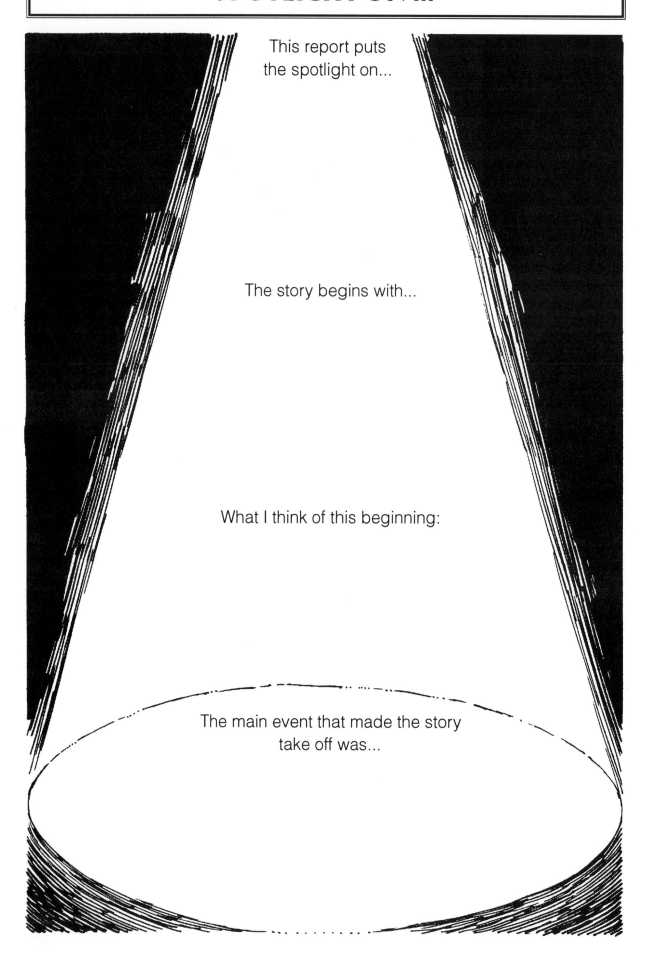

This report puts
the spotlight on...

The story begins with...

What I think of this beginning:

The main event that made the story
take off was...

Scholastic
IMAGINATIVE WRITING
Workshop

A HAND ON YOUR SHOULDER

1. Is the child a boy or a girl?

2. How old is the child?

3. Where is the forbidden place?
    (Add some descriptive detail. Remember it may be a sinister, frightening place in keeping with an alarming adventure *or* a beautiful, peaceful place which will provide a contrast to the fierce hand and make this a strong turning point.)

4. Whose hand is this? (add a few descriptive notes.)

5. How does the child escape?

Four starting points

Name of writer

1. Description of the child   _____

2. Description of the place   _____

3. One thing that is shouted or said
   by the child or the other character   _____

4. Description of the chase   _____

THEY ALL LIVED HAPPILY EVER AFTER

◆ Write the final paragraph of the story of *Cinderella*. Use the starter sentence below and try to make sure that all the questions are answered.

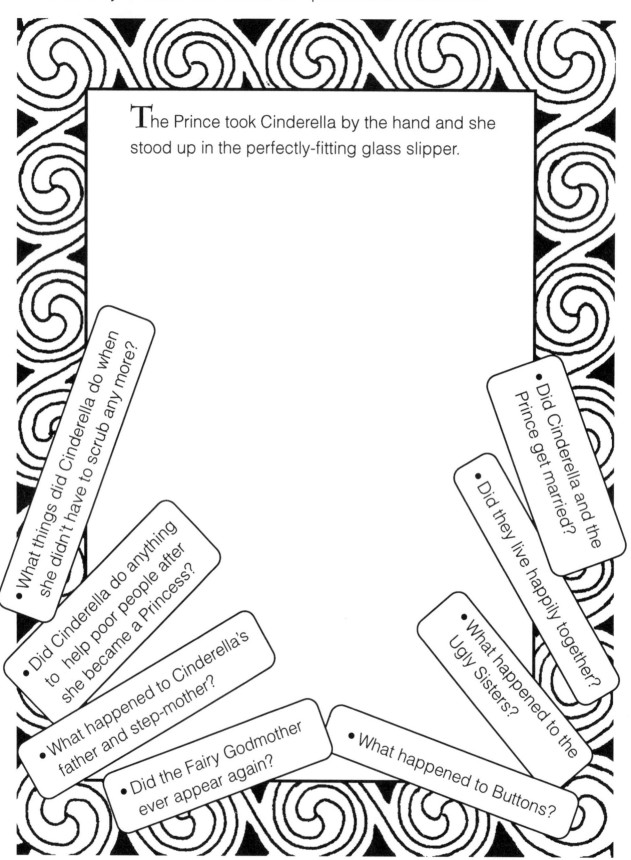

The Prince took Cinderella by the hand and she stood up in the perfectly-fitting glass slipper.

- What things did Cinderella do when she didn't have to scrub any more?

- Did Cinderella do anything to help poor people after she became a Princess?

- What happened to Cinderella's father and step-mother?

- Did the Fairy Godmother ever appear again?

- What happened to Buttons?

- Did Cinderella and the Prince get married?

- Did they live happily together?

- What happened to the Ugly Sisters?

THE END

◆ There are several different ways of ending a story. These are some of the options.

1. Signing off, telling the reader directly that the story has finished.

2. One character speaking of what they will all do in the future.

3. Characters looking ahead to an unknown future.

4. A summary of what happens to all the characters at the end.

5. A tantalising hint that we too may travel to magical lands.

6. A character arrives who knows nothing of the exciting adventures that have happened and assumes that life has been going on just as normal.

7. A character looking back over events that have unfolded in the story.

NAME

THE END

◆ There are several different ways of ending a story. These are some of the options.

1. Signing off, telling the reader directly that the story has finished.

2. One character speaking of what they will all do in the future.

3. Characters looking ahead to an unknown future.

4. A summary of what happens to all the characters at the end.

5. A tantalising hint that we too may travel to magical lands.

6. A character arrives who knows nothing of the exciting adventures that have happened and assumes that life has been going on just as normal.

7. A character looking back over events that have unfolded in the story.

THE LOST KITTEN

◆ Read the following openings to the story of the lost kitten and decide which character is narrating.

It was a frosty night, when no clouds floated between me and the Earth that I saw the little lost kitten. I twinkled as brightly as I possibly could so that...
Who am I?

The strange noises around me made me shiver with fear as well as cold! Why didn't my best friend answer when I called with my scared 'meow'?
Who am I?

'Yum! Yum!' I laughed quietly as I silently stalked the delicious treat I was to have for my supper.
Who am I?

Desperately I called my kitten's name as I plunged through the wet undergrowth.
Who am I?

Scholastic
IMAGINATIVE WRITING
Workshop

PERSPECTIVES ON A PLACE

◆ Choose one of the characters listed below and answer the questions from the point of view of your chosen character.

Pick-pocket
Owner of a successful ride
Stray cat
Rat
Owner of a ride that nobody likes
Lost child
Escaped prisoner

My feelings about the fair

(please tick) ☐ ☐ ☐ ☐ ☐ ☐
love like okay dislike hate loathe

Smells I particularly adore

Smells I hate

Sounds that I love

Sounds that frighten or alarm me

Things I hope to do

Things I hope won't happen

'SAVE MY PUPPY!'

◆ Rewrite this dialogue as a short narrative using some of the alternatives to 'said' from the list.

Fireman: Are you sure there's a dog in there?

John: Yes! Yes! Please save him. He's my puppy. I got him for my birthday. He's in there, honest.

Fireman: I'm sorry son. I'm being driven back by the smoke. Maybe he got out of a window.

John: None of the windows will open. They're all stuck up with paint. Please mister. I'm desperate. Save my dog!

Fireman: I've tried every room upstairs. I was driven back down the stairs by flames but he's not up there, I know it. I even looked under the beds.

John: He'll be in the kitchen. I know it. I'll try myself.

Fireman: Back you come son. Now! Now!

John: Thanks. Thanks mister. Where were you hiding, you silly puppy? Oh, thanks mister.

Alternatives to 'said'

shouted

           sobbed

commanded

           whispered

groaned

           begged

choked

           pleaded

wept

           demanded

A PUBLISHER DROPS THE PAGES

◆ Cut out the following statements and arrange them in the correct order to tell the story of *Sleeping Beauty*.

Everyone was preparing for the birthday party.

The Prince chops his way through the forest.

The Wicked Fairy makes a wish.

The Princess pricks her finger on a spinning wheel.

The Prince kisses Sleeping Beauty.

Every person in the palace falls asleep.

A beautiful baby is born to the King and Queen.

Fairies make lovely wishes at the christening.

One hundred years later a travelling Prince finds a thick forest.

There is a big party for the baby's christening.

The Princess grows up to be happy and talented.

Sleeping Beauty marries the Prince.

Now, divide your story into three sections and give each one a chapter heading

CHAPTER ONE	CHAPTER TWO	CHAPTER THREE

TITLES TO MAKE YOU READ ON

◆ Write each of these book titles in the column you think most appropriate.

Strong titles	Weak titles

'BILLY GOAT FOOTSTEPS...'

◆ Read the following list of refrains from traditional fairy tales. For each one answer the following questions:

1. Which story does the refrain come from?

2. How many times is it repeated and when does it occur?

3. Does it rhyme?

Little pig, little pig let me come in.

Rapunzel, Rapunzel, let down your hair.

Someone's been sleeping in *my* bed.

Grandma, what big ears you have.
All the better to hear you with...

Princess, will you let me eat from your golden plate and drink from your golden cup;
will you let me lie in your bed with my head upon your pillow?

Fee fi fo fum, I smell the blood of an Englishman;
Be he alive or be he dead, I'll grind his bones to make my bread.

Then I'll huff and I'll puff and I'll blow your house down.

Who's been eating *my* porridge?

Run, run, as fast as you can, you can't catch
me, I'm the Gingerbread man.

'Not I' said the dog;
'Not I' said the cat;
'Not I' said the pig.

LAYOUT AND LETTERING

◆ Choose one of the following passages to copy out and illustrate.

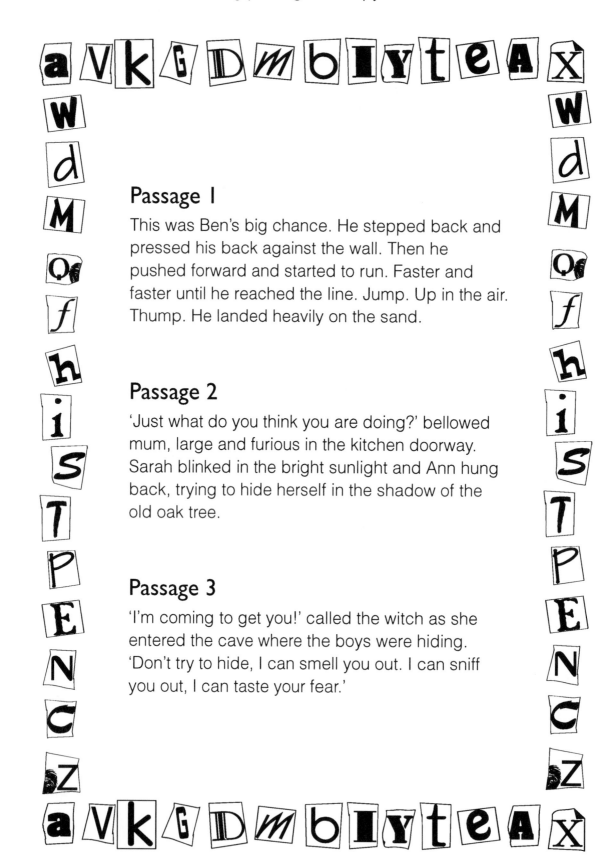

Passage 1

This was Ben's big chance. He stepped back and pressed his back against the wall. Then he pushed forward and started to run. Faster and faster until he reached the line. Jump. Up in the air. Thump. He landed heavily on the sand.

Passage 2

'Just what do you think you are doing?' bellowed mum, large and furious in the kitchen doorway. Sarah blinked in the bright sunlight and Ann hung back, trying to hide herself in the shadow of the old oak tree.

Passage 3

'I'm coming to get you!' called the witch as she entered the cave where the boys were hiding. 'Don't try to hide, I can smell you out. I can sniff you out, I can taste your fear.'

DOORS INTO NEW WORLDS

◆ Look at the first pages of 'Nice Neighbours' and 'Nasty Neighbours' and imagine what kind of hallway you would find behind these front doors. Write brief notes for each of the following categories.

	 Nice Neighbours	 Nasty Neighbours
What items of furniture would be in the hall?		
What other items may be in the hall?		
Describe the wallpaper. What pictures or mirrors would hang on the walls?		
What would you smell as the door opened?		
What sounds could be heard coming from the other rooms in the house?		

EDITORS IN ACTION

◆ The stories 'Nice Neighbours' and 'Nasty Neighbours' have been divided into chapters. Give each chapter an appropriate title.

Nasty Neighbours	Nice Neighbours
INTRODUCTION	CHAPTER 1
From 'The McNasty family was like any other family...' to '...the McNasty family were very happy.' Title:	From 'There was no place quite like the O'Naice home...' to '...feeling happy... proud... and bored.' Title:
PROBLEM	CHAPTER 2
From 'In fact, they only had one problem...' to '...this was the last straw.' Title:	From 'Of course, it wasn't always quiet...' to '...a hundred and fifty million times.' Title:
SOLVING THE PROBLEM	CHAPTER 3
From 'From that fateful day...' to '...the O'Naice family emerged.' Title:	From 'Then one evening...' to '...most helpful children on the street.' Title:
BILLY AND LOUISE CHANGE	CHAPTER 4
From 'It was time for...' to '...and all the children cheered.' Title:	From 'So, the next day...' to '"Or maybe William McNastikov..."' Title:
THE END	CHAPTER 5
Middle page Title:	Middle page Title:

Scholastic **IMAGINATIVE WRITING** Workshop

SUPERMARKET MAYHEM

◆ Cut out these speech bubbles and stick them in the appropriate column.

Careful where you walk –
I've just ironed the bathmat.

Who asked you in here, eh?

Oh no, I've dropped the bottle.
Quick, round the corner before
anyone sees us!

Out of my way! You're blocking
the passage way.

So sorry! Did my trolley run over
your foot? Hope you're all right.

Oh dear! I've dented that tin.
We'll have to pay for it.

These flowers will do nicely for
that poor old lady down the road.

Hey, watch your trolley,
mate! You need L-plates.

Nice Neighbours   ## Nasty Neighbours

ENDINGS AND BEGINNINGS

◆ For each of these passages from *Matthew and the Sea Singer*, decide where one chapter ends and the next one starts.

"I don't know whose fault it is" said Papajack "but I know a hungry child when I see one."

And Birdy took her birthday shilling out of her apron pocket, and bought Matthew on the spot. Next morning, Birdy woke up hearing something new. There was the wind scraping itself on the sharp corners of the house and whining a bit over it, as it often and often did.

"Keep your shilling, and give Matthew a day in the week to play with me," said Birdy, and it was agreed. Time went by and by and Matthew learned tunes with his notes and words with his tunes. He learned to sing the Sunday music in Zennor church. He had a voice that might have been an angel's voice.

And people began saying that on Sundays when the service started at Zennor, the birds on the bush fell silent, and the wheeling gulls stopped screaming, and the seal-folk and mermaids gathered on the rocks below the church, hoping to catch, drifting down to them on the wind, the faint sound of Matthew singing. Then one day Matthew went missing. All day Birdy thought the parson had kept Matthew, and the parson thought he was with Birdy. They didn't find out they were wrong till Matthew had been gone many hours.

Hadn't they been lumbering out of the water and waiting for the wind to bring voices down to them? Specially one voice?

Suddenly Birdy knew where Matthew was. Getting him back, though, was another matter.

WORD DETECTIVE

◆ Examine this opening sentence to *Matthew and the Sea Singer*, then discuss the following questions.

> Once there was a little girl called Birdy who paid a shilling for a living boy.
> Birdy's father, Papajack, was a ferryman, rowing travellers across the river.

What characters are introduced at the beginning of this story?

Write their names, if you are told them, or a short description if you don't know this. Next to each, write what you know about each character.

Where do you think this story will be set?

How do you know?

At roughly what time in history do you think this story is set?

What makes you think this?

What questions are generated by this opening?

◆ Look at the list showing types of story. What type of story do you think this is going to be? Tick which you think it could be and why.

Story type	Yes	No	Why?
A detective story			
A school story			
A space adventure			
A monster story			
A folk tale			
A fairy tale			
A murder mystery			

Does everyone in the group want to read on? Why?

THE DRY SIDE OF THE WATER'S EDGE

The water

Character 1 _____

Character 2 _____

Two thoughts provoked by
Pagan's singing (pages 40–41)

1

2

Feelings inspired by Pagan's
singing (page 44)

The dry side

Character 1 _____

Character 2 _____

Two thoughts provoked by
Matthew's singing (pages 13–14)

1

2

Feelings inspired by Matthew's
singing (page 44)

◆ Read the last paragraph of the story. Write here the sentence that best
sums up the meeting of the two worlds.

Chapter Six

THE WRITING PROCESS

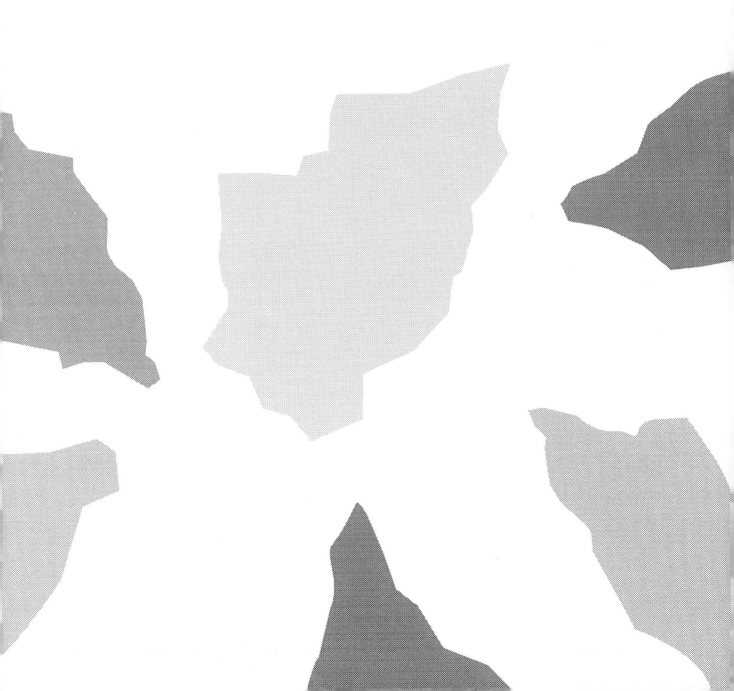

INTRODUCTION

*There is no greater gift a writing teacher
can give than to help another person know
he or she has a story to tell. (Lucy Calkins, 1986)*

The writing process approach

The writing process approach as advocated by Lucy Calkins and Donald Graves involves considering why and how children produce the stories they do. It is only when teachers pay attention to why children write and how they work – what they find difficult and easy and what they themselves identify as strengths and weaknesses – that they can hope to target their teaching effectively. By working with and through each child's current understanding and motivation teachers can help children to develop more complex and sophisticated understandings and thus improve their work.

However, the writing process approach also embodies a notion of 'process as content'. In helping children to craft effective stories, teachers need to teach specific techniques but also to introduce children to effective ways of working. This requires them to have a familiarity with some of the writing processes used by successful writers (for example, story planning, drafting, editing).

The writing process and the teacher

It is difficult to teach any subject effectively without finding out what motivates the children, how they conceive the task, what they perceive as triumphs or failures and what they find easy and difficult. In teaching mathematics, teachers constantly check the children's understanding – asking them to explain how they arrived at an answer. By watching and listening the teacher finds out how the child thinks and why errors occur, and can pitch the teaching to ensure that explanations make sense, build on relevant understandings and counter misunderstandings.

Teachers need this same information in teaching children how to write stories. The teacher needs to know the criteria the child uses to judge the story and how far these match the teacher's own. The teacher also needs to know how the child composed and wrote the story. It is only when the teacher knows which parts make the child proud, what came easily and what was problematic, that she can use her knowledge to help the child.

The writing process and the children

The writing process approach empowers children in two ways. Firstly, it makes them more aware of what they know, of how they work, and of what is effective (or not effective) about their work habits. This knowledge helps them to work more efficiently in the future.

Secondly, it makes children more aware of the learning process in general and of what they have learned in particular. This encourages children to become more reflective, self-directed and analytical in all aspects of their work.

The writing process model

The writing process focuses on how writers go about writing. It can be framed in various ways. Calkins advocates Donald Murray's model of rehearsal, drafting, revision and editing. By rehearsal he means 'stories happen to those who tell them': that writers are aware of, and looking for, the story potential in everyday incidents and often discover potential through talking, observing and reading. Drafting refers to the first, tentative, efforts to get the story down on paper and leads to revision: re-living the story as a reader and re-writing to make it more effective. All of the UK national curricula encourage the teaching of the writing process.

Teaching the writing process

The 'writing process' provides a focus for thinking about aspects of a complex activity rather than a description of what writers do. There is no single 'correct' way to write and there is no 'correct' process that children must be taught. Moreover, the needs and behaviours of individual children differ from each other and may differ in important ways from those of an adult. It is the teacher's job to notice how children write and help individuals to work in the way that they find most helpful. Knowledge of the writing process components should inform, not enslave, the teaching of writing.

Process cannot be divorced and taught separately from context and content. Children should be encouraged to write, first and foremost. Only then can they talk about their writing and work to improve it. Through this they learn about the processes. Teaching of process needs a light touch to avoid becoming boring and mechanistic.

Well taught, the writing process makes children more aware of the possibilities and encourages them to experiment with ways to get ideas, plan, draft, revise and edit their work. Because children are individuals, each child will arrive at an individual solution. Over-prescriptive methodologies that force children to work in particular ways create more problems than they solve.

The activities in this section, therefore, do not provide a linear 'step-by-step' guide to teaching the process aspects of writing, but a bank of resources which should be used sensitively and flexibly to make children aware of the different aspects and to encourage them to become experimental, reflective writers.

Meaningful contexts: prerequisite for teaching about the writing process

There is no point in asking children to behave like writers unless the classroom ethos and conditions make this possible. Children have to write for real reasons. It may be that they are driven by a sense of audience – they know that someone (beyond the teacher) will want to read their work, and are excited by the thought of the reader's response. It may be that they are driven by a desire to get the story down on paper. For many children, writing for themselves is just as important as the thought of writing for others. The important message is that children need time to work on their stories and to become emotionally involved with them.

The *Scholastic Writing Workshop* activities, particularly the writing projects help teachers to establish such conditions. They introduce a variety of ways for children to get ideas, plan, draft, review, edit and present their work, providing rich experiences for reflection.

COLLABORATIVE WORK

Why do collaborative work?

• It is fun to work with friends and it can make the work less daunting. The confidence, enthusiasm and self-esteem that this work can promote is in itself a powerful justification.
• Children appreciate the importance of writing clear and interesting stories when they see other people reading their work. Through talking about their stories and watching others read them, children develop a sense of audience that is real and personal; it goes beyond simply knowing who will read their work and becomes a question of 'How can I control what the reader will think?'

• Collaborative work deepens children's learning because it encourages them to re-explain ideas in their own words and to link new ideas to existing understandings. This helps them to use new knowledge and strategies and also makes them aware of what they know and what and how, they have learned.
• Collaborative work makes for an efficient and practical way to organise the classroom. Instead of 33 children seeking help from one teacher, there are 33 teachers in the class. It can help children to become more self-directed and independent learners and it also promotes and develops a range of desirable social skills.

Teaching through collaborative work: prerequisite knowledge

When implementing any collaborative approach to learning, teachers should take care not to overload the children. They need to balance the demands that any collaborative task makes in terms of the children's social skills with their familiarity with the content knowledge. It is unreasonable to expect children to succeed in tasks in which both the level of content knowledge and the social skills required challenge their abilities. For successful collaborative work, teachers need to know their classes well, to be aware of those children who require help with either the content or the social skills and to tailor tasks accordingly. They also need to ensure that the children are aware of their own strengths and failings in working collaboratively. If some children find it difficult to work with others, suggest they form pairs, or that they work with children who are skilled group workers.

CONTENTS AND ORGANISATION

Activities in this chapter focus on three aspects:

The writer's self-knowledge

By encouraging children to analyse their own writing and their work habits, the activities:
• raise awareness of the children's interests and preferred topics;
• raise awareness of which writing processes they use;
• analyse their strengths and weaknesses.
In doing this, children will become more aware

of their own motivations and the strategies open to them and can reflect on how and when these may be useful.

Because the activities ask children to reflect on their current attitudes, skills and strategies as writers, some are particularly appropriate to be done with a class that is fairly new to the teacher. They yield information about each child's reactions to previous writing experiences that can provide insights into how best to teach and contextualise the work for each child.

Aspects of process

These activities target strategies that underpin aspects of the writing process. They are designed to make children more aware of particular aspects and to expose some of the decision-making, the work habits and the skills that help writers to:
• generate ideas;
• select and sequence ideas to plan, draft and review their work;

• edit and proof read effectively.

Some of these activities use poetry to exemplify certain aspects of the writing process, since poems are short and therefore easily tackled in a single session.

Helping each other

These activities raise children's awareness of when, how and why collaboration may be valuable to writers. Children are asked to consider:
• when they may find collaboration helpful in their writing and why. It is unlikely that it will be useful at the same points to everyone, but each child needs to know how working with others may help them to generate, clarify or understand ideas and provide feedback on their work;
• how to be a good collaborator: what sort of advice and comment is helpful/unhelpful;
• their own skills and attitudes towards working collaboratively.

Activity	Teaching Content	Star rating	Group size	Photo copiable
SELF-KNOWLEDGE				
1 My history as a writer	To highlight attitudes and feelings about writing and possible reasons for them	✶⇨✶✶✶	Ⓦ⇨1	✓
2 Picture a writer: picture me	Raising awareness of different work patterns	✶✶	1⇨3	✓
3 The stories I tell	Reading/writing links	✶✶	1	✓
4 It's a good story because ...	Discussion of the criteria used to judge work and why	✶✶	4⇨Ⓦ	✓
5 That's easy, that's hard!	Reflecting on individual strengths and weaknesses	✶⇨✶✶	1⇨4	
6 Ideas analysis	Raising awareness of possible sources for ideas; reflecting on the most common sources	✶✶	4	✓
7 Common errors	To make teachers aware of how children feel about the errors they make	✶✶✶	1	✓
ASPECTS OF PROCESS				
8 The story ideas bank	Story ideas come from different sources; writers keep a bank of ideas which they add to and draw on	✶✶	1	
9 My poem's a bit like your poem	Drafting - sequencing ideas	✶✶	Ⓦ⇨2	
10 Five line poems	Drafting - selecting ideas	✶✶	Ⓦ⇨1	
11 Only you	Drafting - selecting and sequencing ideas	✶✶	1	
12 Music poems	Using music as a stimulus for ideas; drafting-ordering ideas for best effect	✶✶✶	Ⓦ⇨4	
13 Responding to writing	How to improve a story	✶✶✶	2	
14 Proof-reading for errors	Proof-reading and how it differs from other reading behaviours	✶✶	1	✓
15 Find the error	Proof-reading practice	✶✶✶	1	✓
16 How do you feel?	Children feel differently about different aspects of their work	✶⇨✶✶✶	1⇨2/3	✓✓
HELPING EACH OTHER				
17 Reading for a friend	The role of a writing partner when reading another's story	✶✶	1⇨4	✓
18 The perfect writing partner	Personal preferences for writing partners; reflecting on helpful/unhelpful behaviours in a writing partner	✶✶	1⇨4	✓
19 Writing partner comments	Providing helpful feedback as a writing partner	✶✶	4⇨1	
20 When to talk	When is it helpful to consult others?	✶✶	1⇨4	✓
21 What I learn from others	Working with others provides opportunities to learn	✶✶✶	Ⓦ⇨1	

A = anthology page
Ⓦ = whole group

MY HISTORY AS A WRITER

What you need
Chalkboard, writing materials, photocopiable page 188 (optional).

Teaching content
To highlight attitudes and feelings about writing and possible reasons for them.

What to do
Explain that you are interested in how the children feel about writing, and why they feel this way.

List the following questions on the board and use them as the basis for a class discussion.
• Do you like writing stories? Explain your answer.
• Have you always felt the same way about writing stories? If not, when did your feelings begin to change? Why?
• What is your earliest memory of writing a story?
• What is the best story you have written? Why is it the best?
• What is the worst experience you have had of writing a story? Why?

After the discussion, ask the children to write a short piece about their own experiences of, and feelings about, writing. Again, the questions can be used as a prompt or to help the children structure their writing. Photocopiable page 188 provides more support for those children who may feel daunted by having to produce a passage of writing. The information this activity yields will help you teach in a way that is enjoyable and appropriate, but it will also help the children to begin to see, and to understand, themselves as writers.

PICTURE A WRITER: PICTURE ME

Teaching content
Raising awareness of different work patterns.

What you need
Photocopiable page 189, writing materials, chalkboard.

What to do
Ask the children to consider the most recent story they have written and to think about how they went about their work. How did they start? Which parts did they find difficult? Did they talk to anyone about their work? If so, when?

If the children are not used to thinking about their work in this way, they may find this quite difficult. Give them a few minutes in which to think, then ask them to put up their hands if they found it easy to remember. (Make a mental note of these children.)

Then give each child a copy of photocopiable page 189 and explain that it contains five brief descriptions of different writers and the way they work. Tell the children to read each description and to tick the one which they think is most like themselves. Explain that they will probably not find one that describes them exactly. Having identified the one that is nearest to themselves, however, ask them to consider the following questions (write them on the board):
• Are you totally like this?
• Which bits are most like you?
• Which bits are least like you?
• Are you always like this?

Now ask the children to work in groups of three. The children should take each describe themselves briefly as a writer to the other two memberof the group, then the group should discuss what has been said. How are they similar? How are they different? Did they hear anything that surprised them? Finish with a brief class discussion to emphasise the different needs of individual writers, the different ways in which they work and the various factors that may affect this: for example, individual skills, attitudes and work patterns, the subject matter, the context, the purpose for writing, the time available and so on.

Development/homework task

• Ask the children each to write a short description, following the models on the photocopiable sheet, of their own typical working pattern. Make these into a class book.

• Ask the children to consider what the 'perfect' writer might be like, if such a thing is possible.

3

THE STORIES I TELL

Teaching content
Reading/writing links.

What you need
Photocopiable page 190, writing materials.

What to do
The stories that children enjoy reading, listening to or watching on television can influence what they want to write and what they find easy to write. By reflecting on their own preferences, children realise that they are unique writers, who will produce a unique body of work. This activity also helps them to recognise their versatility as writers and can provide a good starting point for encouraging children to read and write different types of story.

From the teacher's point of view, it would seem helpful to know children's personal experiences and preferences about stories before asking them to write: no child is going to be enthusiastic about writing a story that they would not personally enjoy reading. Moreover, children who, for example, enjoy watching stories on television but who do not read them, may need particular kinds of support to help motivate them and to appreciate the difference between watching television and reading stories.

Introduce the lesson by explaining that this is an activity to get the children to think about the type of stories they enjoy writing and why this might be so. Explain that, although the children will get an opportunity to discuss what they have found later, the first part of the activity must be done without discussion. Give each child a copy of photocopiable page 190 and ask them to consider the first two columns together, ignoring, for the moment, the third and fourth columns. Ask them to:

• tick each story type they enjoy reading/watching;

• put a cross against those they hate reading/watching;

• put a question mark against those they sometimes enjoy reading/watching.

Then, ask the children to consider the third and fourth columns. For the third column ask them to think about the stories they have written, both at school and at home. For the fourth column, ask them to think about the stories they enjoy talking about with their friends and the stories they invent when they day-dream and when they play (alone and with others). Tell the children to use the same code of ticks, crosses and question marks to record their preferences.

Now, ask the children to examine their sheets. What patterns and gaps can they see? This part of the activity may be done in pairs if preferred. The questions at the bottom of the photocopiable sheet may help to focus their attention.

Finally, ask the children to write a short paragraph describing themselves as writers.

4

IT'S A GOOD STORY BECAUSE...

Teaching content
Discussion of the criteria used to judge work and why.

What you need
Photocopiable page 191, scissors.

What to do
Children need opportunities to discuss the criteria on which they believe different people judge their stories. They need to explore whether the differences are real or merely perceived and whether they are constant, applied to all stories in all circumstances, or variable.

Give each group a copy of photocopiable page 191 and ask the children to cut out and sort the statements into two columns: 'Important for me' and 'Important for the teacher'. Where they feel that the statement is equally important for both, it should be placed across both columns.

Then, hold a class discussion to compare how each group has classified the statements and why. The following questions may be useful to direct the discussion:
• Did all the groups agree on what was important for the teacher?
• Why do they think these are important?
• Are the children's views of the teacher's criteria accurrate?
• Did all the children agree about what was important for themselves? Why?
• How far do the teacher's and the children's concerns concur?

Finally, it may be interesting for children to consider whether they use the same criteria to assess their own stories as they would use to assess the work of professional authors. Do children see themselves as less able to write particular types of stories than professional authors? Do they perceive professional authors as sharing any problems with themselves or not?

Development/homework task

This activity can be repeated, asking children to consider the headings 'Important for me' and 'Important for my parents'. The children can interview their parents to see how far they were correct and then write a short report to go in a class book

5
THAT'S EASY, THAT'S HARD!

Teaching content
To reflect on individual difficulties and strengths.

What you need
Chalkboard, writing materials.

What to do
Teachers and children need to identify which aspects of the writing process can be problematic for individuals and why. Such analysis enables solutions to be found.

Explain that all writers have different strengths. Just as writers all work in different ways, so they find different things easy or difficult. Some aspects of writing are easy for some writers and not for others. This activity enables the children to reflect on their own strengths as writers.

Write the following list on the board.
1. Getting ideas for characters
2. Deciding how to start
3. Deciding what will happen
4. Getting the story on to the page
5. Making the story exciting/funny/scary/interesting
6. Thinking of a title
7. Writing neatly
8. Choosing which bits to illustrate
9. Deciding what to put in/leave out
10. Deciding how to end the story
11. Working alone when writing
12. Punctuation and spelling
13. Knowing which bits of the story are most important to tell
14. Telling the story clearly so that others know what you mean

Ask the children to write down the three activities that, generally, they find easiest. You may need to explain that sometimes people find things so easy that they do them automatically without thinking. Then, ask the children to write down the three that, generally, they find most difficult. If this is too hard for some children, ask them just to look at the first seven points and to note down *two* that they find easy and *two* they find difficult.

Arrange the children in groups of four and ask them to share their strengths and weaknesses. Ask them to talk about particular examples of when they found things hard and to try to get the group to identify why. Finally, ask the children to discuss who is best placed to help them with the things they find difficult: is it the teacher, another child or a parent/friend outside school? Explain that the children are not looking for someone to do the difficult parts for them, but for someone who can help them to do them more easily – by explaining things, encouraging them, demonstrating or practising with them. If it is helpful to work with other children, would they prefer to work with someone who has the same difficulties as them, or with someone who doesn't? Does it matter?

Ask each group to make brief notes about their discussion, identifying what people found difficult and report back on what they think could be done about it.

IDEAS ANALYSIS

* * 👤👤👤👤 ⏱30

Teaching content

• Raising awareness of possible sources for ideas.
• Reflecting on the most common sources.

What you need

Photocopiable page 192, writing materials.

What to do

Arrange the children in groups of four and give each group a copy of photocopiable page 192. Ask the children to think about the stories they have written in the past and how or where they got the ideas on which they were based. Explain that ideas for stories can come from anywhere, then go over the list of possibilities on the photocopiable sheet, getting the class to add any further suggestions on to the bottom of the list.

Now ask the children to consider each ideas-source and to decide whether they each use it frequently, sometimes or never, recording this by writing their initials under the appropriate heading.

Then, ask each group to discuss what they have indicated on the sheet. What is the most common source of ideas? Are they happy with this? Why do they think that some sources are never used? Are there any sources that they hadn't thought of using before? Are there any that would not be useful at all? Why? Hold a class discussion on the issues raised.

COMMON ERRORS

* * 👤 ⏱25

Teaching content

To make teachers aware of how children think and feel about the errors they make.

What you need

Photocopiable page 193, writing materials.

What to do

It is important that children engage in self-evaluation and analysis of their work. Self-esteem and confidence must arise from the satisfaction children get from their work and cannot be based on comparisons with others. Teachers need to encourage self-assessment and to be aware of how children feel about their work.

Give each child a copy of photocopiable page 193. Ask them to read the list of possible errors and, for each error, to tick whether they:
• make that type of error more often than other people in the class;
• make that type of error about as frequently as other people in the class;
• make that type of error less often than other people in the class;
• never make that type of error.

Finally, ask them to add to the list any errors not mentioned and tick the most appropriate column.

Children's view of their work may or may not tally with that of the teacher. Some children are over-critical of their stories and feel that they make more mistakes or find things more difficult than their peers. Others are over-confident and set themselves low standards. It is obviously not desirable that children should be overly competitive in their work. However, children are often acutely aware of how their work compares with that of their peers.

THE STORY IDEAS BANK

Teaching content
- Story ideas come from different sources.
- Writers keep a bank of ideas, which they periodically add to and draw on.

What you need
Chalkboard, writing materials.

What to do
Writers devise different ways of remembering good ideas for future use. Some writers jot down ideas for stories whenever they occur to them and keep them for future reference. Sometimes the ideas may not get used for years or a story may combine two or three ideas.

Suggest that the children may like to start up their own ideas bank for stories. They can use it for stories they write at home or at school. The most important thing is that the ideas should be kept somewhere safe and not be lost. The back page of a writing jotter is a good place in that it is unlikely to be misplaced.

Frequently it is quite small events that spark a good idea for a story. Talk to the children about when good ideas come to them. Often it is when they are on their own, relaxing in the bath, lying in bed or playing quietly. The poet Benjamin Zephania insists that good ideas frequently come to him when he is sitting on the loo!

Introduce the notion of an ideas bank and explain how it may be useful. List the following prompts on the board.

Inspirations from my life
- two interesting people I know
- two events that have happened to me
- two places I have visited
- two memories I have

Inspirations from books/television
- two characters and what I admire/hate/enjoy about them
- two animals I like
- two unfinished stories where I don't know what happens

Inspiration from play
- two of my toys
- two games I play alone
- two games I play with friends

Explain that the children are going to spend 10–15 minutes today using the prompts to generate a few ideas to get the ideas bank started. Tell the children not to worry if they draw a blank on one prompt but to move on to the next. Once children have finished this exercise, they may choose to share their ideas with others, or not if they prefer.

As further ideas occur to them in the future, they should jot them down and increase their bank of ideas.

MY POEM'S A BIT LIKE YOUR POEM

Teaching content
Drafting: sequencing ideas.

What you need
View from classroom window or large picture/poster, chalkboard, writing materials.

What to do
Many children find it difficult to distance themselves from the initial composing process sufficiently to re-draft their work.

Tell the children to look at the poster, or out of the window, and to call out some of the things they can see. List these down the middle of the board. When you have about five or six, take the first object on the list and ask the children to tell you a bit more about it. Make whatever they say into a possible line of poetry (beginning with a capital letter, omitting the function words and so on). For example, if a child says 'The black railings are wet and shiny,' write 'Black railings, wet and shiny'. Do the same for each object on the list, until you have five or six complete lines.

Now, explain that the class has the raw material for a poem. However, this is not finished and needs re-drafting. Explain that the children can alter the sequence and content of the poem. They may think that the first line is not the best starting point and choose another. They may like to change some words, omit some lines altogether, or add new ones.

Tell the children to work in pairs to decide what they would like to change, omit or add to any of the lines and how to sequence them. Once finished, ask some pairs to read out their final poem and to explain the decisions they made and why.

The children will be interested to compare their own poems with those of other pairs and to hear about how and why changes were made.

Development/homework task

Get one child in each pair to copy out their version of the poem in beautiful handwriting. The other child can write a short paragraph explaining how and why they chose to change it from the original draft. These can be compiled into a class book or displayed around a copy of the first draft of the poem.

FIVE LINE POEMS

Teaching content
Drafting: selecting ideas.

What you need
Writing materials.

What to do
The first part of this activity can be done as a class or in groups, as long as all the children have recently experienced a similar special event.

Ask the children to think of a type of event that they have all attended at some point – it might be a firework display, a party, a wedding or a school trip. Ask them to brainstorm what happened, what they saw, what they thought, what they said (aloud or to themselves) and what they heard others saying.

When they have a good selection of ideas, explain that each child is going to write a poem, but that the poem cannot be longer than five lines. They must read the list of suggestions carefully and select the five ideas that best reflect their own experience of the event. They may use ideas not in the brainstorm if they wish. Emphasise that because the poem is only going to be five lines long, the choice of ideas is vital.

Once finished, ask some children to read out their work to the rest of the class and explain why they chose as they did.

ONLY YOU

Teaching content
Drafting: selecting and sequencing ideas.

What you need
Writing and art materials.

What to do
Ask the children to think of someone that is important to them. It may be a parent, grandparent, neighbour, brother, sister or friend. Ask them to think of, and write down, six things that they admire, appreciate or love about this person.

Then, ask the children to select the four things that most capture the essence of the person and to re-draft and sequence them into a poem.

Once finished, the poem can be written out and decorated as a gift for the person in question.

MUSIC POEMS

Teaching content
• Using music as a stimulus for ideas.
• Drafting: ordering ideas for the best effect.

What you need
Large strips of paper, music cassette, cassette player, writing materials, marker pens, scissors, adhesive, A2 sugar paper.

What to do
To do this activity, the children must be familiar with the format and structure of a list poem.

Choose a time for this work when the class is in a sensible, thoughtful mood. Tell the children that you are going to play some music.

Choose a piece of music that the children will find evocative in some way, for example, Vaughan Williams' *The Lark Ascending*, 'Mars' from Holst's *Planets Suite*, 'Morning' from Grieg's *Peer Gynt Suite*, Tchaikovsky's *1812 Overture* and almost anything from Saint-Saens's *Carnival of the Animals*. It is helpful to choose music that the children will find accessible but not necessarily familiar. Dukas's *The Sorcerer's Apprentice* is a wonderful piece of music, but if the children are familiar with the Disney cartoon version, it may hinder them giving an original interpretation.

Explain that often, when people listen to music, especially when they listen with their eyes closed and let their minds 'wander', all sorts of thoughts and pictures come into their heads. Sometimes they imagine a whole scene, sometimes just colours, shapes, a word or an image or sometimes they remember an event from the past.

Explain that you want the children to listen to the music (with their eyes closed if they prefer) and to let their minds drift. Whenever an image, phrase, word or colour comes into their head, they should quietly open their eyes and write it down quickly on the paper in front of them, before closing their eyes again and continuing to listen

Play the music until you are sure that all the children have at least two different words or images on their paper. Then, stop the music and ask them to read silently what they have written and to try to compose two lines of poetry from their jotted notes. Emphasise that a line of poetry may consist of one word, or it may be longer. The lines do not have to follow on from each other or be related in any way. Once they have composed two lines, ask them to write them on the strips of paper using the marker pens – one line on each strip. (You may need to remind the children that, in a poem, each new line usually begins with a capital letter.)

Now ask the children to form groups of three or four. Explain that they are going to make a list poem by combining the lines of poetry which have been written by all the individual group members. Give the groups time to read each other's lines and decide in which order they should be placed. Suggest that the groups begin by discussing which line would make the best beginning. Which line should follow next? Remind the children that although poems have a 'shape', they do not need to develop a coherent 'storyline'. Poems can be effective

when similar images are clustered together, or when opposing images are juxtaposed.

Once the sequence of lines has been decided, the group should think of a title for the poem and write this at the top of the sugar paper before gluing the lines in their chosen sequence. Make a space for each group to display their work. Suggest that each group chooses a reader and a spokesperson. The reader should read the poem to the rest of the class and the spokesperson should explain how and why they decided on the sequence.

RESPONDING TO WRITING

13

*** †† ④⓪

Teaching content
How to improve a story.

What you need
An old story written by one of the pair, writing materials.

What to do
The day before you intend to do this activity arrange the children in pairs and ask them to find an old story, maybe written the previous year, that they could work on together. It should not be too long. Explain that the children are going to re-work this story. Because it was written some time ago, the children will be reading it with fresh eyes and new insights.

Ask the children to use a different coloured pen from that in which the story has been written. Tell them to read through the story together and, as they read, to:
• tick those sections which they think are particularly good or effective,

• write down any questions that occur to them about what the characters or the setting is like, what happens, why things happen and so on;
• put a vertical line in the margin to identify the parts that are less effective or not so good.

Now ask the children to discuss as a group how the story could be improved. Are there any sections which they feel need to be changed, re-ordered, expanded or perhaps left out altogether? Let the children work together to re-write the story.

Development/homework task

The children can mount and display a photocopy of the original story and the re-write, along with a short paragraph saying which sections they improved and why they made the changes they did.

PROOF-READING FOR ERRORS

Teaching content

Proof-reading and how it differs from other reading behaviours.

What you need

Photocopiable page 194, short piece of writing (well within everyone's reading ability) on the board, chalk, writing materials.

What to do

Give each child a copy of photocopiable page 194 and tell them to begin reading it immediately. After 2–3 minutes discuss the children's reaction to this first exercise. Did they spot all three errors at first reading? If not, did their reading behaviour change when they read the sentence a second time? Did they read at the same speed? Did they use their eyes differently? Did they think about the writing differently? Explain that the second sort of reading is the one that people use when they proof-read work for errors and that proof-reading is a skill – it gets better with practice.

Read the passage on the board with the children. Explain that it is an error-free piece of work. Ask the children to copy this on to paper, introducing into their copy the following errors (list them on the board):

• 5 spelling mistakes
• 3 repeated words
• 3 left out words
• 5 punctuation mistakes

Emphasise that the children may be as inventive as they like about their errors, but that the best hidden errors (the ones that are hardest to spot) are the subtlest ones.

Then, take in all the error-riddled work and re-distribute it, so that everyone has a piece of work that is not their own. Ask the children to select a different coloured pen from that in which the work has been written and to proof-read it, circling each error they notice. Time the children as they work.

This activity should be repeated periodically. With practice, children will get faster and more accurate.

FIND THE ERROR

Teaching content

Proof-reading practice.

What you need

Photocopiable page 195, chalkboard, writing materials.

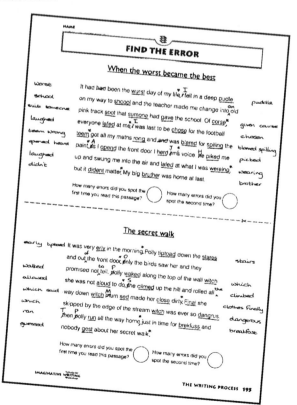

What to do

Give each child a copy of one of the exercises on photocopiable page 195 and explain that it is full of errors. Ask the children to proof-read it, correcting as many mistakes as possible. It is important that the children have an agreed code for corrections. If you do not have an agreed code, write the following points on the board for the children to refer to as they are proof-reading:

- *spelling mistakes* – underline and write the correct spelling in the margin
- *extra words* – cross out with a diagonal line
- *punctuation errors* – mark with an asterisk and write in the correction
- *missed capital letters* – cross through the letter and write the capital above
- *missing words* – mark with a 'tent' and write the word above it

The illustration shows a corrected version of photocopiable page 195 using this code.

How many errors did the children spot the first time? Ask them to write this in the first circle at the bottom of the page. Ask the children to re-read the passage, looking for more errors. How many errors did they spot the second time? Tell them to write this number in the second circle. If appropriate, allow the children to work in pairs to find and correct all the errors.

many reasons: because children lack strategies to complete the task effectively; because they do not understand how their work will be judged; because they have not been made aware of their progress in this area, or many other reasons. Teachers need to understand why children feel as they do about tasks and take steps to ensure a positive experience for each child in the future.

Give each child a copy of either photocopiable page 196 or photocopiable page 197 (easier version) and ask them to complete it, rating their feelings according to the scale shown. Once completed, use the sheets as a basis for discussion, in pairs or small groups, about why children feel as they do. Make sure children are in groups according to the sheet they are using.

Tell the groups to begin the discussion by taking each question in turn and comparing how each member rated their feelings and why. It may be that there are similar ratings but for different reasons, or dissimilar ratings and reasons. Ask the children to discuss with the group the reasons for their own reactions and to try to determine what could be done to change their attitudes to those tasks they dislike. Are any of the reasons that underpin their answers for different questions related? Each child should note brief solutions or recommendations below the relevant questions.

HOW DO YOU FEEL?

Teaching content
How children feel about writing.

What you need
Photocopiable page 196 and/or 197 (these are differentiated versions of the same idea), writing materials.

What to do
Children's feelings about composing and sharing writing in different ways can influence their willingness to engage in such tasks. Both teachers and children benefit from understanding more about how individuals feel about particular types of tasks, and why. If certain tasks are not enjoyed, it may be for

READING FOR A FRIEND

Teaching content
The role of a writing partner when reading another's story.

What you need
Photocopiable page 198, writing materials.

What to do
Before children do this activity, they need some experience of reading another's work and responding to it in a helpful way.

Give out copies of photocopiable page 198 and ask the children to read each statement and tick whether they agree, disagree or are not sure about it. They should do this alone with no discussion.

Then put the children into groups of four to six. Ask them to take each statement in turn and compare what they thought, explaining their reasons and giving examples where appropriate.

Then, ask children to re-consider their original judgements. Have they changed their minds about anything? If so, ask them to select a different coloured pencil/pen and to record their new opinion by ticking the appropriate box.

18

THE PERFECT WRITING PARTNER

Teaching content
• Reflecting on personal preferences for writing partners.
• Reflecting on helpful/unhelpful behaviours in a writing partner.

What you need
Photocopiable page 199, writing materials.

What to do
Explain that, often, people like to work in different ways. They have their own preferences and have different styles when they work with others. Behaviour or advice that one person thinks is clear and helpful, another might find overpoweringly bossy.

Give each child a copy of photocopiable page 199 and ask them to imagine that they have asked a friend to comment on a story they have written. Ask them to consider the different behaviours listed on the photocopiable page and, for each one, to decide whether they would find it helpful, sometimes helpful or unhelpful.

They should write beneath each statement 'helpful because...', 'unhelpful because...' or 'sometimes helpful because...' and complete each sentence.

Then ask the children to compare what they have written in groups of four to six, discussing their different decisions and the reasons behind them.

End the lesson by reminding the class that everyone has individual preferences and, when they work with others, they must be sensitive to these.

19

WRITING PARTNER COMMENTS

Teaching content
Providing helpful feedback as a writing partner.

What you need
Writing materials, ruler.

What to do
Before children do this activity, they need to have commented on the work of others and had their own work commented on.

Arrange the children in groups of four. Ask them to draw a line down the centre of a piece of paper making two columns. They should label one column 'Most useful comments' and the other 'Least useful comments'. Each group should then brainstorm comments that they have either offered or received, decide whether they were useful and productive or not and then write them in the appropriate column.

When they have finished, display the papers and ask each group to choose a spokesperson to read out and explain what they have written.

Finally, ask each individual to think of and write down one way in which they will try to improve the usefulness of the feedback they give in the future. Some children need help to think of constructive things to say about another's work. The lists generated can be typed and kept in the classroom to be used as 'memory-joggers' for writing partners.

20
WHEN TO TALK

Teaching content
When is it helpful to consult others?

What you need
Photocopiable page 200, writing materials.

What to do
During this activity, children are asked to think about how discussion with other children can help them during particular stages of the writing process and when discussion may be detrimental. Begin by asking the children whether they ever discuss their writing with others in the class, or with people outside school. If they do, what sort of things do they talk about and at what point do they talk (or when would they like to be able to talk) to others during the story-writing process?

Give each child a copy of photocopiable page 200 and ask the children to complete it by ticking the column they feel is most appropriate for each statement. Then, arrange the children in groups of four and ask them to compare their responses and the reasons for them. Give each group a fresh photocopiable sheet and ask them to agree a group response to each statement.

Finally, ask each group to appoint a spokesperson to report to the rest of the class on when, and in what circumstances, they find it helpful to talk to a friend about their work.

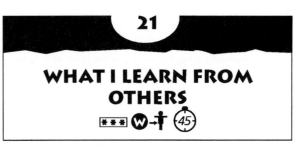

21
WHAT I LEARN FROM OTHERS

Teaching content
Working with others provides opportunities to learn.

What you need
Chalkboard, strips of paper (approximately 10 x 30cm), marker pens, adhesive, poster-sized paper.

What to do
Brainstorm with the whole class recent occasions when they have been involved in working collaboratively, either with one other person, or as part of a larger group. Ask the children to consider in which tasks they would have achieved the same results working alone. Are there any tasks they could have completed more effectively working alone? Why? Ask the children to think about specific things they learned from working with others on the tasks, and make a list on the board.

Now ask the children to think about writing tasks in particular. Can they identify a recent writing task in which they worked with others? What was the task about and what did they do? Now, ask them to think hard and to try to remember which parts of the task they found difficult or daunting. Was there any point at which someone explained something to them? Did they explain anything to someone else? Was there any point at which someone did something differently from how they would have done it? Were they surprised at any point by the results that someone achieved.

Explain that these all provide different opportunities for us to learn. We learn when people explain things to us, but we also learn when we explain things to others, when we watch how others do things and when we consider other people's ideas.

Give each child a strip of paper. Ask them to think hard about their most recent collaborative writing experience and to use a marker pen to write on their strip one thing they learned from working with another person. Finally, ask children to stick their strips on to the poster paper to make a record of what they have recently taught each other.

MY HISTORY AS A WRITER

When I was younger I used to feel like this about writing stories
(tick the appropriate face):

Now, when I write stories I feel (tick the appropriate figure):

Yippee!   Okay   Oh no   Angry   Other
(draw a simple picture
to show how you feel)

My best story was...

I hated writing when...

PICTURE A WRITER: PICTURE ME

◆ Read the following descriptions of writers and tick the one that best fits you.

☐ I get ideas easily, begin writing immediately and write quite quickly, knowing exactly what I am going to say. I rarely pause to make corrections or to re-read what I have written. I enjoy talking about the story I've written more than I enjoy watching others read it.

☐ I spend a long time deciding on a story idea and then I don't know how to start the story off. Usually, once I've started, I work quite hard, occasionally re-reading what I've written so far and checking spellings. When the story is finished, I am quite keen to hear what other people think about it.

☐ I can never think of what to say or how to write the words. I put off starting to write by taking ages to find my pen, pencil and paper. Then, I chat to the person next to me or take a while to sharpen a pencil. When forced to begin writing, the first line is often messed up in some way and has to be rubbed or crossed out. I nearly always begin writing without thinking about what is going to happen in the story, or how it will end. I am easily distracted and my stories are rarely finished. I give the impression of not really trying too hard at writing.

☐ I enjoy writing, but like everything to be correct and neat. I concentrate hard and get more satisfaction from producing neat work than from telling the story. I usually get one idea for a story and begin writing straight away. My stories are always short to medium length and I enjoy doing a picture at the end.

☐ I feel slightly anxious when asked to write a story. I worry that I won't get any good ideas, but when I do, I work quite hard. My handwriting isn't very tidy and I don't write words I can't spell. My story is never quite as exciting or as neat as other people's.

THE STORIES I TELL

◆ Tick each type of story you enjoy; put a cross against those you hate; put a question mark against those which you sometimes enjoy.

Type of story	Reading stories	Watching stories (television and film)	Writing stories	Talking/ playing stories
Fairy tales				
Real life				
Mystery				
School				
Personal experience				
Funny				
Horror				
Adventure				

◆ Now answer the following questions.

1. Which types of story do you enjoy reading, watching and playing, but have never tried to write?

2. Are there any types of story that you enjoy writing about, but have never read?

IT'S A GOOD STORY BECAUSE...

◆ Cut out the following statements and arrange them in two columns: things that are important to you and things that you think are important to your teacher. Place any statements that you think are important for both you and your teacher in the middle so that they touch both columns.

It has a good beginning.

It has long words in it.

The spelling and punctuation are correct all the way through.

The handwriting is neat.

Exciting things happen.

Reading it makes the reader want to meet the writer.

It is quite short.

It is quite long.

It makes the reader react – feel happy, sad, frightened, sorry...

The characters are believable.

It is simple and clear.

It surprises the reader.

It makes the reader think about it later on in the day/week.

It has lots of description.

It is funny.

There is plenty of action.

There is plenty of speech.

IDEAS ANALYSIS

◆ Read the following list of ideas-sources. For each one, decide whether you use it frequently, sometimes or never and write your initials in the appropriate column.

	Frequently	Sometimes	Never
Things that have happened to me in real life			
Stories I have read			
Things I have seen on television or in films			
Games I have played with friends			
People I have met in real life			
Things I have talked about with a friend in class			
A place I have been to in real life			
Things I have talked about with a friend outside class			
Things I have talked about or heard in a class discussion			
Things the teacher has talked about			
Things I have talked about at home			

Scholastic
IMAGINATIVE WRITING
Workshop

COMMON ERRORS

◆ How often do you make each of these errors? Put a tick in the appropriate column.

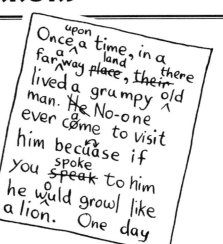

	More often than others	As often as others	Less often than others	Never
Weak beginning				
Weak ending				
Spelling errors				
Grammatical errors				
Weak characterisation				
Disjointed story				
Unclear story				
Boring story				
Repeating words				
Nonsensical sentence				
Weak title				

PROOF-READING FOR ERRORS

◆ Read this sentence:

Sometimes it is easy to see when

mistakkes have beenn made, but at

at other times it is much more difficult to spot them.

Did you spot the THREE deliberate errors in the sentence above?
If not, read the sentence again.
Did you read the sentence differently the second time? How?

Did you read at the same speed?

Did you use your eyes differently?

Did you think about different things as you read?

---✂----------

PROOF-READING FOR ERRORS

◆ Read this sentence

Sometimes it is easy to see when

mistakkes have beenn made, but at

at other times it is much more difficult to spot them.

Did you spot the THREE deliberate errors in the sentence above?
If not, read the sentence again.
Did you read the sentence differently the second time? How?

Did you read at the same speed?

Did you use your eyes differently?

Did you think about different things as you read?

Scholastic
IMAGINATIVE WRITING
Workshop

FIND THE ERROR

When the worst became the best

It had had been the wurst day of my life i fell in a deep pudle
on my way to shcool and the teacher made me change into old
pink track soot that sumone had gave the school. Of corse
everyone lafed at me i was last to be chose for the football
teem got all my maths rong and and was blamd for spiling the
paint as I opend the front door I herd jims voice. he piked me
up and swung me into the air and lafed at what I was wereing
but it dident matter My big bruther was home at last.

How many errors did you spot the first time you read this passage? ◯

How many errors did you spot the second time? ◯

✂ - - - - - -

The secret walk

It was very erly in the morning Polly tiptoad down the stares
and out the front door only the birds saw her and they
promised not tell. polly waked along the top of the wall witch
she was not aloud to do she climed up the hill and rolled all
way down witch mum sed made her close dirty Final she
skipped by the edge of the stream witch was ever so dangrus.
then polly run all the way home just in time for brekfuss and
nobody gest about her secret walk

How many errors did you spot the first time you read this passage? ◯

How many errors did you spot the second time? ◯

HOW DO YOU FEEL?

◆ Rate your feelings for each of the situations listed according to the scale at the top of the page.

Oh No!   1   2   3   4   Yippee!

How do you feel when...

Writing

...you have to write a story alone?	1	2	3	4
...you have to write a story with a friend?	1	2	3	4

Talking about writing

...you have to talk with a friend about what you have written?	1	2	3	4
...you have to talk with the teacher about what you have written?	1	2	3	4
...you have to talk with a group about what you have written?	1	2	3	4
...you have to talk with a friend about what he or she has written?	1	2	3	4
...you have to talk in a group about what a friend has written?	1	2	3	4
...you have to talk with the teacher about what a professional author has written?	1	2	3	4
...you have to talk about a professional author's work with a friend?	1	2	3	4

Reading stories

...you see friends reading your story?	1	2	3	4
...you see parents reading your story?	1	2	3	4
...you see the teacher reading your story?	1	2	3	4
...you read a story written by a friend?	1	2	3	4

HOW DO YOU FEEL?

◆ Answer each of the questions by circling the appropriate picture.

1. How do you feel when you are asked to write a story alone?

2. How do you feel when you are asked to write a story with a friend?

3. How do you feel about writing stories for fun at home?

4. How do you feel when your teacher reads your story?

5. How do you feel when you are asked to read your story to the teacher?

6. How do you feel when you are asked to read your story to a friend?

READING FOR A FRIEND

◆ Read the following statements about being a writing partner. For each one, decide whether you agree, disagree or are not sure about the statement. Place a tick in the appropriate column.

	Agree	Disagree	Not sure/ undecided
It is important for the reader to say what he or she likes about the story.			
A reader is most helpful because they can help the writer by talking about the story or the ideas.			
A reader is most helpful because they can correct the spelling, grammar and punctuation.			
Other people look first of all for mistakes when they read.			
A reader shouldn't worry about hurting the writer's feelings: it is important to say what you think no matter what.			
A reader should be better than the writer whose work they are reading.			
It is best if the reader is a friend of the writer.			
My job as a reader is to look for mistakes when reading.			
It only works if the reader is interested in the story.			
It is impossible to read someone's work and help them if you don't like them.			
It is better for the author to read the story aloud to the reader.			
It is better for the readers to read the story themselves.			
Reading another person's work can help you with your own.			
Reading another person's work can make it more difficult to work on your own.			
You should never say anything that you don't like or understand about a story in case you hurt the writer's feelings.			

Scholastic
IMAGINATIVE WRITING
Workshop

THE PERFECT WRITING PARTNER

◆ This is a list of things that a writing partner might do when asked to comment on your work. For each one, say whether it is helpful or unhelpful, and why.

When a writing partner...

...immediately tells me what she would change about my work it is

...asks me which bits I like best it is

...tells me which bits they like best it is

...explains what was difficult to read or understand it is

...asks me about the background to the story it is

...tells me what is wrong with my story it is

...compares my story to her own it is

...writes a bit of my story for me it is

...asks me about the setting, characters or events in my story it is

WHEN TO TALK

◆ When is it helpful to talk to a friend about your story? Put a tick in the relevant column for each statement.

	Always	Sometimes	Never	Not applicable
Before you even think about any ideas.				
When you've thought of lots of ideas but haven't decided which to go for.				
When you've decided what will happen in your story, but not how to tell it.				
When you can't decide how to begin.				
When you've written a beginning and know what you're going to say next.				
When you can't decide what will happen next.				
When you've written quite a lot and your hand hurts.				
When you've written most of the story and are getting a bit tired of it.				
When you're nearly at the end.				
When you've finished writing the story, but it's still in rough.				
When you've finished the story and published it.				

Scholastic WRITING Workshop

Chapter Seven

ANTHOLOGY

IDENTITY PARADE

When he got close, Andrew realised that Victor was not fat at all. On the contrary, he was exceptionally thin; all of him, not just his head and legs. The fat part was made up of clothes. Andrew could see a white T-shirt, a red shirt, a blue sweater and a red sweater. Further down he wore a pair of black jeans with orange patches sewn over the knees and yellow patches on the hip pockets. Over it all he had an anorak so covered in badges and buttons that it was difficult to tell what colour it was.

In fact, he was not so much dressed as camouflaged. Even his hair seemed to be some part of a disguise, more like a wig than live hair, dusty black as if it had been kicked round the floor before being put on. It was so long at the front that Victor was actually looking through it. His ears stuck out cheerfully, like a Radar device.

From Thunder and Lightnings by Jan Mark

Col. Grangerford was very tall and very slim, and had a darkish-paly complexion, not a sign of red in it anywheres; he was clean-shaven every morning, all over his thin face, and he had the thinnest kind of lips, and the thinnest kind of nostrils, and a high nose, and heavy eyebrows, and the blackest kind of eyes, sunk so deep back that they seemed like they were looking out of caverns at you, as you may say. His forehead was high, and his hair was black and straight, and hung to his shoulders. His hands were long and thin, and every day of his life he put on a clean shirt and a full suit from head to foot made out of linen so white it hurt your eyes to look at it; and on Sundays he wore a blue tail-coat with brass buttons on it. He carried a mahogany cane with a silver head to it.

From The Adventures of Huckleberry Finn by Mark Twain

He was short and slender. He wore overalls and heavy working boots that laced up the front. The shirt under his overalls was dark blue with fancy red and yellow flowers printed all over it. His face was square and blunt; he had grey hair that he brushed back off his forehead and thin, straight eyebrows over cold eyes. He moved towards the Tillermans without hesitating, without hurrying, and stood silent before them. His skin was tanned and leathery. Deep lines ran across his forehead. He reached his napkin up and wiped his mouth.

'Yeah,' he said.

From Homecoming by Cynthia Voigt

EYES – WINDOWS ON TO THE SOUL

The eye-smiler

You might think, if you didn't know him well, that he was a stern and serious man. He wasn't. He was actually a wildly funny person. What made him appear so serious was the fact that he never smiled with his mouth. He did it all with his eyes. He had brilliant blue eyes and when he thought of something funny, his eyes would flash and if you looked carefully, you could actually see a tiny little golden spark dancing in the middle of each eye. But the mouth never moved.

I was glad my father was an eye-smiler. It meant he never gave me a fake smile because it's impossible to make your eyes twinkle if you aren't feeling twinkly yourself. A mouth-smile is different. You can fake a mouth-smile any time you want, simply by moving your lips. I've also learned that a real mouth-smile always has an eye-smile to go with it, so watch out, I say, when someone smiles at you with his mouth but the eyes stay the same. It's sure to be bogus.

From *Danny The Champion of the World* by Roald Dahl

FAIRY-TALE APPEARANCES

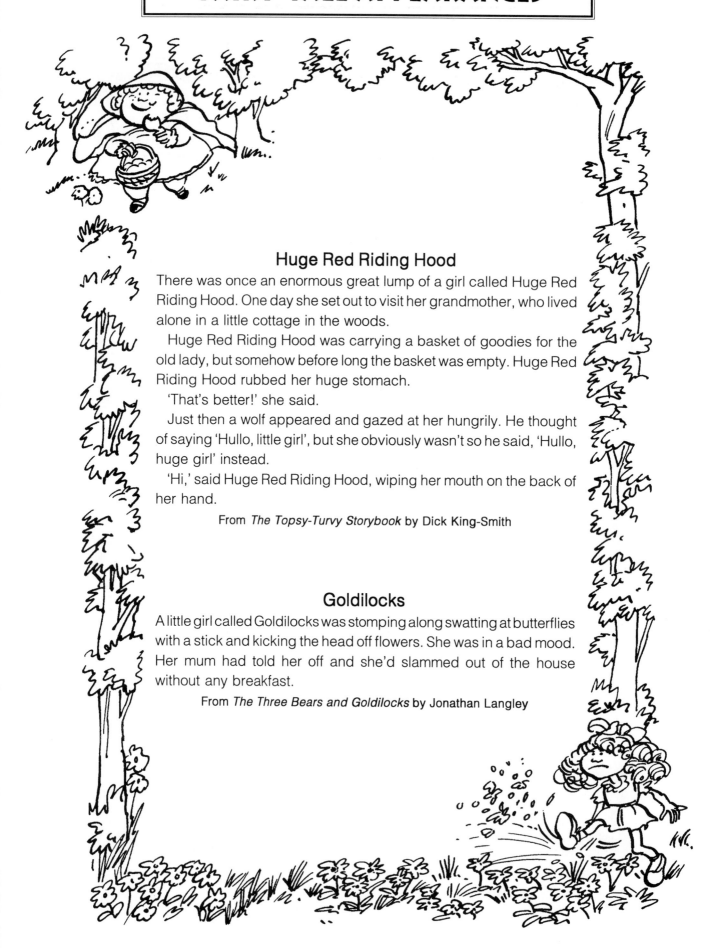

Huge Red Riding Hood

There was once an enormous great lump of a girl called Huge Red Riding Hood. One day she set out to visit her grandmother, who lived alone in a little cottage in the woods.

Huge Red Riding Hood was carrying a basket of goodies for the old lady, but somehow before long the basket was empty. Huge Red Riding Hood rubbed her huge stomach.

'That's better!' she said.

Just then a wolf appeared and gazed at her hungrily. He thought of saying 'Hullo, little girl', but she obviously wasn't so he said, 'Hullo, huge girl' instead.

'Hi,' said Huge Red Riding Hood, wiping her mouth on the back of her hand.

From *The Topsy-Turvy Storybook* by Dick King-Smith

Goldilocks

A little girl called Goldilocks was stomping along swatting at butterflies with a stick and kicking the head off flowers. She was in a bad mood. Her mum had told her off and she'd slammed out of the house without any breakfast.

From *The Three Bears and Goldilocks* by Jonathan Langley

WHAT ARE THEY LIKE?

Jack Bobbin

Jack Bobbin was a neat little boy. His hair was neat and his shoes were neat. His house was neat and his room was neat. Above all, his mother was neat.

"What I like," said Mrs Bobbin, "is order. I can't abide a muddle."

So Jack could always find his pencils and his ruler, and always knew where he had put his football boots.

From *Jack Bobbin* by J. Bennett

Lizzie Dripping

This is how our Lizzie Dripping was. She walked about with her head in the clouds and was always trying to make life more exciting, more full of shivers and panics and laughter than it is if you leave it to itself. It often looked as if she was telling what most people would call fibs. She wasn't, of course. She was just making things up as she went along – and that is quite a different thing.

From *Lizzie Dripping and the Orphans* by Helen Cresswell

Angela Mitchell

I don't think Angela always means to be bad. It just sort of happens. And it seems to happen most often when she's with me. I once wrote in a composition at school, "Angela Mitchell is my very best FIEND". It was a stupid spelling mistake, and everybody laughed like mad. But my dad says there's many a true word spoken in jest and if anybody deserves to be called a fiend it's Angela. I don't know why I bother with her, sometimes. And then at other times she can be really nice. You never know where you are. But you're never bored, that's for sure.

From *The Fiend Next Door* by Sheila Lavelle

Lenny Fraser

Lenny Fraser is a boy in my class. Well, he's a boy in my class when he comes. But to tell the truth, he doesn't come very often. He stays away from school for a week at a time, and I'll tell you where he is. He's at the shops, stealing things sometimes, but mainly just opening the doors for people. He does it to keep himself warm. I've seen him in our shop. When he opens the door for someone, he stands around inside till he gets sent out. Of course, it's quite warm enough in school, but he hates coming.

From 'Lenny's Red-Letter Day' by Bernard Ashley

After the quarrel

Laura walked on ahead. Oliver followed more slowly, scuffing the sodden mulch of leaves and kicking clumps of it aside as he walked. He didn't feel good about the quarrel. Not that you expect to feel good about a quarrel, exactly; but Oliver was at least used to feeling he was completely in the right. This time he didn't, and the whole business made him rather uncomfortable.

So Laura hadn't told him about the mistake. But why not? Maybe because he'd kicked up such a storm when, in all cheerful innocence, she'd written the first Lady Melody letter. He'd practically bitten her head off. And yet he knew that Laura was what Mrs Coverley always referred to as a 'sensitive plant'. Maybe he should have been a bit more careful about what he'd said, and how forcibly he'd said it.

Without realising what he was doing, Oliver speeded his pace a little.

A few yards ahead, Laura was feeling terrible. Oh, why had she been so snappy and horrid with Oliver? It wasn't his fault he'd been brought up to get in such a tizzy about these things! And it wasn't fair not to tell someone exactly what had happened, and then go and bite their head off when they misunderstood.

Unwittingly, she slowed her pace.

The two of them came together at the corner. Laura stopped for a bicycle that was miles away and Oliver chose to cross at the very same place.

From *A Pack of Liars* by Anne Fine

INSIDE OUT

Dumb insolence

I'm big for ten years old
Maybe that's why they get at me

Teachers, parents, cops
Always getting at me

When they get at me

I don't hit em
They can do you for that

I don't swear at em
They can do you for that

I stick my hands in my pockets
And stare at them

And while I stare at them
I think about sick

They call it dumb insolence

They don't like it
But they can't do you for it

Adrian Mitchell

The woodland meeting

'I don't believe it,' said Grey Squirrel.

'Load of rubbish!' cried Stoat.

Rabbit merely giggled and nudged his girl-friend. 'Let's go somewhere quiet,' he whispered.

Weasel rippled his slim body angrily. 'I'm telling you the truth,' he snapped. 'Saw 'em with me own eyes, I did. Ruddy great yellow machines.'

Stonechat bobbed his white rump and flicked his tail nervously. 'P... Perhaps we ... ought to see ... I ... I ... mean ... It wouldn't do any harm ... would it?'

They all turned to stare at Stonechat, who bobbed and twitched hysterically under their steady gaze.

Badger scraped at his snout with one sharp claw. 'It could be true,' he growled, 'we all know how nosey Weasel is.'

'Quite,' sneered Fox, 'and it will be the death of him one day.'

Rook gave his usual bronchitic wheeze. 'Not if he sees you first,' he said and immediately broke into a fit of coughing.

They all glared at him.

'Comes of sleeping in perishing draughty nests,' observed Thrush.

'What I want to know,' said Tawny Owl in his sleepy, breathless voice, 'is what you think we can do about it if they are there, heh?'

'They wouldn't dare!' shouted Stoat.

'Don't be an idiot,' snorted Brown Rat, 'they do whatever they like and you can't stop 'em.'

From The Battle for Badger's Wood by Frederick Covins

BEDROOMS

Uncle Owen's room

Uncle Owen Bowen was hovering outside his room at the top of the house, waiting to welcome them. What a relief it was to be there. Inside, with the door shut, there was no smell at all except for a pleasant whiff of oil paint and turpentine. It was a lovely room. From the balcony outside you could see right up to the great iron bridge with its fairy-tale towers, and the moored barges, and the river slipping past. Near the window Uncle Owen Bowen had his easel and his paints and brushes, neatly arranged upright in big jars. Charlie had never seen so many interesting objects collected in one room. There was the stuffed pike in a glass case, the brass letter-scales, the fourteen old clocks (none of them going), the banjo, the tailor's dummy and the model ship. There were also stacks and stacks of pictures, framed and unframed, not only hung all over the walls but leaning up against them too. Uncle Owen had painted quite a few of these himself. Hanging over the massive sideboard was a birdcage, inside which lived, not a parrot or a budgie, but Uncle Owen's best false teeth and his gold-rimmed glasses. His sight was bad, so he kept them there for safety in case he lost them.

From *Charlie Moon and the Big Bonanza Bust Up* by Shirley Hughes

PICTURE POEM

Snow

No breath of wind,
No gleam of sun –
Still the white snow
Whirls softly down –
Twig and bough
And blade and thorn
All in an icy
Quiet, forlorn.
Whispering, rustling,
Through the air,
On sill and stone,
Roof – everywhere,
It heaps its powdery
Crystal flakes,
Of every tree
A mountain makes;
Till pale and faint
At shut of day
Stoops from the West
One wintry ray.
And, feathered in fire,
Where ghosts the moon,
A robin shrills
His lonely tune.

Walter de la Mare

Scholastic
IMAGINATIVE WRITING
Workshop

Salford Road

Salford Road, Salford Road,
Is the place where I was born,
With a green front gate, a red brick wall
And hydrangeas round a lawn.

Salford Road, Salford Road,
Is the road where we would play
Where the sky lay over the roof tops
Like a friend who'd come to stay.

The Gardeners lived at fifty-five,
The Lunds with the willow tree,
Mr Pool with the flag and the garden pond
And the Harndens at fifty-three.

There was riding bikes and laughing
Till we couldn't laugh any more,
And bilberries picked on the hillside
And picnics on the shore.

I lay in bed when I was four
As the sunlight turned to grey
And heard the train through my pillow
And the seagulls far away.

And I rose to look out of my window
For I knew that someone was there
And a man stood as sad as nevermore
And didn't see me there.

And when I stand in Salford Road
And think of the boy who was me
I feel that from one of the windows
Someone is looking at me.

My friends walked out one Summer day,
Walked singing down the lane,
My friends walked into a wood called Time
And never came out again.

We live in a land called Gone-Today
That's made of bricks and straw
But Salford Road runs through my head
To a land called Evermore.

Gareth Owen

PREPARATIONS

A Fine Christmas Dinner

Scrooge is peering through the Cratchits' window. Master Peter has just returned with the goose.

Such a bustle ensued that you might have thought a goose the rarest of all birds; a feathered phenomenon, to which a black swan was a matter of course: and in truth it was something very like it in that house. Mrs Cratchit made the gravy (ready beforehand in a little saucepan) hissing hot; Master Peter mashed the potatoes with incredible vigour; Miss Belinda sweetened up the apple-sauce; Martha dusted the hot plates; Bob took Tiny Tim beside him in a tiny corner at the table; the two young Cratchits set chairs for everybody, not forgetting themselves, and mounting guard upon their posts, crammed spoons into their mouths, lest they should shriek for goose before their turn came to be helped. At last the dishes were set on, and grace was said. It was succeeded by a breathless pause, as Mrs Cratchit, looking slowly all along the carving-knife, prepared to plunge it in the breast; but when she did, and when the long expected gush of stuffing issued forth, one murmur of delight arose all round the board, and even Tiny Tim, excited by the two young Cratchits, beat on the table with the handle of his knife, and feebly cried Hurrah!

From *A Christmas Carol* by Charles Dickens

FRESH EYES ON FAMILIAR PLACES

Mrs Cole's house

The lights were on all over the house even though it was daytime. There was music blaring out, and a dog barking, and children shouting. Mrs Cole was still in the window. I could see her making toast and frying eggs, and she still carried the baby in her arm.

So she hadn't boiled it after all.

I stood waiting on the grim grey street. I wanted to run away. But I didn't know where to go. Then Mrs Cole came.

I wondered if it was a trick, if Mrs Cole was really a child-catcher by trade, and once I stepped inside her smile would vanish and a net would drop on me from the ceiling, and no one would ever know where I'd gone.

But the street was cold. Mrs Cole smelled of bacon, and her house looked warm. She took my hand and we went inside.

In the hall there was a pile of dirty washing, a broken pram, half a scooter, a pyjama leg, and three shoes: one red, one brown, one blue.

In the kitchen at the table was a big boy with a small boy on his head.

There were three cats among the dishes on the table, and one on the window-sill who watched the goldfish swimming in the tank. A terrapin sat on a stone and stretched his neck.

In the corner a black dog lay dozing in a cardboard box while four puppies were feeding from her teats.

Two cages hung from the ceiling. In one was a yellow canary who sang. In the other, two budgies, one blue, one green, who chirruped and kissed.

On an old settee a girl and boy were eating toast, talking with their mouths full, and dropping crumbs. But Mrs Cole never told them off.

The baby lay on the settee without a nappy on, kicking its legs.

The oven door was open and the oven was on to make the kitchen warm. Mrs Cole sang a song with a singer on the radio, and it didn't give her a headache. She made me a bacon butty and a cup of tea.

"How many sugars?" she asked.

"Three," I said.

And she gave me three. (My mum only lets me have one.)

From I'll take you to Mrs Cole! by Nigel Gray and Michael Foreman

THE PLAY PARK

Rain

Suddenly, in one huge downpour, the sky shed its burden of rain. It lashed the lake and beat upon their bare heads and soaked them to the skin. In great blinding sheets it fell, so that they could not see where they were. Their ankles were deep in water. Had they stumbled into the lake, or was the shore flooding?

From *The Silver Sword* by Ian Serraillier

Night

The moon dimmed and disappeared into the depths of a bigger cloud, so that only a dim luminous glow from the stars gave shape to anything at all. They went gingerly through the darkness, feeling that at any moment they might collide with something unseen...

They were right among the standing stones now, and they could feel rather than see the black rock pillars rearing up around them. The wind blew gustily, singing through the grass, and again they heard the owl cry below them out of the dark. They moved slowly together, straining their eyes to peer ahead. Then the ragged cloud turned silver again, and the moon came sailing out through the flying wisps at its edge; and in the same moment they became aware of a tall dark shape looming up before them where no stone had been before.

From *Over Sea Under Stone* by Susan Cooper

Fog

The fog was much thicker now. The air smelled riverish and the streets had turned narrow and steep. He kept catching glimpses of huge, threatening gates, and gaunt cranes, grazing hopelessly over wastelands of rubbish, as if for worms. He must have been very near the river, as he could hear water, muttering and sighing.

He saw a faint stain of coloured light in the air, and walked towards it. It turned into a small public house, standing forlornly by itself, as if all the other houses had crept away while it had been asleep.

From *The Wedding Ghost* by Leon Garfield

Scholastic
IMAGINATIVE WRITING
Workshop

THE SUN HAS GOT HIS HAT ON

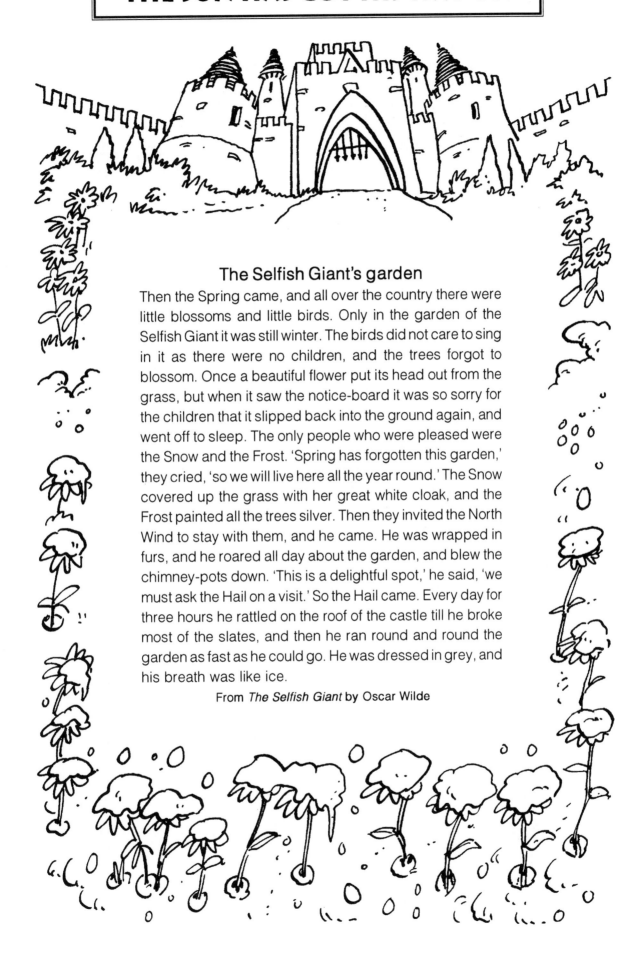

The Selfish Giant's garden

Then the Spring came, and all over the country there were little blossoms and little birds. Only in the garden of the Selfish Giant it was still winter. The birds did not care to sing in it as there were no children, and the trees forgot to blossom. Once a beautiful flower put its head out from the grass, but when it saw the notice-board it was so sorry for the children that it slipped back into the ground again, and went off to sleep. The only people who were pleased were the Snow and the Frost. 'Spring has forgotten this garden,' they cried, 'so we will live here all the year round.' The Snow covered up the grass with her great white cloak, and the Frost painted all the trees silver. Then they invited the North Wind to stay with them, and he came. He was wrapped in furs, and he roared all day about the garden, and blew the chimney-pots down. 'This is a delightful spot,' he said, 'we must ask the Hail on a visit.' So the Hail came. Every day for three hours he rattled on the roof of the castle till he broke most of the slates, and then he ran round and round the garden as fast as he could go. He was dressed in grey, and his breath was like ice.

From *The Selfish Giant* by Oscar Wilde

WHO AM I?

The Old Field

The old field is sad
Now the children have gone home.
They have played with him all afternoon,
Kicking the ball to him, and him
Kicking it back.

But now it is growing cold and dark.
He thinks of their warm breath, and their
Feet like little hot-water bottles.
A bit rough, some of them, but still...

And now, he thinks, there's not even a dog
To tickle me.
The gates are locked.
The birds don't like this nasty sneaking wind,
And nor does he.

D.J. Enright

SNOW

On the mountain

There was a blizzard on the mountain. The wind and snow lashed his face and he had to screw up his eyes and look down at his boots in order to make any headway...

The spider rolled off Gwyn's hand and drifted up into the snow. He watched her, shining silver, amongst the white flakes, and then he had to shut his eyes against the blizzard. When he opened them the spider had gone, and already the wind had slackened. There was a sudden stillness as the mountain held its breath. Clouds of snow began to gather on the summit; they intensified and rolled downwards in a vast, ever-thickening ice-cold wave. In a few seconds Gwyn could hardly see his hands...

He called his friend's name, again and again as he ran, until he was hoarse. The snow had become a fog, still and heavy, like a blanket, smothering any sound.

From *The Snow Spider* by Jenny Nimmo

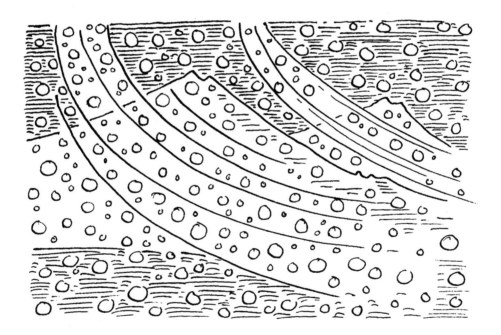

Whitewash

'But that was not the same snow,' I say. 'Our snow was not only shaken from whitewash buckets down the sky, it came shawling out of the ground and swam and drifted out of the arms and hands and bodies of the trees; snow grew overnight on the roofs of the houses like a pure and grandfather moss, minutely white-ivied the walls and settled on the postman, opening the gate, like a dumb, numb thunderstorm of white, torn Christmas cards.'

From *A Child's Christmas in Wales* by Dylan Thomas

GOING FOR A DIP

Daddy Fell into the Pond

Everyone grumbled. The sky was grey.
We had nothing to do and nothing to say.
We were nearing the end of a dismal day.
And there seemed to be nothing beyond,
   Then
      Daddy fell into the pond!

And everyone's face grew merry and bright,
And Timothy danced for sheer delight.
'Give me the camera, quick, oh quick!
He's crawling out of the duckweed!' Click!

Then the gardener suddenly slapped his knee,
And doubled up, shaking silently,
And the ducks all quacked as if they were daft,
And it sounded as if the old drake laughed.
Oh, there wasn't a thing that didn't respond
   When
      Daddy fell into the pond!

Alfred Noyes

Scholastic
IMAGINATIVE WRITING
Workshop

IT'S A CRACKING BEGINNING

Grace was a girl who loved stories.

She didn't mind if they were read to her or told to her or made up in her own head. She didn't care if they were from books or on TV or in films or on the video or out of Nana's long memory. Grace just loved stories.

From *Amazing Grace* by Mary Hoffmann and Caroline Binch

Sid lived at number one, Aristotle Street.

He also lived at number two, number three, number four, number five and number six.

From *Six Dinner Sid* by Inga Moore

When the swimming-pool lights were turned out and Colonel and Mrs Roberts had gone to bed, the Anderson kids came out of the bushes in their underwear. They moved silently over the moss-smooth lawn, across the Moroccan tiled terrace.

From *The Night Swimmers* by Betsy Byars

Just as Sam is short for Samuel, so Samuel was short for a boy. Very short. When he fetched the dishes in, all you could see was roast goose and legs. When he took the dishes out, all you could see were dirty plates and legs. The most you ever saw of his other end was a tuft of hair sticking up over the top of sprouts or dumplings, like a sprig of black parsley. He was a nothing, a nobody; he was a kitchen-boy in Babylon, and he was rushed off his feet.

From *The Writing on the Wall* by Leon Garfield and Michael Bragg

All Jilly wanted in the world was a dragon. Luckily, it was her birthday next month. She would be seven.

From *Dragon Ride* by Helen Cresswell

'Where's Papa going with that axe?' said Fern to her mother as they were setting the table for breakfast.

From *Charlotte's Web* by E.B. White

Silence. Except for her footsteps, except for the soft thunk of mussels dropped on to the rocks by gulls, except for the wind that moved murmuring through the distant trees above her, there was silence.

From *Tree by Leaf* by Cynthia Voigt

Once upon a time, long ago, when the world was not as it always has been and rivers flowed uphill as well as down, there lived a king who had seven daughters.

From *The Princess and the Frog* by Jonathan Langley

THE END

My troubles are all over, and I am at home; and often before I am quite awake, I fancy I am still in the orchard at Birtwick, standing with my old friends under the apple trees.

From *Black Beauty* by Anna Sewell

Away to the south a black cloud rolled. There was joy and many tears. And this tale is called the Weirdstone of Brisingamen. And here is an end of it.

From *The Weirdstone of Brisingamen* by Alan Garner

If you ever have the luck to go to Narnia yourself, do not forget to have a look at those caves.

From *The Silver Chair* by C.S. Lewis

His father came up. 'You will need to teach me how those things work, son,' he said, peering into the box. Simon lifted Jessica up and sat her on top of the box. 'Mustn't leave you out,' he said. 'From now on we do everything together in this family.'

From *Simon's Challenge* by Theresa Breslin

She filled the kettle and brought out the teapot, glancing brightly from one to the other of them. 'Nothing much has happened here, I suppose? We've only been away such a little time, haven't we? By the way, where's Hannah?'

From *The Sea Witch* by Joan G. Robertson

The past was clear and colourful as a tapestry as they gazed out across the sea that was shrouded and misty as the future. THE CURTAIN FALLS

From *The Swish of the Curtain* by Pamela Brown

Only two more things need to be told. One is that Caspian and his men all came safely back to Ramandu's Island. And the three lords woke from their sleep. Caspian married Ramandu's daughter and they all reached Narnia in the end, and she became a great queen and the mother and grandmother of great kings.The other is that back in our own world everyone soon started saying how Eustace had improved, and how 'You'd never know him for the same boy': everyone except Aunt Alberta, who said he had become very commonplace and tiresome and it must have been the influence of those Pevensie children.

From *Voyage of the Dawn Treader* by C.S. Lewis

INSIDE A BEAR'S SKIN

Once there was an old mother pig who had three little pigs, but she had not enough money to keep them. So she sent them out to seek their fortune.

From *The Three Little Pigs* by Val Biro

Three little pigs – that's what they told you did they? Yeah, I get it. You haven't actually met these three 'little' pigs, have you? Never seen them? Nope, I didn't think so. Because if you did, then you just might come round to my way of seeing things. Everyone thinks I'm the bad guy around here. The villain of the piece you might say, but I'm sick of taking the rap. You think that BB stands for 'Big Bad' don't you? Well, do you want to know what it really stands for? You won't believe me but I'll tell you anyway. It's 'Basically Bashful' actually. Oh yeah, I'm cool, I'm a dude, but I'm not big or bad. Hey – I'm a nice guy and everyone deserves a chance. Let me tell you how it really happened.

From *BB Wolf – My Story* by Jane Wright

HOW WOULD YOU SAY IT?

If you don't put your shoes on before I count fifteen then we won't go to the woods to climb the chestnut
one
But I can't find them
Two
I can't
They're under the sofa three
No
O yes
Four five six
Stop – they've got knots they've got knots
You should untie the laces when you take your shoes off seven
Will you do one shoe while I do the other then?
Eight but that would be cheating
Please
All right
It always...
Nine
It always sticks – I'll use my teeth
Ten
It won't it won't
It has – look.
Eleven
I'm not wearing any socks
Twelve
Stop counting stop counting. Mum where are my socks mum
They're in your shoes. Where you left them.
I didn't

Scholastic
IMAGINATIVE WRITING
Workshop

Thirteen
    O they're inside out and upside down and bundled up
Fourteen
    Have you done the knot on the shoe you were...
Yes
Put it on the right foot
    But socks don't have right and wrong foot
The shoes silly
Fourteen and a half
    I am I am. Wait.
    Don't go to the woods without me
    Look that's one shoe already
Fourteen and threequarters
    There
You haven't tied the bows yet
    We could do them on the way there
No we won't fourteen and seven eights
    Help me then
    You know I'm not fast at bows
Fourteen and fifteen sixteeeenths
    A single bow is all right isn't it
Fifteen we're off
    See I did it.
    Didn't I?

From *Mind Your Own Business* by Michael Rosen

HOW WOULD YOU SAY IT?

Father says
Never
let
me
see
you
doing
that
again
father says
tell you once
tell you a thousand times
come hell or high water
his finger drills my shoulder
never let me see you doing that again

My brother knows all his phrases off by heart
so we practise them in bed at night.

From *Mind Your Own Business* by Michael Rosen